## DATE DUE

| | |
|---|---|
| OCT 2 6 2013 | |
| DEC 2 3 2013 | |
| FEB 2 2 2014 | |
| | |
| | |
| | |
| | |
| | |
| | |
| | |
| | |
| | |
| | |
| | |
| | |
| | |

# THE MESS WE'RE IN

# THE **MESS** WE'RE IN

## WHY POLITICIANS

## CAN'T FIX

## FINANCIAL CRISES

GUY FRASER-SAMPSON

First published 2012 by Elliott and Thompson Limited
27 John Street, London WC1N 2BX
www.eandtbooks.com

ISBN: 978-1-908739-06-3

Text © Guy Fraser-Sampson 2012

9 8 7 6 5 4 3 2 1

A CIP catalogue record for this book is available from the British Library.

Printed and bound in the UK by CPI Group (UK) Ltd, Croydon, CR0 4YY

Typeset by Marie Doherty

# CONTENTS

# ONE

Stability is necessary for our future economic success.
The British economy of the future must be built not on
the shifting sands of boom and bust, but on the bedrock
of prudent and wise economic management for the long
term. It is only on these firm foundations that we can raise
Britain's underlying economic performance.

GORDON BROWN, 1997

# 'Just why are we in this mess?'

It was really all Peter's fault. I was sitting in a beach hut restaurant in Goa, enjoying that feeling of deep contentment with the world that only chicken achari, garlic naan and several cold beers can induce, when he piped up with his question.

Peter is not his real name, by the way. If anybody is going to get the blame for this book then it clearly should be me, not him. After all, I wrote it.

Peter is a hugely intelligent and highly educated man, a professor no less, and a Fellow and gold medal winner of the Royal Society. When he addresses a subject you would be well advised to listen carefully, for what comes forth tends to be pure, condensed wisdom. Which also makes it rather unsettling when it is your opinion on a matter that he is requesting, since you know that your answer will be weighed in the white heat of his intellect, and quite possibly found wanting.

'So just why are we in this mess?' he enquired.

'What mess?' I queried. Surely we had enough cash on us to pay for the meal?

'Oh, you know, the financial crisis,' he said, with a grandiloquent gesture that the waiter happily interpreted as an order for two more beers. 'The banks, Greece, pensions, all that sort of stuff.'

'Ah, that,' I said, giving myself time to think. I suppose I had brought this on myself, since I had recently been featured on various television programmes on the subject, claiming to know what I was talking about. Fortunately, most of these sort of appearances are so short that there is rarely time for the limits to one's knowledge to be exposed. This occasion would be different. The baking hot afternoon stretched ahead of me and just across the table a razor-sharp mind lay in wait.

'The main difficulty,' I began, 'is that it isn't really just one problem at all. It's actually at least five different problems, all of which have become tangled together like a big knot, and if you really want to understand what's going on then you need to unpick the knot and examine each of the strands separately.'

'Go on,' he said, lighting a cigarette. An avowed non-smoker, he was trying unsuccessfully to limit himself to twenty a day.

'In no particular order,' I went on, 'there are five of them.'

I started ticking them off on my fingers.

'First, there is the aftermath of the banking crisis of 2007 and 2008. Governments need to work out how they are going to manage the banking sector so as to minimise the chance of having to use public money again in the future to rescue banks which get into trouble.'

'Second, there is the question of governments around the world running budget deficits and as a result having higher and higher levels of national debt. That's what has happened in Greece, but it's a problem everywhere, not least in the USA, as well as most European countries.'

'Third, there is the threat of recession, and what governments might do to try to avoid this by boosting the economy.'

'Fourth, as yet largely confined to the UK, there is the problem of pension funding. As you know, many schemes are in deficit, that is to say they simply don't have enough money to meet their obligations.'

'Fifth, and this may come as a surprise since it doesn't seem an obvious point to make from an economic point of view, there is the whole question of how our political system works, and in particular how it works in making economic decisions.'

I checked my hand. Five digits, five issues. So far, so good. Thank goodness I couldn't think of a sixth.

In fact, writers being the slippery customers they are, I have taken certain liberties with my account so far. Not only names have been changed, but also the chronology, though only slightly. This conversation did indeed take place one long afternoon in a beach hut in Goa, but by then I had already embarked on the odyssey that would lead to this book.

It would prove to be a journey of more than two years' duration as I wrestled to analyse what was going on in the world of finance. In the meantime, many books were published claiming to have all the answers about how the financial crisis had happened, but I wasn't really interested in 'how' things had happened so much as 'why'. The distinction is subtle, but highly significant. I was not so much interested in the crisis as in understanding the economic framework within which events had unfolded. This brought a very different perspective to the situation.

For instance, most writers seemed to be treating the crisis as having begun in mid-2007 (though admittedly the various causes which they ascribed to it had happened earlier – most said from about 2003 onwards) and ended some time in 2009. The more I read, the more I realised these views were defective in two respects. First, it seemed to me that the crisis had not ended, but was still with us, though having developed in nature. Second, it seemed to me that its causes had been constant and ongoing for many years, indeed decades.

To some extent, this was because many people appear to have treated the events of recent years as a banking crisis, with bankers, in their various forms, being responsible for it, and an avalanche of future banking regulation as the solution. I beg to differ, believing this to be part, not all, of the problem; only one contributory factor, though a significant one.

Similarly, everyone seemed to agree that what had occurred was a dramatic failure of the financial system, evidenced by banks tumbling like dominos during the dark days of 2008, though they differed as to what precisely had brought it about and when (or indeed whether) it had come to an end.

The conclusion to which my reading and thinking brought me was startlingly different. That what had occurred was in fact a massive and sustained failure of the political system, which had begun many decades ago and been eagerly abetted by just about every prime minister since the Second World War, with Margaret Thatcher perhaps being the only exception and even then only partially.

If this is so, then how is it that so many people have been led to such a profoundly mistaken conclusion?

First, it seems to me that people show a disinclination to examine the past in analysing the present and, in particular, critically to explore the past actions of politicians. It is as if politicians enjoy some sort of privileged status in this regard. If the head of an industrial firm manages it into insolvency then he is blamed and dismissed, though not always in that order. In the public sector, things work differently. The governor of the Bank of England can repeatedly miss his inflation target and yet be praised and rewarded. Politicians move seamlessly on to retirement, board seats and lucrative consultancy contracts, yet never have to face the consequences of whatever damage they may have inflicted. It is as though the day of reckoning can be indefinitely postponed.

This appears to be coupled with an instinctive trust in politicians to do the right thing, a trust which, remarkably, seems to have survived despite the clear evidence to the contrary of the last several decades. In fact, as I will demonstrate, politicians are part of the problem – indeed, they *are* the problem – rather than the bringers of solutions.

This unwillingness logically to analyse a situation based on clear data runs right through every aspect of our present situation. For example, though most people seem to believe that our problems had been caused by a banking crisis, nobody outside the world of academia has actually bothered to enquire into the nature of banking crises. What causes them? Can they be prevented? If so, how? These are all questions that even a commission specifically set up to enquire into banking regulation totally failed to address.

Then there is the related problem that, in order to understand what has happened, using knowledge drawn from only one discipline is no longer sufficient. For example, most people instinctively describe our present circumstances as 'the financial crisis' whereas in fact it is an economic and political crisis; only its symptoms are financial, and even then not all of them.

Again, the writer in me is taking a few liberties. This was not a journey upon which I suddenly embarked two years earlier. As both a reader and writer of history, I was already familiar with the works of Correlli Barnett, to whom I must acknowledge a huge debt. It was his *Pride and Fall* series, upon which I have drawn heavily in this book, which first made me aware that the official version of events should at least be seriously questioned, and that our problems really began several decades ago, not a few years. Going back to reread these was where I began my quest.

In fact, partly thanks to Barnett, the historical side of things was the easy part. I already had several bookshelves (and a few wardrobes) groaning under the weight of a myriad of books on modern history. What I was lacking was a specialist knowledge of economics and I immediately embarked upon a sustained reading spree. I had in fact strongly considered signing up for a degree in economics at one time, but as things turned out I think the fact that I had not previously studied the subject was a strength rather than a weakness, as I was able to come to things with no preconceptions and ramble about at tangents as one book suggested another, rather than having to stick to a pre-set curriculum.

I started off reading about economics from textbooks but soon progressed to reading economics itself, acquiring various rather battered second-hand volumes in the process. It was here that I struck gold.

I had long been aware that post-war economics had featured two rival schools of economic thought: that of socialism, inspired initially by Karl Marx, and that of Keynesianism, named of course after the great economist John Maynard Keynes. I was also aware that British economic policy had featured an uncomfortable mix of these, with different administrations drifting between the right- and left-hand sides of the road.

What I had not previously known was that there was in fact an additional school of thought, to which we might refer loosely as the Austrian School, which was viewed as so deeply subversive that many economics textbooks entirely failed to mention it, preferring to pretend that it had never existed. Yet, on investigation, its subversive tendencies seemed to be based on little more than a passion for personal freedom and a belief that money should actually possess some absolute value, hardly things that struck me as likely to bring about the collapse of civilisation as we know it.

Going back to reread history from the perspective of the Austrian School was a revelation. Suddenly the *real* causes of our current difficulties, the fundamental causes with their roots deep in the past and their consequences glaringly obvious in the present, became clear. What also became clear was that if I was to report them honestly and fully then this was going to be a deeply controversial and provocative book, and certainly in many quarters a deeply unpopular one.

So it is only right that I should acknowledge from the outset that many readers may find what I have to say disturbing. Those with any sort of involvement with the public sector will almost certainly brand it alarmist, cranky, foolish, impractical or even just dangerously insane. In my defence, all I can say is that the historical facts that I state can be checked and that the views that I express seem to me to be logical conclusions drawn from a combination of theory and circumstances, though I freely acknowledge that others may disagree with them. My intention throughout is to attempt to awaken an awareness of past actions and to prompt an informed debate about the present and the future.

One thing seems to me clear, and I take it as my starting point. Whatever approach has been taken in the past has failed. In fact, it has created the present mess. The two points of which I will seek to convince you are firstly that some totally new approach seems to be called for, and secondly that politicians are not the ones to whom we can look to implement it. My central argument will be that it is politicians themselves who have caused our current problems, and that the time has come for them to be called to account. The day of reckoning can be postponed no longer.

# TWO

# The Tangled Knot

Peter is an eminent scientist of international renown, one of the most impressive and intelligent people I have ever met, who has progressed effortlessly over the course of a glittering career from an Oxbridge starred first to the Royal Society's gold medal. Yet he, like so many other people, has no idea exactly why we are being bombarded with daily messages of gloom about the economy, pensions, national debt, budget deficits and threats not just to global growth but apparently even to the world's banking and other financial systems.

Being an essentially modest fellow, Peter puts this down to lack of understanding on his part, coupled with the fact that he has never studied economics. In fact, though, it is debatable just how much such a course of study would assist in the current situation. Of course it would be some help; it would be facile to suggest that after three years at university studying the subject one would not have a better knowledge of economic theory. The problem is that, at least in the present case, it only takes us so far.

First, the problems that we face are only partly economic in nature, representing a melange of issues from economics, finance, politics, psychology and philosophy, to name but five. Economists have long recognised that the world of economic activity is a hybrid one, demanding knowledge from many different fields properly to analyse it, but the levels of pluralism, diversity and complexity appear to have risen sharply in recent years.

Second, economics is not a precise science. Again, this is recognised by most economists, and distinguishes the subject from the study of finance, for example. Finance tends to assume as its starting point when examining any situation that there is one right answer and that it can be calculated. Economists recognise that a more useful and valid approach is to seek to identify trends and interconnections, and to suggest ranges within which possible outcomes may occur. As the late Edgar Fiedler, himself a distinguished economist, said: 'Ask [the same question of] five different economists and you'll get five different answers – six if one of them went to Harvard.'

As so often, a joke relies on a serious point for its humour. Because economists know that economics is not a precise science, and certainly not a predictive one, they will rarely be drawn into giving a definitive answer, preferring instead to suggest a number of alternatives. President Truman famously asked for the White House staff to include a one-armed economist, so frustrated did he become with economists who said 'on the one hand ... but on the other hand...'.

So even if we did spend three years at university learning about economics there is no guarantee at all that we would even be able to come to a firm conclusion ourselves, let alone one that could withstand discussion with other economists.

Third, if we want truly to understand any state of affairs, it is imperative that we know how it came about. The circumstances of today are the result of the circumstances of lots of yesterdays. Unless we study their history, then we can never *understand* them in their overall context; we can at best *observe* them within a temporal vacuum.

As we will see, an added benefit of history for our present purposes is that by looking at what has happened in the past we may be able better to consider what may happen in the future. Of course it is absurd to suggest that the future will exactly mirror the past, so that a record of past events may be taken as a close approximation of future outcomes (though not so absurd that finance theory adopts this assumption as one of its fundamental beliefs). Yet where specific remedies have been applied to particular problems in the past it is surely valuable to know how effective or otherwise they proved, and to note and understand how the present situation may differ from the previous one.

So, in seeking to explain the problems of today, and in tentatively suggesting some possible solutions, this book will look not just at current economic indicators, but also at how present circumstances were created by the unfolding story of history and how real world events influenced, or were in turn influenced by, the development of economic theory.

In looking at the causative factors, the objective will be to bring things together into an amalgam of strands that, when placed together in a certain combination, illuminate the truth. It will be as if a number of different lenses are being tried out by an optician, one on top of another; our vision is hopelessly fogged until the one optimum combination arises, at which point we can see through all the lenses together with perfect clarity.

Yet in analysing the present issues themselves, we first need to do exactly the opposite. They have become hopelessly tangled together and if we are to get anywhere at all we first need to unknot them and set them out singly, so that we may consider each strand individually. Let us do this straight away, since it will help to define our enquiry.

As I explained on the beach to Peter, the present situation represents a combination of issues, of which the following may be identified as the most prominent and/or more serious.

First, there is the ongoing impact on the banking and financial system generally of the crisis which began in 2007. This issue is of international dimensions.

Second, there are the closely related issues of budget deficits and national debt. Again, these are international in scope, though some countries are worse, and more immediately, affected by them than others.

Third, there is the question of the collapse, as yet partial, of the chosen method of occupational pension provision. Thus far, this is an issue that affects largely the United Kingdom, though it may yet become a significant issue in various other countries as well.

Fourth, there are concerns over the strength and robustness of economic growth generally and, indeed, fear of recession. This is a global issue, though certain countries are more susceptible to such vagaries than others.

Fifth, and this may come as a surprise entry into the list to many who have not previously considered it a problem or issue, there is the question of whether the political system within which government has to work in making decisions relevant to the running of the economy is one in which such decisions may be taken and implemented in an optimal manner. In the case of countries such as the UK and others, this question obviously arises at two different levels: domestic and European.

## The aftermath of 2007 and 2008

Some people persist in referring to the period from about September 2007 until the early part of 2009 as 'the crisis', as if it ended as soon as stock markets began to rise again. As we will see when we examine these events in detail, it is strongly arguable that 'the crisis' did indeed begin in 2007 but is still with us, albeit that it may have changed its nature in the interim.

For these introductory purposes, however, let us confine ourselves to what might be called the banking liquidity crisis, which peaked with the collapse of Lehman Brothers in September 2008 (ironically on Battle of Britain Day: 15 September).

The immediate aftermath of these events saw many well-known names disappear, either failing altogether, ceasing to exist as independent entities, and/or being bailed out and recapitalised by their nations' taxpayers. Lehman Brothers, Northern Rock, Nat West, Lloyds TSB, Merrill Lynch, Citibank, Bradford & Bingley, Alliance & Leicester, and the American institutions Fannie Mae and Freddie Mac were all casualties. Others, such as the insurance giant AIG, were struck savage blows from which they are still struggling to recover.

In the process, it became clear that government policy was being made up on an ad hoc basis as they went along, and frequently with little attempt at international cooperation or consistency, a factor that was blamed for the failure of Lehman Brothers. More worrying still, it became clear that governments were often prepared to ride rough-shod over laws and regulations, thus raising significant concerns about the accountability of the executive in supposedly democratic societies. For example, many of the banking mergers that were pushed through almost overnight would have been outlawed by the competition authorities had they been attempted by the banks themselves. In addition, it was subsequently argued that the bans on short selling imposed by France and Germany were illegal under EU regulations, individual governments not having the power to do this unilaterally without consultation. Incidentally, it is strongly arguable that such a ban must create a false market, something that if done by an individual would constitute a serious criminal offence.

As far as the banking sector is concerned, two different but related trends have so far emerged. One is a general psychological aversion to banks and those who run them, a feeling that they were responsible for what occurred but have escaped taking responsibility for their actions. The other is a debate, which has undoubtedly been clouded by the emotions we have just mentioned, into how future financial crises may be averted, with increased regulation of banking activities the prime candidate. In the UK, for example, the government established the Independent Commission on Banking, known as is customary by the name of its chairman, Sir John Vickers, to report on how this might best be achieved. Outside the UK, discussion has focused on the Basel Accords, which we will consider in more detail later, but, briefly, which provide levels of so-called 'capital adequacy' for financial institutions.

In the area of non-banking financial services, such as institutional investment management, similar siren voices have been heard luring the industry onto the rocks of ever-increasing regulation. Chief among these in Europe have been the AIFM[1] regulations emanating from the European Union. In the United States, similar sentiments have driven such measures as the Dodd–Frank Act and the Volcker Rule, which aims to ban various types of speculative activity.

As we will see, this understandable concern on the part of leg-islators and regulators alike to prevent another crisis from occurring has become little short of an obsession, which is unfortunate. People driven by an obsession rarely make good decisions. A need to make at the same time fine-sounding public statements pandering to prevail-ing mass emotions can only make things worse. As a result, regula-tory discussions have been initiated from the wrong starting point and thus, inevitably, have missed the correct target. Rather than asking

---

[1] Alternative Investment Fund Managers Directive.

'how can we control what the banks do?' it would have been infinitely preferable to ask 'what are financial crises and how might they be averted?'

It should be noted that this is a hugely complex area. It would be possible to write an entire book about 'the banking crisis' and still not be able properly to discuss all the relevant issues. Nor is it likely that the authors of even two such books, let alone several, would agree in their description of the current situation or in their analysis of its causes and possible effects.

For the moment let us simply note that, apart from sparking a debate on the regulatory framework within which banks should operate in future, the events of 2007 and 2008 saw one key development, which was a series of events by which many banks were effectively recapitalised at public expense.

## Budget deficits and national debt

If a government spends more than its income, the difference between the two is called a budget deficit. If it spends less than its income, the difference is called a budget surplus. In the case of a budget deficit the shortfall has to be made up somehow or the government would simply run out of money. Just as with individuals, this can only come from debt, from borrowing money from other people.

A government that consistently runs a budget deficit year after year is like a household living on its credit cards. At the end of each year the amount that they have borrowed is added to the running balance and they are then in an even worse position than they were at the end of the previous year because, not only are they going to have to borrow again for the coming year, but the amount of interest that they have to pay to service their debt is rising all the time. First, because they owe more money, so even if the interest rate stays the same the total interest for the year will also be greater than it was before. Second, because, just as with a business, the more money a government owes, the more nervous creditors become about lending them even more money, and so the higher an interest rate they will look to charge. This is exactly what we saw happening during 2011, for example, when the rates that investors required to persuade them to buy the bonds (debt) of various governments rose sharply.

If things get really bad, the household might get to a stage when they cannot even pay the interest on the accumulated debt, and so this too is added to the running balance. In effect, they are now borrowing to pay the interest on their existing debts. Imagine what would happen if they were to go to their local bank manager and ask for a new bank loan to pay the interest on their existing loans. Once he had stopped laughing, he would reach for the phone and speak to his debt recovery department. With credit cards, though, things have worked differently and much more like the way things have worked for governments. Just as the household becomes really desperate because they are running out of room on their credit cards, a letter arrives noting that their credit limit no longer appears adequate for their purposes, and increasing it.

Those who buy government bonds have acted in a similar manner, being prepared always to extend more credit to a government regardless of the state of their existing budget deficits and national debt levels. Incidentally, this tendency goes back a long way. During the fourteenth century, Edward III's Italian bankers, the Bardi family, extended him huge amounts by way of loans to prosecute the early stage of the Hundred Years' War. It may come as a surprise to those who know of the glorious victories of Crécy and Poitiers (Agincourt came much later, under Henry V) to learn that the early part of the war was in fact an abject failure and that, had Edward died young, then he would almost certainly have gone down as one of England's worst kings.

His strategy at that time was to pay other people to do his fighting for him. Predictably, most of them took his money but then found all sorts of reasons for staying at home. His military campaign collapsed, as did the public finances. Unable to service the loans, England went bust. Its immediate aftermath was Europe's first banking failure and financial crisis. The Bardi went bankrupt, because they had borrowed most of the money they had then lent to Edward from other banking houses across present-day northern Italy. Some of these banking houses went bust in turn because they were unable to satisfy *their* creditors. For a while the crisis threatened to engulf even governments and the richest institution in Europe, the Church. Sound familiar?

Then, as now, investors and bankers were forced to learn a salutary lesson. Debts sooner or later have to be repaid and the idea that just because you are lending to a government you are somehow exempt from normal financial consideration is nonsense. It is a lesson that has to be painfully relearned every so often, but this new reality never seems to last for long. Argentina defaulted on its debts in 2001, though according to the IMF creditors eventually got back more than ninety cents in the dollar. Perhaps finding encouragement and comfort in this first foray into national bankruptcy, four years later Argentina had to be rescued again and this time creditors got back less than thirty cents in the dollar.

Since the early part of 2011, recognition has been dawning that some governments are getting into a position from which they may never be able to pay their debts in full, at least without dramatic restructurings and slashed budgets, neither of which do many governments seem able to offer or deliver. This belated realisation of course came at a time when many governments were already stretching their finances to the limit simply to pay interest on existing debt. In the UK, for example, the government is at the time of writing being forced to pay more in interest on its debts than it receives by way of corporation tax.

As an added complication, people began to question whether the conventional way of measuring government debt might not give a dangerously misleading picture. In the UK, for instance, net debt in 2011 was about 60% of GDP, already well above a previous guideline of 40% as the absolute maximum for safe borrowing. However, this did not include the government's contingent liabilities under public sector occupational pension schemes, nor did it include the government's liabilities under PFI contracts.[2] Nor, and this is where the link to our

---

[2] Private Finance Initiative: a way of encouraging private sector capital into key infrastructure projects such as the building of roads, hospitals and railways. More cynically, a way of keeping such projects off the government's balance sheet.

first identified issue emerges, did it include the cost of the government's rescue operations on behalf of the banks, officially known as financial intervention. So it is arguable that, partly because the government continued to run a budget deficit during the meantime, all their intervention really achieved was to transform a bank liquidity crisis into a potential government solvency crisis.

## Occupational pension provision

The extent of change in the circumstances of occupational pension schemes, at least in the UK, has been genuinely revolutionary, but is as yet little understood by the general public.

Traditionally, occupational pension schemes, that is, pension plans provided for their workers either by individual employers or by groups of employers within a single industry, were what in America are called defined benefit (DB) schemes and in the UK final salary schemes. As the British name suggests, these promised to pay a worker during their retirement a sum equivalent to a certain percentage of their salary level on their retirement date. Typically these benefits were index-linked to protect against the effects of inflation and could be extended to the pensioner's partner, though usually at the expense of accepting a slightly lower annual amount.[3]

For reasons that we will later examine, in the UK most DB schemes have now closed, either to new members or altogether, and been replaced by what in America are called defined contribution (DC) schemes and in the UK money purchase schemes. These operate on the same principle as the personal pension plans with which many will already be familiar. Money is paid in during an individual's working lifetime, usually with the benefit of tax relief, and invested, again usually with the benefit of tax relief. On retirement the resulting balance, or much of it, must for most people be used to buy an annuity. An annuity is an annual sum paid by an annuity provider, usually a life

---

[3] This is a deliberately simplified summary. For example, the phrase 'final salary' was often not applied literally.

insurance company. Again, benefits can be index-linked and extended to one's partner, at the cost of a lower annual amount.

This change has radically altered various aspects of pension provision, yet here too realisation is dawning but slowly.

First, the investment risk has passed from the scheme to the individual. In the case of a DB scheme, the trustees are obliged to pay a certain level of benefits regardless of the scheme's investment performance and other financial circumstances. In the case of a DC scheme, the individual will get whatever the final 'pot' might be, and there is absolutely no guarantee that this will have accumulated to an amount sufficient to fund an acceptable level of benefits.

Since the only way in which the payments made into a scheme can grow is by investment performance, this means that the risk of poor performance is now borne by the individual rather than by the scheme itself. Yet in the case of an occupational scheme the individual will often have little or no control over the choice of investments,[4] while even in the case of a personal plan they may be limited to a small number of mutual fund-type vehicles owned by or associated with the scheme manager.

So the individual is now put in the position of having responsibility for a situation yet without having the means to control it. Since nobody would accept such a position within an organisation, it seems strange that nobody has objected to this particular instance of it. This argues strongly that what might be called the 'unethical' aspect of money purchase pensions has not yet been properly appreciated.

Second, the responsibility for payment of the benefits has shifted from the scheme to the insurance industry. Thus pensioners are now effectively in the same position as creditors of a commercial business. Were some future financial crisis to engulf the insurance sector in the same way that the events of 2007 and 2008 engulfed the banking sector, it is entirely possible that many people might be deprived of their pension altogether, despite having purchased an annuity. Again, this aspect of the situation appears to have been largely overlooked.

---

[4] This is much less true in the US with 401(k) type schemes, and some limited flexibility is now also being offered by similar schemes in other countries, including the UK and Australia.

Finally, and most crucially, the level of benefits that a money purchase scheme is likely to provide is very much less than that which people might have been expecting from a final salary scheme. Calculations performed by the writer elsewhere[5] suggest that the annual amount generated by a money purchase scheme may actually only be about one-third of what would otherwise have been payable under a final salary scheme.

We will examine how and why this has come about, but the conclusion seems inescapable: retirees will in future have to put up with a relatively impoverished lifestyle. Some have even questioned whether history will look back on retirement as a novel late twentieth-century experiment.[6]

Even in countries other than the UK, where pension provision may be structured differently, there is yet another issue that does not appear to have been properly appreciated. Pension funds typically hold very high levels of the bonds (debt) issued by their own government. Indeed, in some cases they may be forced to. With the growing recognition of the very real possibility of governments defaulting on their debt, this raises the prospect of a disaster (sovereign debt default) being turned into a tragedy (loss of pension provision).

## Global economic prospects

Economic cycles come and go. We in the UK should be more aware of that than most, since we have witnessed a seemingly endless cycle of boom and bust. This is linked to various of our other issues, most notably that of budget deficits and national debt.

First, as we will see, economic theory strongly suggests (indeed, this should be obvious) that during good times you put something away for a rainy day and then, when that rainy day finally arrives, as arrive it must, you have something to fall back on. In other words, in the 'boom' part of the cycle you run a budget surplus and build up a buffer of cash reserves and/or pay down debt. Then in the 'bust' part

---

[5]  See Guy Fraser-Sampson, *No Fear Finance*, London, Kogan Page, 2011.

[6]  See for example various publications by Professor David Blake of Cass Business School.

of the cycle you will have flexibility to borrow money and/or to use up your accumulated cash reserves.

Sadly, this has not happened, and so governments around the world now find themselves trying to navigate a particularly nasty downward part of the cycle with no safety net.

Second, if you are the government of a heavily indebted nation, then economic growth is the fairy godmother you look for to wave a magic wand and get you out of trouble. With economic growth come both higher taxes (since there is more income and activity to tax) and lower spending (since unemployment will fall, thus reducing the welfare budget). This double whammy will transform both the annual budget and total debt as a proportion of GDP since a budget surplus will allow debt to be paid off, so the level of total debt will be falling at the same time as GDP is rising.

At the end of the Napoleonic wars, for example, Britain, whose strategy once again had been largely to pay huge subsidies to other people to induce them to do the bulk of the fighting (on land, that is), had national debt exceeding 200% of GDP. Luckily Britain then experienced explosive economic growth over the next fifty years or so by virtue of being in the forefront of the industrial revolution. By 1850 debt had halved as a proportion of GDP, and by 1900 it had more than halved again.[7]

Some believe that if all the various elements of UK government debt, which we considered briefly above, were added together they would once again approximate to 200% of GDP. Given that we clearly cannot expect the same explosive economic growth of the nineteenth century, then this may signal a bleak future. The only other time that national debt was at that level was at the end of the Second World War, and by then Britain had already effectively gone bust (that happened in 1941, with Britain able to continue the war only as a credit client of the United States).

At the time of writing it is unclear whether we really are heading into a global recession and, if so, whether it would be anything like as

---

[7] www.ukpublicspending.co.uk

severe or prolonged as the Great Depression of the 1930s, but it does seem that even the most optimistic medium-term forecast is for no more than sluggish growth.

## The political system

It is impossible to separate economics from other fields of study. For example, economic circumstances and outcomes are directly influenced, in some cases even directly caused, by policy decisions. Policy decisions are made by politicians and those advising them, and they do this within the framework of the relevant political system. The question of whether that system helps or hinders optimal decision-making is therefore clearly relevant.

Systems currently in use range from what might be called the western democratic model, slightly different versions of which are employed by countries such as America, Britain, Japan and Germany, to outright dictatorships such as North Korea. Along the way we meet oligarchies such as Russia, benevolent despotisms such as the UAE and totalitarian single-party states such as China.

Politicians from democratic states have regularly bemoaned the phenomenon of boom and bust. Indeed, Gordon Brown even claimed to have halted it but, like Canute holding back the waves, his confidence proved unfounded. This is ironic since arguably political decisions, rather than damping down boom and bust, have in many cases exacerbated it. In 1958, for example, British Prime Minister Harold Macmillan, with an eye to a forthcoming election, wanted increased public spending. His Chancellor of the Exchequer (finance minister), with an eye to inflation and economic cycles, wanted decreased public spending. Macmillan got his way and, most unusually, his entire treasury team (Thorneycroft, Powell and Birch) stuck up for their principles and resigned en masse. Of course this was effectively the end of their careers; nobody likes a politician with principles.

To be effective, economic planning must be long term in nature. It must also embrace other areas, such as technology, innovation, global trading conditions, currency movements, social issues and government policy. One of Macmillan's successors, Harold Wilson, at least recognised this, though he proved unable to put it into practice.

Strategic long-term planning across any discipline, whether it be military, industrial, investment or any other type of strategy, reveals a common and all-pervading principle. Like many common and all-pervading principles it is ignored, or even denied, by those most affected by it, but it is valid nonetheless. It is this: most strategic decisions come down to a trade-off between one choice which has a short-term benefit but a long-term cost, and another choice which has a long-term benefit but a short-term cost.

Within a western democratic system we place our politicians in an impossible situation. We ask them to make decisions with long-term effects, but because they must seek election every few years we more or less force them to consider only the short-term consequences. Thus, like Macmillan in 1958, they will always tend to choose a short-term benefit rather than a short-term cost, almost regardless of the possible consequences in the long term. Is it a coincidence that China, a totalitarian state, has just witnessed a twenty-year economic miracle, while those countries currently struggling with high debt and stagnant growth are all western-style democracies? Or does it speak to the ability of a single-party system to conduct strong, long-term central planning and efficiently oversee its consistent implementation?

To be clear, it is no part of this book's mission to advocate totalitarianism, but it *is* valid to ask whether the system within which we force our politicians to operate fosters good decision-making, and, if not, what we might do to change it while still remaining true to the ideals of democracy.

A good example of this problem may be seen in the UK government's decision to use their Project Merlin initiative (which consisted essentially of taking money from the banks by force) to provide investment capital to private companies. Clear evidence from the United States shows that the most logical place to deploy this would be by way of early-stage venture capital to start-up companies with dynamic growth potential, often based around some proprietary technology application. Studies show that about 20% of American GDP is currently contributed by companies that are, or were, venture-backed.[8] Yet instead, government has chosen to deploy the money to medium-sized companies with limited growth potential, though being careful of course to have their spin doctors apply the word 'growth' to both the fund and its target companies.

Why have they done this? It is obvious where the money should be targeted and that the government has got it wrong. Is government stupid? No, or at least not in this instance. They are simply looking determinedly at the short term. If UK venture performance were to be even a fraction as effective as American, then the benefit to the economy of seeding early-stage companies would be dramatic. Yet it would take at least ten years to show through, whereas it is just possible that they may be able to persuade people that the 'growth' fund is showing some results (perhaps by stating the number of investments made) within the lifetime of a single Parliament.

Politicians are interested in votes, not the long-term national interest, and we should not feel entitled to complain because we force them to act that way. We get the politicians we deserve because we are not prepared to take the trouble to think seriously about political or constitutional reform.

A further problem within countries such as the UK and Germany is of course that national sovereignty has been ceded to the European Union. It is because of this that regulatory regimes are able to be imposed upon countries across a whole range of things from financial services to vitamin pills to light bulbs without the consent of the electorate. Since in cases such as the UK the electorate never got to approve the handover of sovereignty in the first place, this does raise the question of just how 'democratic' such a democracy might be. At the very least, it requires that any review of the political system should be all-embracing; it is no longer sufficient for EU member countries to consider only what takes place domestically.

---

[8] Source: National Venture Capital Association (NVCA).

## The rest of the book

I have now rehearsed briefly what seem to me to be the five main strands of the knot, which we must try to unpick and consider in more detail. Thus far we have focused largely on the current situation and have been content to consider the broad outline of what we can observe. I now need to introduce the economic ideas that I believe will help us understand the issues which we are facing, and the unfolding events that created them.

Once I have done this I will come full circle and, armed with this new-found knowledge, analyse the full extent of our current problems and consider some possible ways in which we might seek to address them.

I could begin this quest just about anywhere. I have already mentioned the Napoleonic wars, and even Edward III, but there is probably no need to go back to the nineteenth century, let alone the fourteenth. Let us start instead with the Treaty of Versailles, which was finally concluded in 1919 after what Edward House called 'eight fateful months'. The Treaty, which of course reshaped the map of Europe after the First World War, sought to deliver 'justice' (in Clemenceau's words) but had many critics. Among them was a man who is destined to play a major part in our story: John Maynard Keynes.

# THREE

# Money and Inflation

John Maynard Keynes was a true Victorian, being born in 1883, by coincidence the same year which marked the passing of Karl Marx. Keynes was to prove at least as influential a thinker, though believing in a very different socioeconomic model.

A childhood prodigy who is said to have puzzled over interest calculations at the age of four, he won a scholarship to Eton, followed in due course by a scholarship to Cambridge, where incidentally his father was a lecturer in 'moral sciences', an academic area which no longer exists but which included – yes, you've guessed it – economics. Incidentally, Keynes was more or less exclusively gay for the first part of his life and his first known love affair occurred at Eton with the older brother of the same Harold Macmillan whom we met in the last chapter.

His gayness is actually relevant to his thought and the impact that this had on his times, since it provided an entrée, through a later lover Lytton Strachey, not just to the hugely influential Bloomsbury Group, but to its innermost circle: people such as Virginia Woolf, Clive and Vanessa Bell, Roger Fry and E.M. Forster. Moving in more distant orbits were the likes of Harold Nicolson (also gay, and husband to Vita Sackville-West), Duff Cooper and the Mitfords, and through them he had access to all the leading politicians of the day, including Winston Churchill.

Not that Keynes probably needed much help, for he rapidly became not just a member of the Apostles, a group to which only the intellectual elite of Cambridge University were invited, but also secretary of the Cambridge Union and president of its Liberal Party (then one of the two parties of government) association. His fellow Apostles' faith in him was not misplaced; he graduated with a first in mathematics in 1904. Membership of the Apostles was for life, by the way, and Keynes maintained an active participation after he left Cambridge.

After a brief and un-enjoyable flirtation with life as a civil servant, during which one of his achievements was to become an expert on the Indian rupee, Keynes returned to Cambridge to concentrate on economics, becoming first a lecturer and then a Fellow. By the end of the First World War he was already established as an economist of repute and, having worked for the Treasury during the war, it was natural that he should have found himself a member of the large advisory team which accompanied the British delegation to the lengthy negotiations that would culminate in the Treaty of Versailles. It was, however, a frustrating experience for Keynes as he was sidelined by the two political heavyweights chosen to front the financial aspects of discussions, Lord Sumner, a Lord of Appeal, and Lord Cunliffe, who was the immediate past governor of the Bank of England, finding himself at odds with their views.

The story of the Treaty of Versailles is well known. Shortly before the end of the war President Wilson had unilaterally issued his 'Fourteen Points', on the basis of which he wished peace to be established and post-war society conducted. Britain and France were taken entirely by surprise, not having been consulted in advance, and the ground was then cut from under their feet when Germany sought peace directly from Wilson expressly on the basis of the Fourteen Points.

The most contentious aspects of the Fourteen Points were Wilson's insistence on the establishment of a League of Nations, which he thought would render future war impossible, and a proposal for (though it was not couched in exactly these terms) self-determination as a general principle. His actual words were 'the adjustment of all colonial claims', which caused the British, with their extensive empire, great concern.

It quickly transpired though that Wilson had intended self-determination to apply only if you were white and European. Britain provided no separate representation for India, and Britain and France together effectively blocked an Arab delegation. Doubtless feeling that Wilson's commitment to self-determinism was literally only skin deep, the Indian poet Tagore would in 1930 tell a US audience including Franklin Roosevelt and Henry Morgenthau that 'a great portion of the world suffers from your civilisation'. Perhaps he was still sore from Wilson, whom he had met on an earlier trip, having rejected his proposed dedication of his book, *Nationalism*.

In similar vein, while in Paris Wilson refused to grant an audience to an importunate young kitchen worker in a borrowed suit who wanted to speak to him about self-determinism in Indochina. It might have saved a lot of trouble had he done so; the young man's name was Ho Chi Minh.

The League of Nations caused Wilson no end of problems as well. Japan, one of the victorious Allies, asked for a racial equality clause, pointing out not unreasonably that this principle was already enshrined in the American constitution. Wilson, who strangely had not anticipated this point, was acutely embarrassed and eventually had them withdraw their request, sowing the first seeds of future US/ Japanese discord. Japan became one of the four permanent council members, but would withdraw in 1933 after disagreements over Manchuria. Had the Japanese delegation known in 1919 that Wilson had at one stage told his cabinet that he thought America should stay out of the war 'to keep the white race strong against the yellow', they might perhaps have been less accommodating.

Ironically, since it was only Wilson who ever really wanted the League, in the event he was unable to persuade Congress to ratify the Treaty of Versailles and so America never became a member.

Crucially, while the Fourteen Points made specific proposals for the return of territory, including the long-disputed Alsace-Lorraine region to France, they were silent on the question of financial compensation and it was in this area that Keynes found himself in disagreement with Sumner and Cunliffe, who quickly became nicknamed 'the heavenly twins' because of the sky-high rates of reparations that they wished to inflict on Germany. In fairness, in doing so they were merely responding to popular sentiment in Britain, which was demanding that Germany 'be squeezed until the pips squeak', and may have felt that politically they had little choice but to go along with this – an early example of politics triumphing over economics.

The French agenda was clear. Having narrowly won the third round of the Franco–German conflict (the first two being the Napoleonic wars and the Franco–Prussian war, both of which France had lost), they were determined that there should never be a fourth. This strategy demanded that Germany be weakened, preferably by being split up into its former constituents such as Bavaria, Saxony and Prussia, by having territory taken away and given to other nations such as Poland and the newly-formed Czechoslovakia, and by swingeing financial obligations that would keep the German economy weak and unable to afford any attempt at rearmament.

In broad terms, a bargain was struck. Wilson was desperate for the League of Nations to be set up and, increasingly, to bring the interminable discussions to an end so he could return to America. He was dubious about reparations, being instinctively inclined to the balance of power, and seeing Germany as an important trading partner of the United States in the post-war world. Britain and France wanted reparations but were cool about the League of Nations. They were both extremely sensitive to his 'adjustment of colonial claims' point, not least because they had concluded the Sykes–Picot Agreement during the war, secretly dividing up the Middle East between them; exactly the sort of treaty that the Fourteen Points sought expressly to ban. They had also concluded a treaty with Italy by which, in return for Italy entering the war on the allied side, she would be given large territorial gains when peace came, largely at Austria's expense. In the end they were unable to move Wilson on this latter point, leaving Italy too with a lasting sense of grievance. Incidentally, the Sykes–Picot Agreement was directly inconsistent with a separate treaty that Britain had signed with King Faisal and various of his Arab allies, which was why they were desperate to deny them a platform at Versailles and were hugely irritated when they attempted to gatecrash the proceedings in the company of their champion, Colonel T.E. Lawrence.

To cut a long story short, Wilson got his League, but Britain and France got their reparations. These were initially set at 226 billion marks, but reduced to 132 billion in 1921. To give some idea of the amounts involved, using figures later quoted by Keynes this was roughly approximate to between ten and fifteen times Germany's post-war annual tax revenues.

To complicate matters further, many reparations were stipulated to be payable *in specie*, as lawyers say, literally in stuff, in things. For example, for many years Germany was obliged to make shipments of coal to France; indeed, France even occupied much of Germany's coal mining region for a while to enforce compliance. Incidentally, one of the 'things' transferred by way of reparations was the patent and formula for aspirin, surely one of the most valuable pieces of intellectual property ever acquired.

As we will see, Germany would shortly find herself in a situation in which all available export goods were desperately needed as a source of foreign currency, yet she was hampered by the fact that a large part of her raw materials were already signed away.

Keynes disagreed deeply with this 'squeeze until the pips squeak' approach. In 1919 he published *The Economic Consequences of the Peace*, which became a best-seller not just in Britain (where it sold an astonishing hundred thousand copies in six months) but around the world, helping to convince many that it had been unwise to burden Germany so heavily. Incidentally, it is said that disenchantment with the Treaty of Versailles caused by the book's publication in America was a major contributory factor in Congress refusing to ratify the Treaty in 1920.

The book was remarkable, not just for its prescience, nor just for its intellectual authority, nor even for its courage in daring to criticise the establishment in a conformist age, but for its style. Perhaps because of his Bloomsbury connections and cultural interests, Keynes wrote at times like a novelist, with moving phrases ('men will not always die quietly'), pithy pen portraits (of Clemenceau: 'he had only one illusion: France, and only one disillusion: mankind') and purple passages ('with what curiosity, anxiety and hope we sought a glimpse of the features and bearing of the man of destiny [Wilson] who, coming from the West, was to bring healing to the wounds of the ancient parent of his civilisation and lay for us the foundations of the future').

Keynes saw the Treaty for what it was: an attempt to break Germany economically and keep her forever weak. He pointed out that this was not only in direct contravention of one of the Fourteen Points, but also a breach of a promise that Wilson had made to Congress that there should be no punitive damages.

He argued that by imposing punitive compensation on Germany rather than an equitable settlement (the Allies ignored, for example, the fact that the Kaiser, who had been primarily responsible for the war, had abdicated and gone into exile while the German people had sought to evolve a new, more democratic system of government), the Allies had probably laid the seeds of a new war rather than laying to rest an old one. Marshal Foch, former allied supreme commander, agreed. 'This is not peace,' he said, 'but an armistice for twenty years.' In the event he would be proved sixty-five days out in his reckoning.

Keynes also argued that, with the very real threat of starvation not just in Germany but across the former Hapsburg possessions, revolution could ensue. In fact, by the time the Treaty was signed various communist republics had already been proclaimed in Germany, including one in Berlin under Rosa Luxemburg and Karl Liebknecht, but the rising petered out after they were both killed by right-wing paramilitaries. A more vigorous one in Munich threatened a permanent socialist state of Bavaria. The Weimar Republic, founded in such turbulent times, was a sickly child and might easily be toppled.

Most of all, Keynes was concerned by the threat of inflation.

Inflation was not something that many worried about at the time, or even properly understood. America had been through a period of sustained low inflation (indeed, even deflation) after the end of the Civil War, and Britain similarly since the end of the Crimean War. Then, as now, because people had experienced a period of low inflation they seemed automatically to assume that it could safely be ignored as a potential problem in the future.

It had always been understood that inflation meant a rise in prices, which could also be described as a fall in the value of money (or, more precisely, in its purchasing power). Originally, in ancient and medieval times, a prime cause was debasement of the coinage. This occurred when a government called in existing coins, melted them down, mixed in a little more base metal and reissued a greater number of coins each containing rather less gold or silver than previously. The benefit that a government receives from such an exercise is called seigniorage and shows why the right to run the mint was highly prized as a privilege and usually restricted to the king himself or a close relative.

This sort of exercise tended to boost inflation in two ways. First, people valued the coins simply because of the precious metal which they contained. We call this commodity money or specie money. The problem here is obvious. If people know, or even suspect, that there is less of the commodity (gold or silver) in each coin than there was before, they will ascribe a lower value to each, regardless of its face value, and will demand more of them in payment for the same thing as they did before.

Incidentally, enterprising private individuals attempted to do the same thing themselves by 'clipping', shaving a small piece of metal off each coin and then melting them down to make new ones. This was understandably viewed very seriously by the authorities, since only they were allowed to devalue the currency, and a lingering and painful death was the most usual punishment for those unlucky enough to be caught. 'Milling', cutting many small grooves into the edges of a coin, a traditional measure shown for nostalgic reasons on the old half-crown, was designed to make clipping more difficult.

The other thing that tended to boost inflation was that there were now more coins in circulation than there were before. In modern economic terms, you would have increased the money supply. As a simple principle of supply and demand, the more of something there is available the less valuable it tends to be. If there are now more coins than there were before but the same number of potatoes, then the price of potatoes will rise. This is the basic foundation of monetarist economic theory, which we will be considering later.

Growth in the money supply had occasionally happened for legitimate reasons. For example, a massive influx of gold and silver from the New World caused rampant inflation in Tudor and Stuart times (the late sixteenth and early seventeenth centuries). Usually, however, it came about through debasement. France continued to play this game well into the eighteenth century. As late as 1785 the French mint reduced the gold content of a Gold Louis from nearly 7.5 grams to just over 7 grams, while keeping the face value the same.

At about this time a general shortage of coins, and particularly silver ones, affected the whole of Europe and this became a particular problem during the Napoleonic wars, leading to difficulties in gathering and transporting enough coins to pay troops. In Britain, for example, experiments were made with 'token' coins, which were sometimes even foreign coins with a British crest stamped onto them. It was understood that such coins did not have the intrinsic commodity value that they purported to represent, but could be taken as representing ones which did. Understandably, this did not prove popular, and the government embarked on a major recoinage exercise as soon as the wars were over.

By this time bank notes had begun to circulate, representing a promise to pay the same amount in gold pounds if the note was presented at the relevant bank. This arrangement was known as the Gold Specie Standard. Gradually the bank notes of banks other than the Bank of England were discouraged and most disappeared from circulation, though this took time. As late as 1851 one would provide a major plot device in Mrs Gaskell's *Cranford*.

By shortly after the time of the Franco–Prussian war in 1870 most major economies had adopted a gold standard, whereby small amounts of notes would be redeemed as gold coins under the existing Gold Specie Standard, but large amounts might be redeemed in bullion. It is this latter arrangement that is the Gold Standard properly so-called, and which led to the expression 'as good as gold' (referring to the British pound).

At the risk of confusing matters further, there was also something called the Gold Exchange Standard, which pegged the value of silver coins to gold. In America, which was late to adopt it, this became a major political issue during the 1896 election campaign, with small-town America pressing for its adoption to halt severe deflation, which was hurting them but benefiting their creditors (the banks). McKinley, the Republican, wanted to keep the pure gold standard. William Jennings Bryan, the Democrat, wanted the Gold Exchange Standard.

Few people realise that *The Wizard of Oz* was actually written at this time by a journalist as a satirical political allegory. As described by Gregory Mankiw:[1]

> it tells the story of Dorothy, a girl lost in a strange land far from her home in Kansas. Dorothy (representing traditional American values) makes three friends: a scarecrow (the farmer), a tin woods-man (the industrial worker) and a lion whose roar exceeds his might (William Jennings Bryant). Together, the four of them make their way along a perilous yellow brick road (the Gold Standard), hoping to find the wizard who will help Dorothy return home. Eventually they arrive in Oz (Washington) where everyone sees the world through green glasses (money). The wizard (McKinley) tries to be all things to all men but turns out to be a fraud. Dorothy's problem is solved only when she remembers the magical power of her silver slippers.

All the major combatants had to abandon the Gold Standard when the First World War came along. Britain, rather sneakily, never officially abolished the Gold Specie Standard, but withdrew all gold coins from circulation and made it clear that anyone who was so unpatriotic as to turn up at the Bank of England with a ten-pound note requesting payment in sovereigns would be publicly debagged and horsewhipped on the steps of his club.

Britain would go back on the Gold Standard in 1925, officially abolishing the Gold Specie Standard at the same time, but would pull out again in 1931. However, even then most countries retained some link with at least the principle of gold convertibility, holding a speci-fied percentage of banknotes in circulation as gold, not least with a view to what might happen if people around the world suddenly took a dislike to their currency.

Keynes understood various aspects of inflation that nobody had yet raised.

---

[1] N. Gregory Mankiw. *Macroeconomics,* New York, Worth Publishers, 2002.

He recognised that a government running a budget deficit for any length of time must itself be inflationary, and the longer and more significant the deficit then the greater this effect would be. For even a government can only borrow so much money, after which it will resort to printing more money, and with more money in circulation its value must surely fall. Germany had actually resorted both to borrowing and printing money to finance its war effort, effectively decoupling the mark from gold in order to do so. Now, according to Keynes, its proposed spending was 25 billion marks *before* payment of any reparations, while it had projected tax revenues of only 10 billion marks. Austria and Hungary were in even worse states; Keynes said neither could really be regarded as having a budget at all.

Keynes realised that, once heavily indebted, a country could slip into a vicious inflationary spiral. If it borrowed in its own currency, then it would need to print more money with which to pay it back and, if it was running a budget deficit, perhaps even to service the interest. If it borrowed in foreign currency, then again it faced the prospect of having to print much more of its own money with which to purchase the foreign currency with which to repay the loan.

He was also concerned about the moral or ethical aspects of inflation, both for society and for the individual. For society, a rising spiral of prices could bring widespread hardship, and even starvation, if for example there should be a disincentive for farmers to release their grain onto the local market because they would be better off exporting it for foreign currency, or waiting a few weeks for a higher price in local currency. For the individual, it was morally objectionable that he should be subjected to a phenomenon the workings of which he did not understand and could not control.

It was the danger of widespread economic hardship leading to social unrest, or even revolution such as the communist uprisings that Germany had already witnessed, to which Keynes was attempting to alert the French and British governments. Incidentally, Keynes is widely credited with saying that the easiest way to undermine a capitalist society is to 'debauch its currency', but in fact he was quoting Lenin, albeit only to agree with him.

Largely as a result of events that were shortly to unfold in the former Central Powers (Germany and Austro-Hungary), the 'debauching' of a country's currency would become viewed as the most unthinkable crime that could be committed, a betrayal of all civilised capitalist values. The Reichsbank reacted with horror to plans to flood Britain with beautifully forged five-pound notes during the Second World War, for instance, and successfully persuaded Hitler to thwart the initiative until much too late for it to have any real effect.

'Shortly', because Keynes's warnings very soon turned out to be not the ranting of a deranged academic whose views had been ignored, as his critics must doubtless have hoped, but a horribly accurate prophesy. One is reminded of the story of Cassandra, who was given the gift of prophecy by Apollo as part of his efforts to seduce her but then also, after she frustratingly and ungratefully rejected his advances, the curse never to be believed.

The seeds of the tragedy that was now rapidly to unfold[2] had already been sown.

As we have already seen, Germany decided to finance the Great War by borrowing, rather than higher taxes. The finance minister, Karl Helfferich, usually gets the blame for what was to ensue, though in fairness he was not in office at the beginning of the war. What German financial policy did seemed breathtakingly simple or, if you were one of its critics such as the banker and economist Hjalmar Schacht, breathtakingly stupid.

Going into the war, Germany had both gold marks and paper marks, paper being freely convertible into gold. To cover such an eventuality, paper marks could only be printed if one-third of their value in gold was sitting in the vaults, plus the remaining two-thirds in 'short' (ninety-day) bonds or bills of exchange, which in turn had to be adequately secured, or discounted in lieu of security. This practice gave the German people as much confidence in their mark as the British had in their pound. As we have seen, the latter gave rise to the

---

[2]  For an illuminating and excellently written account of the relevant events, see Adam Fergusson, *When Money Dies: The Nightmare of the Weimar Hyper-Inflation*, London, Old Street Publishing, 2010 (first published in 1975).

saying 'as good as gold', while of the former the Germans used to say 'Mark gleich Mark', which strictly translated means 'mark equals mark', but more freely as 'one mark [a paper one] is as good as another [a gold one]'.

All of this was quickly swept away. Convertibility was the first thing to go, though the myth of 'Mark gleich Mark' would persist. Then the government authorised the setting up of loan banks to issue credit, both public and private. Where did the money come from to capitalise these banks and fund these loans? The government printed it. In order to facilitate this, they abolished the rule about gold and prime bond backing for new bank notes, stipulating that the loans issued by the savings banks could be held as cover instead. Thus for a secure financial pyramid they substituted either a house of cards or a vicious, self-destructive and ever-expanding circle depending on your point of view. In the event, even this wobbly edifice proved unequal to the task and Germany *did* also have to resort to higher taxation, as well as foreign borrowings secured against pre-war German government bonds held overseas.

By the end of the war, a combination of greatly increased money supply and the scarcity of goods caused by Britain's naval blockade, had already produced rapidly rising prices and social hardship. This was now starting to make itself apparent in other people's view of German currency. Even while the negotiations were continuing in Paris, the value of the mark was falling steadily. Before the war there had been 20 marks to the pound. By the end of the war there were 43. By the time the Treaty was signed in the summer of 1919 there were 60, and by the end of that year 185. When the final compensation figure was set at 132 billion marks in 1921, the Allies were careful to stipulate payment in gold.

The money supply figures during this period tell us all we need to know. At the outbreak of the war, 2.7 billion marks were in circulation. By the end of the war there were 27 billion, a tenfold increase in four years. Two years later there were 77 billion.[3] The currency

---

[3] All figures from *When Money Dies: The Nightmare of the Weimar Hyper-Inflation*, op. cit.

had already been well and truly debauched, but worse, much worse, was still to come. In 1922, with its own printing presses running full time but still unable to keep up with the demand for new money, the government began to license the private printing of *Notgeld*, which would be accepted by the Reichsbank on exactly the same basis as its own notes. '*Mark gleich Mark*' had now taken on a whole new meaning.

Remarkably, despite the fact that there was clearly rampant domestic inflation within Germany, largely driven by an ever-increasing supply of money, the mark enjoyed a brief period of apparent strength on the foreign exchange markets, albeit at around 250 to the pound. This enabled enough gold and acceptable foreign government bonds to be bought to pay the first instalment of reparations (despite rising political protest against the Treaty within Germany) in June 1921. Keynes then predicted that from the following month onwards the mark would fall by an average of one point a day against the pound for the next two or three years; he could see only too clearly what was happening. Sure enough, from July 1921 the steadily weakening mark went into freefall against all major currencies and, significantly, against gold.

The story of the Weimar Republic's hyperinflation is well known. Less so is that of Austria and Hungary, which in fact suffered even worse. Genteel pensioners found the value of their savings stripped away so that they had to sell first their valuables, then their furniture, then finally even their homes just to feed themselves. An obscure economist in Vienna called Friedrich Hayek received two hundred pay increases in eight months.

By the late summer of 1923, German workers were taking wheelbarrows to work to collect their wages. One well-known story told of a returning worker leaving his wheelbarrow of cash outside a shop; when he came out, someone had stolen the wheelbarrow but left the money behind. Bank notes were being used as wallpaper, and burnt as kindling. A recently demobbed serviceman, Adolf Hitler, paid one billion marks for a glass of beer in Munich. Many farmers refused to release their harvest to the towns, leading to widespread hunger and anger. Anger on all sides; as bread prices had risen sharply with inflation, some politicians, in a sadly typical vote-catching gesture, had outlawed further price rises. This meant bakers could not afford to buy flour and millers in turn could not afford to buy grain, while farmers could make huge amounts in local currency by selling it for export.

Inevitably there were some who actually worked out how to profit from the situation, and not only farmers. On a small but widespread scale, gleeful foreign tourists flooded across the borders to enjoy what were to them ridiculously cheap hotels and restaurants. On a larger scale, many Germans worked out that they could borrow heavily in marks, buy foreign currency, then sell it back a month or two later, pay off the loan and perhaps have enough left over to buy a luxury apartment. Repeated on a monthly basis, this could, and did, make some people very wealthy indeed. In a disturbing precursor of later horrors, this gave rise to greatly increased anti-Semitism since many bankers and financiers were Jewish. *Notgeld* was increasingly referred to insultingly as 'Jew confetti'. Chillingly, Keynes had actually predicted exactly this eventuality in *The Economic Consequences of the Peace*: 'Those to whom the system brings windfalls beyond their deserts and even beyond their expectations or desires become "profiteers", who are the object of the hatred of the bourgeoisie, whom the inflation has impoverished, not less than of the proletariat.'

Some important lessons may be gleaned from the Weimar hyperinflation, many of which would have to be painfully relearned in the 1970s.

First, inflation can initially look benign, even attractive. Asset values such as real estate and stock markets can rise dramatically, but only because their denominator is losing value equally dramatically. In 2011, by the same token, there were politicians around the world who were claiming that much recorded inflation was illusory because it was simply a product of rising commodity prices and ignoring the possibility that exactly the opposite might in fact be taking place.

Second, inflation is as much psychological as it is economic; it is as much a state of mind as it is a financial phenomenon. There comes an emotional tipping point when rising prices trigger an irresistible demand for higher wages. In Weimar Germany, people generally complained about not having enough money, rather than that prices were too high. Germany was fortunate that, as we will see, in the hour of her darkest need she found a man who would recognise this and use psychology, rather than finance, to solve her problems.

Third, as Keynes himself said repeatedly, inflation is just plain unfair because it is arbitrary and completely outwith the control of the individual. It is in fact the equivalent of a secret tax: 'By a continuing process of inflation, governments can confiscate, secretly and unobserved, an important part of the wealth of their citizens.'

If you have ten marks in your pocket today and inflation is running at just over 12%, then in a year's time you will only have nine marks in your pocket, in terms of what you can purchase with it compared to what you can purchase today. Should you regard that one missing mark as a secret tax which the government requires you to pay? Yes, said Keynes.

What would he have said, one wonders, had he known that in the UK by 2011 there would be a specific tax (capital gains tax) on inflation? So, not only does the government have a direct incentive to fail to keep inflation under control, but is levying a tax on a tax. Perhaps it is fortunate for the government that Keynes is no longer around and that so few of the electorate understand inflation.

Keynes was right too about the possibility of social upheaval and revolution growing out of the misery of hunger and unemployment, though when it happened the attempt came from the right, not the left. Hitler's Beer Hall Putsch in Munich collapsed humiliatingly in less than twenty-four hours in November 1923, though ten years later he would sweep to power.

Desperate for somebody to wave a magic wand and make the bad things stop, Germany turned to the man who had been so critical of the policies which had done so much to create their problems in the first place: Hjalmar Schacht. Cometh the hour, cometh the man.

He ordered the Reichsbank to stop issuing new banknotes; at that time newly printed ones would apparently have filled three hundred railway wagons. In the teeth of strong opposition from industrialists who had grown accustomed to printing their own money, he decreed that the Reichsbank would not honour any new issues of *Notgeld*.

This at least staunched the flow of new notes flooding into the money supply. At the same time, he ordered all banks to withdraw credit from anyone dealing in foreign currency. The speculators, many of whom had leveraged themselves many times with debt, were forced to cease their activities; some were even ruined. The 'grey' market in foreign currency collapsed. As exchange rates stabilised, then for the first time since the war the balance tipped in favour of foreign currency being sold for marks, rather than vice versa.

These measures, significant though they were, might be compared to the equivalent of cutting off the enemy's supply of reinforcements, thus preventing the situation from getting any more out of hand than it already was. The situation itself still had to be dealt with. The way in which Schacht chose to do so was a masterly coup; perhaps the greatest confidence trick ever perpetrated.

The idea of a Rentenbank, a bank which lent money to farmers on the security of their land, had already been floated. Schacht made it a reality, the idea being that any bond or debt issued by it would be secured by legal charges, mortgages, over property with a clear market value. These new instruments would be called Rentenmarks and Schacht's initial imperative was to have them accepted by the farmers; unless this happened they would continue to hoard their harvest or, worse, sell it abroad and the country would starve. He was hoping that the knowledge that the new notes were secured by mortgages, over the land of fellow farmers, would do the trick.

The Rentenmark was not currency, in the sense of legal tender, but it was an instrument of value. Schacht's stroke of genius was to ordain that 500 Rentenmarks could be converted into a government bond of 500 gold marks. As we have already noted, this was a blatant bluff. Germany had no gold reserves left, thus the gold mark was itself a purely notional concept. Even if someone had converted 500 Rentenmarks into a 500 gold mark bond and then presented this, the Reichsbank would have been unable to produce the necessary gold.

Yet the bluff worked, outrageous though it was. The mere thought that a paper instrument was at least pegged to *something*, made people turn to it in preference to their worthless banknotes. The farmers accepted the Rentenmark and released their harvests. It was not yet a return to normality, but it was at least an end to the madness. Schacht held his breath and his nerve. In 1924 a new mark, the Reichsmark, was introduced. For each one, a German had to exchange either one Rentenmark or one billion of the old banknotes.

Schacht had rescued Germany from the abyss, perhaps at the last possible moment, but inflation had inflicted some shocking body blows to the economy and society alike. Industry would struggle to recover, with appalling unemployment the inevitable cost. Much of the middle class was permanently impoverished, leaving bewilderment and a bitter taste in the mouth, both of which the Nazis would exploit all too efficiently. Politics polarised increasingly into left and right, with the middle ground steadily squeezed.

Fate had not finished with the German people, however. Even as the dark shadows of the Nazis began to fall across the land, a fresh hammer blow was struck, initially in far-off America, a hammer blow that would lay waste the strongest and most resilient economies in the world. Its effect on one still struggling to recover from a near-worthless currency, industrial stagnation and crippling unemployment may easily be imagined. It was a hammer blow whose aftermath would bring misery and suffering for years to hundreds of millions of people around the world. Almost its only saving grace was that it would prompt from John Maynard Keynes a fresh flurry of intellectual activity and economic insight.

In 1929 equity markets in America suddenly crashed, ushering in a period of several years that would go down in history as the economic equivalent of the Black Death. It would become known as the Great Depression.

# FOUR

# Markets and Crashes

1776 was a momentous year for various reasons. Everyone will instantly recognise it as the year in which the United States of America declared independence on 4 July. It also marked the publication of three of the most influential books ever written: Thomas Paine's *Common Sense*, Edward Gibbon's *Decline and Fall of the Roman Empire* and Adam Smith's *An Inquiry into the Nature and Causes of the Wealth of Nations*, usually abbreviated to just the last four words of the title.

*The Wealth of Nations* was a remarkable book and may be said to be the starting point of modern economic theory, although the word 'economics' would not be adopted until the early twentieth century. In it, Smith conducted a thorough review of how trade took place within a modern manufacturing society and, in particular, how markets operated.

His world view can be summed up as containing three main principles: division of labour, free trade and self-interest.

He recognised that the ongoing industrial revolution allowed one man to specialise in a specific task and that by combining these together great efficiencies could be achieved. He gave the famous example of how many different callings went into the manufacture of a woollen coat: shepherd, shearer, wool-sorter, carder, dyer, scribbler, spinner, weaver, fuller, tailor, etc., and that is before you even begin to think about the buttons that secure the coat, or the cotton thread which holds it together. For any one person to produce such a coat themself might be almost a lifetime's labour. Yet the division of labour enables a labourer to go out and buy a coat to keep him warm, paying for it with the value of his labour supplied in a different area.

Incidentally, it may surprise those who have come to see Smith as a darling of the right (Margaret Thatcher claimed Paine and Smith as two of her intellectual guides, while Ronald Reagan wore an Adam Smith tie) that he was a liberal and a humanist who recognised that the division of labour could reduce the working day to a depressing and monotonous grind in a noisy factory and agonised over how the impact of all this might be alleviated. The fact that he advocated compulsory worker education, paid for by the employer, rather than extra tea breaks or paid holidays, might however better explain his Thatcherite credentials.

Like the division of labour, he saw free trade as benefiting everybody. His example here was wine. If English people could buy wine in France more cheaply than manufacturing it themselves, then it benefited both them and the French wine trade for them to do so. The English could then in turn devote their energies to producing something else that they could manufacture more cheaply than the French.

This would in fact later become a major political issue when in 1815 the British government introduced the Corn Laws to keep the price of grain artificially high. David Ricardo, in many ways Smith's intellectual heir, would use *The Wealth of Nations* to argue unsuccessfully for their repeal. In no area has there been such a consistent mismatch between economic theory and political practice over the years. Today even that supposed champion of free market capitalism, the United States, maintains many trade tariffs to protect domestic producers. It has been argued, for example, that its lengthy campaign against sugar from Central and South America may have been instrumental in persuading many frustrated farmers to turn from growing sugar, which was legal but for which there was no market, to coca, which was illegal but for which there was a ready market.[1]

Sadly, governments around the world have largely ignored Smith's theories, even while paying lip service to them. Ronald Reagan kept import tariffs despite his Adam Smith tie. The effects have ranged from unfortunate, since intervening in what would otherwise be a free market to disrupt its normal workings must always come at some cost, to downright disastrous.

As we will see later, Attlee's Labour government, which took office in Britain after the Second World War, nationalised huge chunks

---

[1]  Todd Buchholz, *New Ideas from Dead Economists*, New York, Penguin, 1989.

of British industry as part of preparing a centrally planned economy along socialist lines, including both the railways and road haulage. A Conservative government subsequently privatised road haulage, but not the railways. A free market was thus restored for carriers by road, who were free to compete for business against each other on price. The railways, however, were *not* free to negotiate, having to quote a standard rate-card that was fixed by a Parliamentary committee. As a result, freight business flooded away from the railways and onto the roads at an enormous social cost that continues to be felt to this day. Road congestion was, and continues to be, far worse than it need have been, even given major motorway building programmes, while much of Britain's network of branch railway lines, which had been viable only because of the freight it carried, was subsequently closed down, leaving many areas, including some large towns, without any railway access at all.

A free market, said Smith and his successors, must always produce an equilibrium between supply and demand, which must by definition be a fair result. In practice, problems have arisen either where people are not prepared to accept a result that is fair but which they find for some reason unpalatable, or where government has been unable to resist an opportunity for raising revenue, or seeking electoral popularity, for example by import tariffs or indirect taxation. We are talking here about where markets do operate freely. Where they do not, then, says Smith, government should intervene to resolve the problem, but should undertake the bare minimum necessary to do so.

It is Smith's work on markets, then, for which he is best remembered and we have yet to see how the third element of his approach, self-interest, comes into play. Smith knew that human beings were selfish rather than altruistic. He knew that left to their own devices they would strive always for their own best interests. Very well, he said, let them. If you have both producers and consumers acting freely, then the market will effectively regulate itself. The counterbalancing effects of producers wanting to sell their goods at as high a price as possible, consumers wanting to buy at as low a price as possible, and producers having to compete against each other for the custom of the consumers will act as an 'invisible hand' that will always move the market price to what economists call equilibrium, the price that represents the perfect balance between supply and demand.

Smith's invisible hand is perhaps the most influential concept ever produced by an economist, and probably the most often quoted. Anytime you hear someone today saying 'just leave it to the market', it is Adam Smith's invisible hand to which they are referring. Free market theory flourishes, though its political adoption, or even acceptance, waxes and wanes. Its opponents point to the fact that he was writing in a pre-corporate age, when it was not necessary to be so vigilant as to the possibility of market abuse by dominant players, though to be fair Smith did expressly acknowledge that whenever producers were allowed to gather together, the first item on their agenda would be price fixing.

More fundamentally, they argue, free market proponents are trying to apply Smith's ideas to areas that they do not believe should be considered as 'markets' at all, such as health, welfare, education and even pollution. *Their* opponents would argue in turn that opening up such areas to market forces increases consumer choice (both as between competing suppliers as well as between different priorities for expenditure) and also focuses the attention of both suppliers (government) and consumers (the public) on the true cost of what is being offered, thus improving efficiency.

So what Smith had done was to lay the foundations for present theories on supply and demand, which would be developed further by later economists such as Alfred Marshall, teacher and mentor of John Maynard Keynes. It is, however, important that we should note a few reservations about Smith's theories, for they seemed unable to explain what would start unfolding in 1929.

As we have just seen, they did not envisage a situation where a market might be dominated by one or two very large players ('price makers' rather than 'price takers'). Even here, though, there is some leeway. Competition policy in the United States has tended to be concerned not with the size of a player's market share, but with what they do with it. They are relatively relaxed if a market is dominated by one or two large players so long as there is no evidence that they are making unfair use of it. Europe, by contrast, has tended to assume that dominance by market share will always lead inevitably to price abuse and thus has striven to prevent large market shares from occurring in the first place. This explains why some firms, such as Microsoft, have experienced very different treatment in Europe to that which they have encountered in America.

Nor did Smith's theories envisage a market that was no longer free as a result of government action. This might take the form of regulating prices in response to market dominance of some kind (many utility markets are regulated in this way, for example), or of import tariffs or sales taxes. The first form of intervention is likely to keep prices artificially low, while the second is likely to keep them artificially high.

Also, what Smith had in mind was a market for either finished goods, such as chocolate bars, or for raw materials, such as cocoa. In other words, a market in which the only players were suppliers and consumers. He does not seem to have dealt with the situation of investors entering the market to buy or sell purely for speculative purposes, nor with people who might buy to hoard rather than buy to consume. For some goods there may also be both a spot market and a futures market, with each price exerting an influence on the other. If the future price rises, then people will be more inclined to buy now, leading to upward pressure on the spot price, and vice versa.

Markets today are almost certainly more complex than the ones that Smith had available for study; certainly this applies to financial, rather than industrial, markets. Yet there was one final, glaring omission from Smith's work that left observers baffled by the events of 1929. Perhaps inevitably, it was left to Keynes to articulate it.

Smith assumed that market participants would always behave rationally, driven solely by their material self-interest. If this assumption should seem in any way suspect, it should be noted that it is one that is routinely used as part of the bedrock of what people persist in calling 'modern' portfolio theory, despite the fact that much of it evolved in the 1950s and 1960s. Deny the idea of the rational investor and much of modern portfolio theory ceases to have any validity. Keynes recognised this, though strangely Markowitz and the other pioneers of modern portfolio theory, who were writing two decades *after* Keynes, did not.

Keynes noted that markets were not rational, probably not ever, and certainly not all the time. First, he said, there was instability resulting from speculation. Second, there was instability resulting from what we would today call market sentiment, the prevailing levels of fear and greed, but which Keynes in a characteristically memorable phrase referred to as 'animal spirits'. He categorically rejected the view that it was possible to build mathematical models that could predict, or even significantly influence, future investor actions:

> [it is a] characteristic of human nature that a large proportion of our positive activities depend on spontaneous optimism rather than mathematical expectations... Our decisions to do something ... can only be taken as the result of animal spirits ... and not as the outcome of a weighted average of quantitative benefits multiplied by quantitative probabilities.[2]

After a brief recession in 1920–21, the US economy had shown strong growth from 1922 onwards; GDP, the standard measure of economic activity, rose by an average of 4.7% a year after inflation,[3] though the increase per capita was lower, showing that (particularly between 1922 and 1925) a large number of new immigrants were attracted to the United States. Incidentally, compared with the period before the First World War, these were now predominantly from Central and South America, rather than Eastern and Southern Europe.

Economic expansion was driven by two main developments: the spread of electricity and the spread of motor cars. As the electric grid

---

[2] John Maynard Keynes, *The General Theory of Employment, Interest and Money*, London, Macmillan, 1936.
[3] All numbers in this section are from eh.net's encyclopaedia and/or Historical Statistics of the United States.

spread rapidly across the country, new suburbs sprang up and factories were able to install the latest electrically operated plant and machinery. Between 1922 and 1929 the number of American homes with electricity grew dramatically. That this was largely an urban phenomenon is, however, shown by the fact that the comparable figure for farm dwellings remained very low. At the same time, an ongoing shift from coal to natural gas, oil and hydro plants actually drove down the cost of electricity.

The rapidly expanding availability of motor cars prompted not just increased production within the motor industry, but the wholescale building of new, metalled roads linking America's towns. So important a part did the motor industry play in the American economy that when Ford closed its plants for six months for retooling in 1927 to switch manufacturing from the Model T to the Model A, it badly impacted the economy as a whole.

Technical developments and growing consumer purchasing power also made this the dawn of the modern age of media and communication. By 1929 40% of households had a radio and 4.5 million radios a year were being manufactured. In Britain, by contrast, most families still had neither a radio nor a telephone. Even as late as 1971 nearly a third of British homes were without a telephone.[4]

However, this economic good fortune, which understandably led to the decade becoming known in America as the Roaring Twenties, was not shared elsewhere in the world. During this period, unemployment in America was generally around or below 5% and, given illness, disability and a steady growth in the labour force as a result of immigration, this is usually reckoned a period of nearly full employment. Britain, by contrast, had over one million men out of work throughout the 1920s.

Rather than financing the war by borrowing or printing money as Germany had done, or largely with taxes as France had done, Britain had resorted to selling off many of her extensive foreign assets. This left her needing to invest heavily to re-enter overseas markets. As an

---

[4] localhistories.org

added burden, in a sad foreshadowing of the next war, about 40% of Britain's merchant fleet, at that time the biggest in the world, had been lost to U-boat attacks. This gave rise to a need for yet more investment and problems with exports while shipping was replaced.

At the same time, overseas markets for basic goods such as coal, iron and steel, which had formed much of Britain's pre-war exports, had fallen off and Britain's elderly factories struggled to compete with brand-new American plants in producing the sophisticated finished goods for which there was now so much global demand, cars and radios being but two obvious examples.

This was in part due to the traditional attitude of British manufacturing, enshrined in 'craft' trade unions, that individual workers' skills must be used and protected, restricting work in certain areas to those who had served time under an existing craftsman, and more or less forcing factories to adopt batch production rather than, as in America, the much more cost-efficient continuous process (the production line, such as had been pioneered by Ford before the war). Ironically, though, in the most vital craft of all, the cutting of the jigs and dies needed for machine tools actually to produce something, Britain lagged woefully behind both America and Germany, and would continue to do so. British rearmament in the 1930s would be badly hampered by the lack of these specialist items and the need to use scarce foreign currency to source them from abroad as well as by batch production, which hampered both production output and standardisation. The fact that both of these problems had first become apparent in 1914 is sad evidence of British resistance to change.

Things were harmed further when Winston Churchill, as Chancellor of the Exchequer, reintroduced sterling to the Gold Standard in 1925, but pegged to the pre-war rate of the pound against the dollar, which in retrospect can be seen to have been much higher than the relative economic strength of the two countries now warranted. With their products now being priced expensively in export markets, British manufacturers struggled to compete. Desperately trying to lower their cost base, they cut wages, leading to much hardship and the General Strike of 1926.

So, the British economy can be said to have gone into the doldrums in 1918, certainly if measured by GDP per capita,[5] and to have remained in them until very shortly before the next war. What economic improvement there was in the 1930s would be led partly by rearmament and partly by the growth of the motor car, a decade later than in America.

Then one day in October 1929 the roof fell in. For some days the American stock market on Wall Street had been showing increasing volatility (the extent to which prices move up or down), as well as increasing deal volumes (in other words, more and more shares were being bought and sold each day). Suddenly, on what would become known as 'Black Thursday', 24 October, the market crashed, losing 11% of its value in one day. In an effort to stabilise the market, representatives of both the Exchange and various banks agreed deliberately to place 'buy' orders in various blue-chip stocks at prices above their current trading levels.

This is an interesting example of how people are prepared to 'let the market take care of it' when they like the results, but not when they find the results disagreeable or even alarming. Margaret Thatcher famously declared 'you can't buck the market', but many politicians and regulators have ignored her advice, usually at great cost, and rarely to themselves.

Over the weekend, investors had a chance to read their newspapers, reflect on what had been done and doubtless wonder if they really wanted to hold stocks in what was probably now a false market, a market that was no longer composed just of buyers and sellers, but also contained market manipulators, people who were attempting to be price makers, rather than price takers.

Their response was unanimous: sell. On Black Monday the market lost 13% and on, yes you've guessed it, Black Tuesday it lost another 12%. The trading volumes on Black Tuesday established a record that would stand for forty years. During the day another large group of investors, headed by no less than the Rockefellers, attempted to drive

---

[5] *A Century of Change*, House of Commons research paper 99/111, December 1999.

prices up but to no avail. In just two days, 30 billion dollars had been wiped off the value of shares (stocks). Other markets around the world saw similar falls. Stockbrokers and investors who had been ruined overnight jumped to their deaths from skyscrapers. Perhaps ironically, one prominent victim (though not a suicide) was Winston Churchill, who with characteristic but misguided combativeness, decided to buy while everyone else was selling. Another was John Maynard Keynes who, unlike Churchill, would go on to rebuild his fortune.

Incidentally, in more recent years, a branch of economic thought known as the rational expectations school has been gaining ground. Though originally put forward in the 1960s, it only really became influential a decade or so later, when considered by the likes of Nobel Prize winner Robert Lucas Jr, one of the many leading economists to have been based at the University of Chicago.

The particular piece of rational expectations thinking that we need to examine is called the efficient-market hypothesis. This says that the price of any publicly traded instrument such as a stock (share) or a bond already has factored into it all the relevant information known to the market. Thus, if interest rates rise, but this has been anticipated for some time, then bond prices will not change on the day the rate rise is announced because the market will have been already expecting the announcement and taking it into account for some time when deciding at what price to buy and sell such bonds.

Thus it is not possible for the value of a stock to be different from its market price unless there is some piece of relevant information out there that is unknown to the market, and which therefore comes as a surprise when it is announced.

This is a compelling argument when viewing any individual stock, but seems inconsistent with what we have just witnessed happening in 1929. After all, if a stock can only be overvalued if there is some unknown information in existence, then its price can only fall if the information is suddenly announced and takes the market by surprise. For a stock market as a whole to fall, and go on falling, not just for one day but for days, weeks or even months, then for the efficient-market hypothesis to be valid, surprise information about every single stock quoted on the Exchange would have to come to light on a daily basis for a protracted period and this is clearly not a feasible possibility.

Proponents of the rational expectation approach would doubtless argue that the market price incorporates not just all known and anticipated information, but also people's *expectations*. These could change, even if the circumstances of the stock did not. For example, if stock market prices fell rapidly then investors' expectations of the riskiness of holding stocks relative to holding, say, gold or bonds or real estate might change, prompting them to expect a higher return to compensate them for this extra risk, and the only way this higher return could be achieved would be by paying a lower price for the stock in the first place.

Yet one of the intellectual attractions of economics as a field of study compared to, say, finance, is that it defies rigid categorisation into black and white. Instead, one is forced to recognise only shades of grey and conflicting alternatives, hence Harry Truman's quest for a one-armed economist. Yes, on the one hand risk and return expectations might change in response to a sudden and unexpected fall in prices, but on the other hand why should such a sudden and unexpected fall occur in the first place, if the efficient-market hypothesis holds true?

Perhaps what has happened here is that a good principle has been turned into a bad rule by being stretched beyond its natural span. The idea that the market price of a stock must incorporate all known and anticipated relevant information seems both intellectually attractive and consistent with actual experience. Certainly in today's highly regulated and information-efficient markets, opportunities for arbitrage (an opportunity to benefit from incorrect or inefficient pricing) seem to be rare, limited in scope and short in duration.

However, perhaps this holds true only to the extent of the way the price of the stock moves relative to the market as a whole. When it comes to the way in which that whole market moves, what the financial community calls market beta, then Keynes's animal spirits seem to provide at least some of the explanation. Research studies by academics pursuing the study of behavioural finance have revealed that, when it comes to making investment decisions and processing financial data, human beings do so subject to what are called cognitive biases, which hamper our ability to act rationally. Thus, as Keynes divined, markets are driven by buy and sell decisions made by human beings, and logic is only partly responsible for making those decisions. Perception and emotion also play a part.

The animal spirits roamed Wall Street for many years. Not until 1955 would the Dow Jones index regain its pre-Crash peak, and this takes no account of inflation during the intervening period. It is arguable that had you invested at the peak of the market in 1929, then you might have had to wait until the 1990s to get back your starting capital in real terms.

Since it may be useful later to attempt to compare and contrast the circumstances of the Wall Street Crash of 1929 with those of subsequent financial crises, let us take a closer look at some of the factors that may have played a part.

The most obvious thing to note is that there had been a huge and sustained rise in asset values, in this case stock prices, to levels well beyond historic comparison or common sense evaluation. The p/e (price to earnings) ratio of the market peaked at 32.6 in September 1929. It would not achieve these levels again until the late 1990s, peaking in 2001 just before another market crash.

The p/e index is a useful measure to watch out for and can be obtained for an individual stock, a market sector or, as here, for the market as a whole. It measures the number of times you would have to multiply the most recent earnings in order to arrive at the market price. To put these figures in context, if you assume that the value of a stock is represented by the present value of its future dividend streams, and that a company will pay out half its earnings each year by way of dividends, then at a p/e ratio of 31 you would have to wait sixty-two years just to get back your purchase price. That is without considering inflation. If inflation were to run at 3% a year, then believe it or not it would take more than 200 years to get your money back. That is before you even start to think about making a profit.

Of course this is an artificial calculation. In practice, earnings are likely to grow over time rather than stay the same. Also (another point that is ignored by much of financial theory), most investors buy equities in the hope of capital gain at least as much as in the expectation of income. Yet it shows just what exaggerated ambitions are implicit in being prepared to pay a p/e ratio of 31. Hardly 'rational expectations'!

We know that in the late 1990s stock prices were driven higher on a tidal wave of exuberance and optimism based on rapid technological progress, which prompted investors to talk of 'a new paradigm' and to reject traditional valuation methods such as p/e ratios as hopelessly outdated. What happened in the 1920s?

The answer is debt. Investors were borrowing money to buy shares, either directly from banks or indirectly from brokers by means of margin trading, under which clients were required to deposit only part of the value of a trade. By October 1929 more money had been lent by US banks than the value of all the US dollars then in circulation. When markets collapsed, investors were unable to repay their bank loans or settle their margin calls. About 4,000 American banks and other lenders would go bust in the course of the next few years.

The American Dream, typified by the Roaring Twenties, was over. The long nightmare of the Great Depression was just beginning.

# FIVE

# Keynes and the Great Depression

The Wall Street Crash seems to most historians to have flowed seam-lessly into the Great Depression. This may be partly because much economic writing is US-centric. In America, as we have seen, things seemed to be not just alright but positively booming before the autumn of 1929, and pretty horrible thereafter. To regard the Crash as the cause of the Depression may therefore have seemed a natural conclusion to draw, though it is hardly a scientific one. It disregards the constant warning which runs through universities worldwide: 'cor-relation is not causation'. Just because the Crash occurred at what appeared to be the onset of the Depression does not necessarily mean that the one caused the other. They may simply have coincided.

This raises a very important issue and, since it underlies much of what we will be discussing in this book, it is worth exploring in a little more detail before we continue with the historical narrative.

Economists are fond of plotting two sets of related data and then drawing conclusions from the way in which they are seen to move over time relative to each other. If they tend to get bigger or smaller at the same time as each other, they are said to be correlated, or to have high correlation. If they seem to move in opposite directions, they are said to be negatively correlated. If there is no apparent pattern to be discerned at all, then they are said to be uncorrelated. To be fair, not only economists but also those in many other disciplines, such as finance and marketing, do exactly the same.

Given the rush of excitement when you finally find an apparent pattern after perhaps months of trying, it is tempting to assume that you have stumbled on something hugely significant, a major discovery that the whole world is waiting for you to unveil as modestly as you are able, the Nobel Prize committee watching approvingly from the wings. Tempting, but very dangerous, hence the warning. Yes, you may well have stumbled upon a causative relationship, but there are three other separate scenarios that you need to consider and, if possible, test before you start writing up your findings.

First, the two data sets may bear no real relation to each other at all, but be purely coincidental; two similar patterns that are produced at the same time quite by chance. For example, if it emerged that a recent increase in the consumption of ice cream in a particular neighbourhood was seen to coincide with an increase in traffic levels in the same area, then if we knew nothing about ice cream or traffic we may be tempted to suggest a causal connection. Of course, it is always possible that part of the increase in traffic has taken the form of the introduction of ice cream vans selling ice cream at the roadside, but this is something we would have to research further; we could not just assume it to be the case.

Second, we would have to consider the possibility of a third, unknown, variable that might be operating on the other two. For example, if our neighbourhood lay on the route to a beach or swimming pool, then a period of fine weather could cause both ice cream consumption and traffic density to increase, yet neither would be causing the other; they would both be consequences of the fine weather. This situation is probably more dangerous from an intellectual point of view than the first, since a period of bad weather would likewise cause both observations to *decrease* simultaneously, thus strengthening the impression that there should be a causal connection between them.

Third, there is the problem of reverse causation. Even if there is indeed a causal link between two sets of observations, which is causing which? Which is the cause and which is the outcome? Suppose that we duly conducted our further research and found that much of the increased traffic was indeed comprised of ice cream vans. We might quite understandably sit back with a contented sigh, having now proved that the increase in ice cream consumption was indeed caused by an increase in traffic levels and, specifically, by an increase in the number of circulating ice cream vans. Yet is it not also possible that extra ice cream vans are being attracted to the area by higher observed demand for ice cream?

This may seem a simple problem, but it represents one of the most frequent stumbling blocks to economic research and analysis. Two real-life examples will suffice, though once we are aware of this particular landmine we will recognise people thoughtlessly stepping on it on almost a daily basis.

In the nineteenth century it was seriously suggested in some quarters that economic cycles were caused by sunspots, since the distance between these was calculated at almost exactly ten and a half years, which was exactly the same interval observed for periods of boom and bust. Lest this seem immediately unbelievable, it should be noted that even two centuries later there are those who believe stock market cycles are affected by, and can be explained by or predicted using, astrology.

This was a classic example of mistaking correlation for causation. Where no possible reason for causation can be logically advanced, then it must be assumed that what you are looking at is coincidence, pure and simple. Sadly, even this proved not to be the case. It turned out that the measurement and observation of sunspots had been incorrect, and should really have shown a result of about eleven years. This difference, though seemingly insignificant, was enough to destroy the apparent correlation after only a couple of iterations. Thus the economic significance of sunspots faded into the history of an era in which it was believed that the shape of your skull could determine your intelligence and personality, that deaths from septicaemia in childbirth could not be reduced by doctors washing their hands and that it could be fatal for a woman to take a hot bath at certain times in her menstrual cycle.

More recently, and as already noted in a previous chapter, it seemed to become the established party line among politicians and central bankers sometime around 2011 that we could safely ignore inflation since it was being caused by rising commodity prices. Yet wasn't it just faintly possible that rising commodity prices were being caused by inflation? Central bankers and finance ministers were perhaps fortunate that nobody in their respective audiences seemed to have heard of reverse causation.

The notion that the Wall Street Crash caused the Great Depression has the status of an established truth in America and, given the circumstances of the domestic environment, one that is difficult to challenge. However, as so often, American writers seem to deal with what is happening elsewhere in the world largely by ignoring it. As we have already seen, for example, Britain had been stagnating since the end of the First World War.

Let us deliberately avoid the use of the word 'recession', since this has a precise meaning for economists and there were certainly times between the two world wars when British GDP increased year on year. However, if we look at GDP per capita, perhaps a more meaningful measure, it was roughly the same in 1938 as it had been in 1918.[1] Thus, across the twenty-year period as a whole, Britain had struggled to make any real progress. As an added indicator of just how bad things really were, unemployment rose from close to nothing before the First World War to 16% by 1921, would peak at more than 20% a few years later and would drop to less than 5% only just before the next war, with the advent of rearmament.[2] So, whatever terminology one chooses to use, it is quite clear that the British economy had already been in terrible trouble for a decade before the Crash and would remain in similar trouble for most of the next decade as well. Hardly the best preparation for a new and lengthy global conflict that would have tested even a more robust economy to destruction.

One of the most worrying things about the Great Depression was that it appeared to fly in the face of a lot of what has since become known as classical economic theory, which we might describe as the theory which had seemed largely to explain things during the nineteenth century.

As we have already seen, classical theory held that any market left to its own devices would automatically find its point of natural equilibrium, the price at which supply perfectly balanced demand. The supply of labour by members of the public was seen as a market just as much as the market for, say, steel, or indeed ice cream. If workers

---

[1] House of Commons Research Paper 99/111.
[2] Ibid.

asked too much for their services, then there would come a point when it was no longer profitable for factories to produce, and so the workers would be turned away and the factory closed down or put to other uses. If the factory owners offered too little, then there would come a point when the workers could no longer feed their families and would leave to seek work either in another factory or even in a different industry altogether. Thus there must logically be a price point for wages at which maximum production can be balanced by maximum employment.

The classical model also envisaged full employment and it was a central belief that, if the economy was working to its full efficiency, then full employment could be achieved. It may be worth noting at this stage that the phrase 'full employment' can be misleading. There will at any time be some people looking for work even under the classical model. For example, people will be constantly leaving school or university and unless they have a job to start on the very next day they will fall into the unemployment statistics. So will those looking to return from sickness or injury and those who may have moved to a new geographic area. This unemployment caused by the time lag between people looking for a job and starting it is called frictional unemployment and is recognised to be a normal part of the system, even if it is functioning properly. Thus, in the US in the Roaring Twenties, there was effectively full employment despite the statistics. What the figures were mostly representing was the time lag between immigrants arriving in the country, or students leaving school or college, and them beginning employment.

The ideas that the labour market left to its own devices would operate at full efficiency, and that an economy operating at full efficiency would generate full employment were central to the classical view. Thus if unemployment was present, then this could only be because the labour market was not operating properly, either at national or local level. Local efficiencies would be corrected in time by labour mobility. In Britain during the nineteenth century and in the US during the early twentieth, large numbers of workers moved from the land to the cities in search of employment. Constant improvements in farming technology meant that, not only was agricultural production not impaired, but it actually rose significantly. Economists pointed to the natural workings of the labour and production markets in both farming and manufacture, and rubbed their hands contentedly.

There is a final, third, element that we need to understand properly to round out the classical model. This is something that became known as Say's law, formulated by the Frenchman Jean-Baptiste Say as early as 1803. Say's law effectively states that production naturally produces its own demand. In order for a factory to produce goods, it must employ workers and pay them wages. Those workers will then go out and spend their wages on the products of this factory and other factories, all of which are employing other workers. Thus the factories are constantly pushing out into the economy the money, in the form of wages, that will be used to purchase their own goods. Under Say's law any disturbance to this cosy system can only be caused by temporary overproduction of one good relative to another, something that will promptly be corrected as a simple matter of industrial management.

It took Keynes to point out the obvious. Say's law said that prolonged recessions were impossible. Yet Britain and most of the world were in a prolonged recession. Therefore Say's law could not possibly be true. Ironically, other people would in due course adopt a similar brutally effective approach to Keynesian thought, but let us not get ahead of ourselves.

If the classical model had ever been valid, Keynes argued in his great work, *The General Theory of Employment, Interest and Money* (understandably usually referred to only by the first three words),[3] then it was no longer so, since it modelled a world that had passed away almost unnoticed. It had been based upon observation of factors that may have occurred in a certain way in the nineteenth century, but now occurred differently. There may have been elements of it that still held true, at least in part, but as a total worldview it had to be abandoned.

---

[3] John Maynard Keynes, *The General Theory of Employment, Interest and Money*, London, Macmillan, 1936.

Keynes began his revision of the system by examining unemployment. He cites *The Theory of Employment*[4] by his friend Arthur Pigou, who despite his name was an Englishman, as setting out the classical view. Frictional unemployment could be reduced only by making the unemployment and employment processes more efficient, by reducing the marginal cost to the manufacturer of employing one more worker or by increasing the marginal output of that one extra worker. In addition to frictional unemployment there was also voluntary unemployment, representing people who chose not to work despite employers offering a fair wage (because the labour market always found its natural point of equilibrium).

Incidentally, this latter type of unemployment has always been particularly vilified in the United States, an attitude that exists to this day and which can represent one of the main cultural differences between Americans and Europeans. Should European entrepreneurs make enough money on which to live comfortably for the rest of their lives, they tend to retire, probably to sip rosé du Provence in the south of France. When American entrepreneurs find themselves in the same situation, they tend to carry on working since they rate sitting idly in the shade almost as sinful as sipping rosé du Provence. It might be said that Europeans work to live whereas Americans live to work.

Having stated his friend's views, Keynes proceeded to demolish them. It was not very plausible to assert that current unemployment in the United States:

> was due either to labour obstinately refusing to accept a reduction of money-wages, or to its obstinately demanding a real wage beyond what the productivity of the economic machine was capable of furnishing. Wide variations are experienced in the volume of employment without any apparent change either in the minimum real demands of labour or in its productivity. Labour is not more truculent in the depression than in the boom – far from it. Nor is its physical productivity less.

---

[4] Arthur Pigou, *Theory of Employment*, London, Macmillan, 1933.

These facts from experience are a prima facie ground for ques‐
tioning the adequacy of the classical analysis.[5]

Incidentally, the explicit reference to the United States was almost
certainly deliberate. In Great Britain, the General Strike of 1926 was
still a bitter memory on all sides.

As Keynes so eloquently put it, the classical model was no longer
'adequate'. With regard to unemployment, it posits that this can only
be either frictional or voluntary but the reality, says Keynes, is that
much unemployment may actually be involuntary, representing people
who want to work but are unable to do so because there simply is not
enough supply of jobs to go round. If full employment had ever been a
valid concept, it was now nothing more than a myth. Unemployment
reached 25% in America and even more in other parts of the world.

Exploding this myth caused fatal collateral damage to the rest of
the system. It had assumed that the labour market would find its nat‐
ural point of equilibrium at the maximum wage compatible with
full employment. In reality it had found a wage point far below full
employment. It was also evident that manufacturers had not been
nearly as ruthless as the operation of a free market would assume. As
Keynes pointed out, wage rates should sink to a point below which
there would be no more potential employees willing to work, whereas
in fact there were many potential employees willing to work even *at*
the current rate. (As we will see when we consider Karl Marx, this was
to prove yet another area in which reality stubbornly refused to act in
conformity with his theories.)

Keynes argued that economists and politicians should plan for a
world that included involuntary unemployment. Instead of clinging
to the belief that employment was driven by production, which was
in turn driven in an unending circle by employment, as under Say's
law, so that a properly functioning economy would always generate
full employment, a grimmer but more realistic view was required.
Employment was indeed driven by production, but production was

---

[5] Keynes, op. cit.

driven by what he called aggregate demand, and so unemployment was driven ultimately not by imperfections or inefficiencies in the labour market, but by lack of demand for goods and services. This may seem a fairly obvious point to a modern audience, but at the time it was revolutionary. It was to form the cornerstone of what would become known as Keynesian economics, a school of thought that would dominate global thinking for nearly half a century.

We will turn shortly to the remedy that he proposed, based on his new approach, for insufficient demand. However, let us first examine another aspect of Smith's theory of markets that is highly relevant to what occurred as the recession gathered pace in the USA.

As we have seen, Smith's disciple, Ricardo, argued vigorously for free trade and this had become, by and large, a rallying cry of the classical economists. Free trade, they said, made everyone better off. For the opponents of free trade, this seemed a strange assertion. Suppose that Ruritanian factories produced cars more expensively than did more efficient Freedonian ones, and thus had to sell them at a higher price? Surely customers in Ruritania would simply buy Freedonian cars rather than Ruritanian ones, leaving the Ruritanian manufacturers much worse off and, indeed, threatened with bankruptcy? In these circumstances the natural reaction of those Ruritanian car manufacturers would be to lobby their government to introduce import tariffs on Freedonian cars, thus ensuring that they had to be sold at the same price as home-produced ones. In countries where an industry is still growing, opponents of free trade would argue, there is surely a case for protection, while the tender child is allowed to grow up unmolested. This is known as the 'infant industry' argument. Ricardo, however, would not agree.

Bad move, says Ricardo. For example, Freedonia might have what is called a comparative advantage in cars, but Ruritania might enjoy one in tractors. Suppose that each Freedonian car costs 4 units of production whereas each Ruritanian one costs 5, but that for tractors the costs are 14 and 12, respectively. Now if each country devotes its production equally to both cars and tractors, then for each thousand units of production Freedonia will produce 125 cars and about 36 tractors, whereas Ruritania will produce 120 cars and about 42 tractors. That's a total of 225 cars and 78 tractors.

Suppose now that each does what it is best at. Freedonia manufactures only cars, producing 250, while Ruritania produces only tractors, manufacturing about 83. If they trade freely amongst themselves they will actually have more goods available that can either be sold more cheaply, or generate more profit. If, on the other hand, they resort to trade tariffs (for Freedonia will surely retaliate by imposing a tariff on Ruritanian tractors), then the result is both less production and higher prices.

Of course this approach can be argued to be somewhat simplistic, particularly in the modern industrialised world. For example, it assumes that Ruritania's car factories are less efficient while its tractor factories are more so. If not, then the only way this equation can work out is if Ruritanian workers are prepared to labour many more hours for the same wages, which may or may not be the case. Even then, it assumes that total demand is at least as great as the combined production of both countries. Finally, perhaps most unrealistically of all, it assumes that left to their own devices governments would eschew tariffs as an obstacle to free trade, rather than welcoming them as a source of both income and domestic political popularity. Thus, while Ricardo remains revered by economists, his pronouncements on free trade are now treated with a certain degree of caution. Even the influential American economist Greg Mankiw is careful to frame the appropriate one of his famed Ten Principles: 'trade *can* make everyone better off', which is really saying nothing meaningful at all. Truman would probably have had one of his arms chopped off by executive order.

Whatever the case, domestic political popularity prevailed and in 1930 the American government made what was already a dire situation very much worse by enacting the Smoot–Hawley Tariff Act, which on average doubled defensive tariffs against various imports. Other countries promptly responded in kind.

America's exports at this time were small compared to the proportion of the economy that they would assume after the Second World War and largely confined to agricultural produce, but their falling off must have had significant impact on the economy even so. Between 1929 and 1933 American exports fell by half in value and two-thirds in volume.

This slowdown in agricultural demand speeded the process of migration from the land to the towns. Many farmers were also destroyed by a prolonged drought which produced what became known as the Dust Bowl, memorably portrayed by John Steinbeck in *The Grapes of Wrath*. Small farmers and the migrant workers who travelled from harvest to harvest were particularly badly hit. Earth turned to dust and simply blew away, covering some East Coast cities in a black cloud, which led to them christening the decade 'The Dirty Thirties'. Many farmers defaulted on their loans, which brought down yet more banks.

The effect was bad enough in America but in other countries more dependent on foreign trade, including Britain, proved much worse. At the very time when government policy should have been looking to promote international trade by cutting or removing tariffs, instead it became focused on imposing or increasing them. It is now generally accepted that in this particular case Mankiw's principle would indeed have held true and that import tariffs both worsened and prolonged the Great Depression.

According to League of Nations statistics from the time, global industrial production increased between 1929 and 1937 by nearly 20%, yet the volume of world trade actually declined during the same period, with British exports falling by 17%.[6] These figures clearly demonstrate that international trade had been choked off when it should have been rising naturally. Further figures from the same source show that Britain's problems had indeed been building for some time. For the period 1913 to 1929 world trade grew by 27%, yet British exports fell by over 13%. Clearly Britain's manufacturing and exporting advantage, which she had held prior to the First World War in the lingering afterglow of her period as the workshop of the world had gone for good, and she had in fact embarked upon a long and steady

---

[6] Alfred Kahn, 'The British Balance of Payments and Problems of Domestic Policy', *Quarterly Journal of Economics*, Volume 61, May 1947, pp. 368–396.

period of decline that persisted, as we have already seen, for more or less the whole of the interwar period.

It was in this unpromising situation that, as we have just seen, Keynes sat down to analyse what had caused the current global economic ills and decide what remedy to prescribe for their relief. The ideas that he formulated would come to dominate the politics of the post-war world, being pursued unquestioningly for the first three decades, and less assuredly but with increasing desperation thereafter. Even today we live not just in their shadow, but in their slipstream.

Back in the recession-ravaged 1930s, however, everything looked very different.

# SIX

# Keynes's General Theory

As we have seen, by the time Black Thursday heralded the end of the Roaring Twenties in America, the British economy had already been languishing in the doldrums for more than ten years. By 1930 there were about two and a half million people out of work (about 12% of the workforce), and the effect of this was worsened by it being uneven. Some shipbuilding centres in Scotland and the north-east became virtual ghost towns.

There were hunger marches on London from all over Britain, organised by the trade unions, in 1929, 1930 and 1932. The last was the biggest of the lot and polarised public opinion when it arrived in London. While it attracted mass support, it was attacked in the newspapers, many of whose owners were close to Stanley Baldwin's Conservative government, as a threat to public order. Its supporters were shabbily treated when their petition, said to contain one million signatures, disappeared in mysterious circumstances on its way to the House of Commons, and there were then indeed serious disturbances. Ronald Kidd, already a veteran civil rights campaigner in his early thirties, was appalled at the treatment of protestors by the police (questions were later asked in Parliament of the Home Secretary, Sir John Gilmour) and would found the Council for Civil Liberty in 1934, largely as a result of the 1932 march. Lest it be thought that this was a cranky fringe organisation, its early members included Clement Attlee, H.G. Wells, J.B. Priestley, Aldous Huxley and Bertrand Russell, while its president was none less than E.M. Forster.

To be fair, the government did what it could, but funds were tight and beyond founding some work camps there was little real response. Further marches would follow in 1934 and 1936, the latter being the famous Jarrow march. Even when recovery did begin to spark, this was confined mostly to the Midlands and south-east, as it was largely a result of the growth of demand for motor cars, which America had witnessed a decade earlier. Most of the areas from which the hunger marchers had come had to wait until the latter part of the decade, as orders for new Royal Navy vessels slowly brought slumbering shipyards back to life.

Passing through a colliery town in south Wales as late as 1936, Edward VIII was approached respectfully by a former soldier and asked if he would inspect a group of veterans of the First World War, who drew themselves to attention as he approached. All of them had survived the horrors of the trenches; many had medals pinned on their shabby clothes. All of them were long-term unemployed. Visibly moved, the King turned away and, looking at the deserted colliery buildings, said 'these works brought these people here. Something must be done to get them at work again.' Reported by the press inevitably with the simple headline 'Something must be done', the episode angered the government, who felt that the King had trespassed on political ground, but gathered a great deal of public sympathy.

It is of course one of the fascinating 'what ifs' of history to wonder what might have happened had Britain stimulated her economy, for example with a naval building programme, in the early 1930s, not least because she would begin the Second World War in 1939 almost totally unequipped to fight the Battle of the Atlantic. Yet such speculation is futile. There appeared no immediate prospect of war even after Hitler took power in Germany in 1933 (in fact, Italy seemed a more immediate enemy when the Abyssinian Crisis broke at the beginning of 1935) and after the First World War Britain enjoyed a lengthy peace dividend, with even the pugnacious Winston Churchill initially espousing the cause of disarmament. In any event, such a rearmament programme would have been very difficult diplomatically as Britain had agreed voluntarily to limit the size of the Royal Navy by signing the Washington Naval Treaty in 1922 and the subsequent Treaties of London in 1930 and 1936 (the Japanese cannily noted that aircraft carriers were not included and set off down the path that would lead inevitably to Pearl Harbor).

Even leaving aside political and strategic considerations, however, there simply would not have been the money available. In recessionary times, government budgets are hit by a 'double whammy': as unemployment rises, tax receipts fall but welfare payments rise and this is exactly what happened to Britain's finances between the wars. Shelling out for a few battleships, or even a few frigates, was simply out of the question.

Such parsimony may seem hard to understand to modern readers reared at least in part under the economic mismanagement of New Labour. Why not just borrow a few more billions? After all, what is debt for but to buy things which you want but cannot afford?

The answer is that during the 1930s governments still believed in balanced budgets. Indeed, it would have been regarded as the height of folly *not* to balance the budget. Keynes himself called any period of budget deficit 'abnormal spending'.[1]

This is a crucially important point, frequently overlooked by present-day politicians eager to pick out the bits of a theory that they like but leave the rest behind. For it was to represent a vital building block in what was to become known as Keynesian economics, a system of thought that would revolutionise the way in which people looked at the world. They key word here is 'system'. Keynes did not intend parts of his thinking to be applied in isolation while the rest of it, the less politically convenient part, was ignored. Let us probe this system a little more deeply.

We have already seen how Keynes rejected Say's law, pointing out that its principle was simply inconsistent with what was happening in real life (sadly, such robust common sense has not always been applied to more recent principles of financial theory). He also rejected the notion that the labour market would always find its point of equilibrium at the market price of full employment. Surely what the present recession demonstrated, he said, was that there could be large numbers of people willing to work at almost any price and yet unable to find a job. Indeed, the hunger marches in the UK demonstrated that, far from withdrawing their labour and moving on when wages fell to too low a level, workers were forced to carry on working, deeply

---

[1] *General Theory*, op. cit.

resenting what they saw as immoral wage cuts. The perfect market theory assumes that everyone has a choice; in a deep recession of the type of the Great Depression, choice disappears.

This might not seem a revolutionary thought today, but it was at the time. What many economists of the time thought was that the labour market had stopped working properly and thus was not producing the desired result. At first sight, this seems an attractive view. Market theory assumes that every market participant is a 'price taker', able to choose freely whether to deal, whether as a buyer or as a seller, at a particular price. Those decisions will drive the price up or down until the equilibrium point is reached at which all demand has been satisfied. Where there is a huge excess of demand for jobs over the supply of available employment, then employers can become 'price makers', particularly if they act in concert with each other, pushing wages down progressively on a 'take it or leave it' basis.

Yet there are problems with such a view. First, as we have already seen, this is not in fact what happened, since at any time there were unemployed workers willing to take work even below the current market price. The demand for jobs had become what economists call price inelastic, at least relative to pre-recessionary times. Where demand is price inelastic it means that it changes little in response to price changes. This is exactly why governments are rightly concerned to regulate the price of essential utilities such as water, electricity and gas. A man dying of thirst will be prepared to pay almost anything for a glass of water.

Second, the labour market does not operate in a vacuum. This truth had been disguised in the period before the First World War since there had generally been an excess of demand over supply for what Britain's factories were producing. Though Britain had already been overtaken by both America and Germany, she was still in the forefront of the relatively few industrialised nations exporting to a largely pre-industrialised world. Her international trading network, though set shortly to decline significantly, was still routing a disproportionate share of world trade to the small island in the Atlantic Ocean. Thus, full demand generally led to full employment. After the First World War this cosy state of affairs ceased to exist, as we have already seen.

What Keynes recognised was that employment was dependent upon output and that output was in turn dependent upon demand, on what he called aggregate demand. Thus, long periods of low aggregate demand would inevitably also be long periods of high unemployment. The phrase 'aggregate demand' has come to have a somewhat specialist meaning that is, in addition, the subject of some argument among economists but let us be content for our purposes with thinking of it as the total demand for all the products and services supplied within a nation.

Incidentally, the words 'within a nation' have been chosen deliberately because the basic Keynesian model takes little account of overseas trade, at least directly. In *The General Theory*,[2] he even tacitly admits that he is not sure how to treat this, though he seems to think it generally benign and that any country will eventually reap some unspecified indirect reward from its people buying imported goods from foreign producers. At the time this probably did not matter too much in practical terms since, as already noted, most developed economies were geared heavily towards domestic trade, relative to our modern, globalised world where imports are commonplace.

However, this would have two important consequences. The first, to which we will shortly return, was that it would colour his thinking on savings and investment. The second was that, as Britain's predicament worsened after the Second World War, it would help to mask the extent to which the basic Keynesian model was becoming unrepresentative of the modern world.

We now have the basic theory in place to be able properly to consider the two main planks of Keynesian thought: the treatment of interest-rate changes (monetary policy, at least in part) and the treatment of government borrowing and spending (fiscal policy).

Remember that Keynes largely ignored the effect of overseas trade. Thus, his model was essentially a hermetically sealed package, with no possibility of leakage in or out. Households were both the suppliers and customers of businesses (what economists call 'firms'). Individual

---

[2] For example, see p. 120 of the 1936 edition.

households supply their labour to firms for money (wages) and then in turn spend their wages on consumption, the purchase of goods and services from firms. So far, so good. Surely this is exactly what Say had in mind? If all capital flows naturally in this circular way, then supply must indeed produce its own supply.

If it did, yes, but it does not. For householders do not go out and spend all their wages. There is a natural propensity to put something aside for a rainy day. In other words, only part of the money paid to households in return for their labour goes for consumption; the rest goes into the bank as savings. The part spent on consuming goods and services relative to the whole is known as the marginal propensity to consume. The part that goes into the bank relative to the whole is known as the marginal propensity to save.

The introduction of the financial sector into the equation changes everything, says Keynes. For some of the fine, circular flow of money, labour and goods that Say envisaged gets diverted into the banks. This also introduces another factor. Firms need periodically to reinvest capital in their operations to keep them efficient and competitive. Much of the time they borrow this money from the banks, intending to pay it off out of future cash flows. Slightly confusingly, economists call this 'investment', which to us today has a rather different flavour. Perhaps it is better to call it 'capital expenditure'. Incidentally, this all has important implications, of which Keynes was well aware, for what has become known as monetarism but let us leave consideration of that to a later chapter.

So, Keynes asks, what can go wrong within this system? Two things. First, people can save too much and spend too little. This leads to reduced demand, which can mean that firms have to lay people off, which in turn leads to yet further reduced demand as there are now fewer people receiving wages, while those who still have a job will probably be panicked into saving even more, and so on. Second, if firms are put off borrowing money for investment in capital expenditure, they will cease to be competitive, in which case purchasers will buy elsewhere, thus leading to reduced demand, and so on. In one or both ways, since in practice these two factors are interlinked, there is clear potential for a downward spiral of reduced demand, reduced employment and reduced investment into a full-blown recession.

Interestingly, Keynes called this gap that could open between consumption and production 'under-consumption', implying that it was always the fault of the consumer for spending too little and saving too much, rather than 'overproduction'. It does not seem to have occurred to him, probably because of the circumstances of his period, that industry might actually just produce more goods than those for which there could be any reasonable demand. This obsession that more production can only ever possibly be a good thing runs like a polyester thread through the factory overalls that are economic theory and would only be questioned much later by J.K. Galbraith.

There is of course another factor that this scenario ignores, yet one which some academics argue may be the most powerful economic driver of all: taxation. Higher taxes mean that firms have lower retained earnings to plough back into the business, while consumers have less money to spend on goods and services. Reducing levels of taxation, they say, may be the most potent weapon that any government has at its disposal to boost economic growth, a belief that half a century later would come to form part of a potent mix of economic policy named after US President Ronald Reagan.

Having analysed the problem, Keynes advocated a tactic that was consistent with his model. By raising interest rates governments could encourage saving (thus reducing consumption) and discourage borrowing for investment, thus slowing down an economy which seemed in danger of overheating, for example one that was exhibiting excessive inflation. By lowering interest rates governments could discourage saving (thus increasing consumption) and encourage investment, thus stimulating a sluggish economy and hopefully stopping it from falling into recession.

These, then, were the basic brake and accelerator pedals that he proposed for a government to regulate the economy. To accelerate, lower interest rates. To brake, raise them. This was revolutionary stuff. Until this time nobody had believed that governments could (or, more importantly, should) intervene actively in this way.

Interest rates, though, have come to be seen as something of a blunt instrument rather than a scalpel and, to be fair to Keynes, he recognised this or at least he recognised that their effects could take some time to become apparent. His recommendation of how to tackle unemployment and recession in the short term was equally radical, if not even more so.

Remember that the accepted view was that governments should never run a budget deficit. Indeed, that governments should never be *allowed* to run a budget deficit, since politicians were inherently untrustworthy and irresponsible and if given the chance to buy themselves some short-term electoral popularity would grasp it with both hands and hang the consequences.

Keynes took a contrary view. The best and most immediate way for governments to boost the economy, he said, was to increase government spending on public works. The money paid out as wages to men who would otherwise be out of work and to contractors for the materials and services required would then be spent in turn by those who received it, creating the effect of what has become known as a Keynesian multiplier, boosting aggregate demand and leading to economic growth.

Crucially, Keynes believed governments should do this even if it meant running a budget deficit for a short period while they did so. He believed that politicians had moved on since the Victorian and Edwardian eras and were now highly principled public servants who had the best long-term interests of society at heart, rather than their own transitory popularity. He was of course to be proved tragically mistaken in this view.

That this was so was due to a fault in the man himself rather than his theory, a fault as it were in his belief system rather than his thought system, if indeed it can be called a fault instinctively to think the best of people. Keynes was someone who reached decisions through logical analysis and assumed that others were the same. This is in fact a well-recognised cognitive bias from which we all suffer known as 'the false consensus effect'; because our own beliefs are our own home territory from which we look out at the world, we tend to assume that they are for other people as well.

Whatever the case, for Keynes there were no bad decisions or bad politicians, just faulty reasoning and he honestly believed that if he could just explain the faults in their logic, then politicians would not only gladly change their minds but would thank him for having enlightened them. Of course, it never worked out like that, but, rather touchingly, to the end of his life he never stopped believing it.

With the bitter benefit of hindsight it can now be clearly seen that in fact all Keynes did in encouraging politicians to run deficits was the equivalent of handing a can of petrol and a box of matches to a pyromaniac and trusting him not to use them. At the time, though, it all seemed very different.

It is difficult to overstate the importance of this sea change in political attitudes. As always, politicians took the piece of the cake they liked ('you can run a budget deficit') and left behind the nasty bits such as 'but only in extraordinary circumstances', 'only for a limited time' and 'provided you make it good by running a surplus in other years'. It is a measure of how deeply embedded such thinking has become and so consequently divorced from reality our politicians, that even in 2012 Sarkozy and Merkel were talking about 'limiting' budget deficits. No recognition there that budget deficit spending was 'abnormal' and should be reversed, or even eliminated, but simply 'limited'. It seems cruel, though necessary, to point out that one cannot have a 'limited' bankruptcy even though the politicians have worked hard on inventing the concept for Greece.

Until the Second World War, governments were slow to adopt Keynes's ideas. Though *The General Theory* was not published until 1936, he had for some years been urging politicians in both the UK and the USA (including Roosevelt) to use a deficit to fund public works. Roosevelt did of course launch his famous 'New Deal', but this was a much tamer version of what Keynes had in mind and Roosevelt still strained to stay within a balanced budget. After Pearl Harbor, of course, America had no choice but to run a deficit and increase borrowing to finance the massive rearmament programme needed to fight a global war.

Ironically in view of what was to come, it was actually the fascist dictatorships of Italy and Germany who would put Keynes's ideas into practice, putting the unemployed to work on ambitious programmes of public works, motorway construction in Germany being a good example.

So it would be after the Second World War and after the great man's death (he died in 1946 having been ill for some time, but without cutting back his hectic schedule) that his policies began to be widely practised by governments. Indeed, they became accepted as economic orthodoxy by politicians of all persuasions, though as we will see, that is not to say that there were no dissenting voices. Yet as we all know, times change and we change with them, or at least we *should* change with them. It was Keynes's misfortune that he did not live to see his ideas gain general acceptance, but his tragedy that when they did he was no longer around to fire off his legendary tracts to the politicians in an effort to keep them on the straight and narrow. For his ideas had been based on a model of the world as it was (or as he believed it to be) in the 1930s, and that world very quickly began to change. It may be convenient to illustrate this by reference to the reservations we mentioned a little earlier.

The first and most important one we have already noted. His work was based on the assumption that government expenditure funded by running a budget deficit was 'abnormal spending', whereas after the Second World War this was sadly no longer the case and budget deficits became the norm rather than the exception.

This also of course gave the lie to Keynes's naive assumption that politicians were principled and trustworthy, and would act rationally in the best long-term interests of the country. This was a disastrous, though rather touching, error and it was future generations who would pay the price.

Nor did it take long for another of his assumptions to fall apart, though he had heavily qualified this one. He had believed that there was nothing inherently wrong with the labour market but had pointed out that workers were disinclined ever to accept lower wages unless and until they could be sure that prices were falling. He also, like other economists before him, pointed to the potential for restrictive practices and collective bargaining to prevent the job market from functioning perfectly. After the Second World War, with demand and output picking up, it would be the trade unions, not a cartel of bosses, who would become the price makers in the UK, with predictable results.

Then there was his belief that increased government spending could boost the economy. It is important to be clear about what he meant here. He had in mind a programme of public works (he mentions specifically building new railways, for example) which would create revenue for the contractors and suppliers involved, and provide jobs and wages for the additional workers that they would have to take on. In other words, government spending would directly and immediately boost aggregate demand as well as providing infrastructure that would hopefully confer some lasting economic benefit.

At this point a twofold economic multiplier would take effect. As people earned money and spent it, the firms from which they bought their consumer items would in turn be able to expand and take on more workers, who would in turn go out and spend their money, and so on. As people saved some of their money, the banks would be able to lend it out several times over to firms for investment in capital expenditure in new plant and machinery, which would itself tend to boost output and require the employment of yet more workers. 'Many times over', since banks are required only to keep a small amount of capital in reserve against amounts which they lend out. This is called fractional reserve banking, and is something to which we will return.

This was in fact already a problem in 1930s America, since the railways and roads had already been built and it was by now difficult to find infrastructure projects on which to put people to work, the Hoover Dam being a significant exception, but even this had been completed by 1935. As time went by after 1945, two things started to happen in parallel. First, it became increasingly difficult, not least because of very high levels of public debt, for governments to spend money on projects such as this. The British railway network, for example, was not only starved of investment but actually significantly reduced by the Beeching cuts of the early 1960s. Roughly a staggering

half of Britain's railway stations would be closed, effectively maroon-
ing whole rural communities. Second, the belief started to spread
that somehow higher government spending must necessarily always
be beneficial for the economy regardless of what it was spent upon.
Increased spending on things such as health and welfare may arguably
make for a better society, but it cannot boost economic activity, except
by a minimal amount, and when it is financed by a budget deficit it
can only possibly be deeply harmful.

Two other points should be briefly noted, the first of which has
already been mentioned.

Keynes largely ignored the effect of international trade. Trade
imbalances were in fact already causing problems for the British government in the 1930s (though Cabinet papers show considerable disagreement as to their precise effects) but would become a major issue
in the 1950s and 1960s. This is partly because of the following point.

Keynes assumed that no government would ever again debauch its
currency after the dreadful example of the Weimar Republic. While he
objected when Winston Churchill reintroduced the Gold Standard, he
did so not so much out of principle but because he specifically disagreed with the rate at which the pound had been fixed. As we will see,
after the Second World War he was party to setting up a monetary system that would formalise this view, with all international obligations
having to be settled either in gold or dollars. By the 1970s, though,
this system had fallen apart, with consequences that are only now
becoming clear.

Before we move on, it may be convenient briefly to summarise the
essence of what has become known as Keynesian economics. These
might be classified as three beliefs, or principles, and one observation.
First, the principles.

To a certain extent interest rates may operate as a self-regulating
mechanism to choke off high levels of either saving or borrowing, but
governments, acting through central banks, can intervene to stimulate or restrain economic growth by actively lowering or raising rates.
However, the effect of such action, though theoretically sound, may be
both delayed and uncertain.

If a government wishes to stimulate economic activity in the short term it may do so by increasing spending on public works, which will have the direct effect of stimulating aggregate demand. Such works may be financed by running a budget deficit but this is an abnormal state of affairs and must be compensated for by running a budget surplus in better times.

Since higher unemployment will tend to have a downward effect on wages, which will in turn tend to have a downward effect on prices, and vice versa, there is a direct trade-off in the medium to long term between unemployment and inflation. Government can seek to reduce unemployment, but only at the expense of higher inflation. Conversely, if a government seeks to curb inflation, it can only do so at the cost of reduced levels of economic activity and thus higher unemployment.

Finally the observation, which we have already noted but which bears repeating since it has become widely ignored in the intervening decades. Running a budget deficit is itself inflationary since it is effectively pushing money out into the system to be spent which would not otherwise be there.

So we arrive rather neatly at 1939, at which point Round Four of the great 'Germany versus France' contest erupted, rapidly spiralling out of control into the Second World War, once again sucking in Britain (sadly and resignedly) after a few hours and the United States (angrily and reluctantly) after a few years.

It is no part of this book's mission to tell the story of the vast human tragedy that ensued. Let us instead skip forward to the postwar period which forms the prelude to the unfolding of our own present situation, which may perhaps most charitably be described as a monumental mess.

# SEVEN

# Marx and the Marshall Plan

The First World War had been a horrific experience that had scarred the collective consciousness of a generation. Yet the horrors had been almost entirely confined to male combatants of six nations (America joined towards the end as a seventh). German troops had committed atrocities behind the lines in Belgium and France, and German Zeppelins and Gothas had dropped a few small bombs on London, but by and large the civilian population had not been directly affected. In addition, some European countries such as the Netherlands, which would later give sanctuary in exile to the deposed Wilhelm II, had even been able to remain resolutely neutral while the fighting ebbed and flowed around them.

Without wishing to diminish in any way the misery and suffering of the First World War, which was magnified in the UK by the policy of allowing young men of the same town to join up together in 'Pals' Battalions' and thus all get killed together, the great influenza epidemic of 1918/19, which would become known to history as Spanish Flu, is estimated to have killed at least 50 million people, which was 3% of the current world population and between three and four times as many as the total service and civilian deaths caused by the war.

The Second World War was different. Neutrality was no defence against being invaded and occupied. Civilian populations were bombed, shot, tortured, raped, robbed, made homeless and abducted for forced labour. The technology of warfare advanced to the stage where finally it was possible to destroy an entire city with one bomb. Yet even this final apocalyptic attack on Japan paled into insignificance compared to what the Allies discovered as they advanced in the final months of the war. When hard evidence of the gassing of millions of people had first reached London in July 1944 it had been greeted with horror and disbelief. By May 1945 there could be no further room for doubt. There had been an awful precedent during the First World War when the Turks had attempted the genocide of the Armenian population, perhaps killing at least one million. Yet what took place in Central Europe during the Second World War was on a different scale, and carried out with cold-blooded efficiency by a process that was almost an assembly line.

The natural reaction to such events, at least in the West, was an overwhelming urge to build a better world for people to live in, a world in which such things could never occur again. At national level this took the form of the election in Britain of a Labour government (which many saw as an act of black ingratitude to Churchill the war leader), committed to a massive house-building programme and the birth of the National Health Service and welfare state. At international level this saw the birth of the United Nations to keep peace between nations, and subsidiary organisations such as the World Health Organisation to promote things such as mass inoculation and research into killer diseases, the Food and Agriculture Organisation to try to prevent famine, and the World Bank and International Monetary Fund to promote economic growth in developing countries and financial stability.

We will in due course examine how the developed nations attempted also to put in place a monetary system that would facilitate international trade while protecting the value and stability of individual currencies, but let us first turn to the other great legacy of the Second World War.

As the victorious Russian troops began advancing through Eastern Europe, Stalin let it be known that they would not be going home again, but would be seeking to bring into the Soviet sphere of influence all the previously sovereign states which they overran. It soon became clear that what Stalin had in mind was the creation of a homogenous communist bloc, based on the installation of puppet governments and the introduction of a single-party system. Thus the only result of the Second World War had for many millions of people been the substitution of one army of foreign occupation with stirring music and fancy uniforms for another.

The situation of Poland in particular, for whom the West had gone to war in the first place, was tragically ironic. Its pro-Western politicians were murdered by the Russians, as, it later transpired, had thousands of captured Polish officers been during the war. In a move of breathtaking cheek that should surely have won the approbation of various later Western politicians, the Soviets attempted to palm off the blame for this onto the Germans by pretending to discover the mass graves and then attempting to lay charges at the Nuremburg war trials. Even at that stage, the British and Americans were deeply unconvinced.

What was clear, however, was that the West was now faced by a concentrated bloc that was both very powerful militarily and deeply inimical to Western-style democracy. It was the great wordsmith Churchill who would coin the phrase 'the Iron Curtain' in 1945, and the even greater one George Orwell 'the Cold War' that same year. The truth was that for the next forty-five years Europe and the United States would live under the constant shadow of war; instant, vicious and potentially totally mutually destructive. Worryingly, it was also very clear that not all the communists were tucked away safely behind the Iron Curtain.

In November 1939 those in charge of protocol within the German government had been faced with a problem. The Soviet foreign minister, Molotov, was due to visit Hitler to discuss how the non-aggression pact that had been entered into in Moscow that August by the German foreign minister, Ribbentrop, might be extended to the two countries' mutual benefit. However, it transpired that German military bands had never been taught the *Internationale* since it was of course the anthem of international socialism and, despite having appropriated the word 'socialist', the Nazis were sworn enemies of the forces of the left. The problem was eventually solved by having one particular band learn the piece and, when Molotov arrived at the railway station, play it very quickly indeed for fear that any passing communist railway workers might be tempted to join in.

The Germans had problems with national anthems throughout the war, actually. When Franco sent some anti-communist volunteers to fight the Russians in 1941 the Germans painstakingly learned the Spanish national anthem, but the wrong one. So it was that the bemused young nationalists found themselves being greeted with the battle hymn of their defeated Republican opponents.[1]

The Ribbentrop pact had stunned the world. It had seemed unthinkable that Germany and Russia should each jump into bed with their fiercest ideological enemy. Almost immediately, in an echo of eighteenth-century statecraft, Germany and Russia had partitioned Poland between them following Germany's invasion and declaration of war. Russia would a few months later fight the 'Winter War' against Finland, a war in which Britain and France were initially disposed to intervene even at the expense of violating Swedish neutrality but these plans were never implemented.

Stalin seems genuinely to have believed that provided Germany could be freely given the agricultural and industrial commodities that she wanted under a trade agreement, then Hitler could have no reason to invade Russia and accordingly would not do so. This is a fascinating example of a form of dissonance, a cognitive bias that affects all human decision-making and whose impact can be seen especially in financial and economic fields.

Dissonance occurs when an individual is exposed either to conflicting ideas or, more usually, to a belief that is seemingly at odds with reality. It seems that in such situations it is less painful to us to change our perception of reality than to change our belief. When people are said to be 'in denial', it is exactly this sort of situation that is being described. Data that would tend to confirm their belief is overemphasised, while that which is inconsistent with it is minimised, discredited or deliberately ignored. This is exactly what Stalin did, brushing aside repeated intelligence and even direct warnings that Hitler intended to invade.

Eventually, when the gap between perception and reality becomes too large, an adjustment has to take place, a change in belief often being accompanied by severe mental distress. Stalin actually had some form of nervous breakdown as the clear evidence of German armoured

---

[1]  Richard J. Evans, *The Third Reich at War*, London, Penguin, 2008.

divisions slashing through the Ukraine finally forced him to admit that he had got things totally wrong and he initially thought that the officials who were visiting him to discuss the situation had come to shoot him (if only!).

While it lasted, the pact was of great assistance to Hitler as all communist parties and networks throughout Europe were instructed to obstruct the allied war effort as much as possible. After June 1941 they were given orders to the contrary and it would be the communists who would provide a major part of the resistance movement in many countries. France was a case in point, where the communist resistance spent as much time fighting the Gaullist resistance as they did fighting either the Germans (in the north) or the Milice, the German-backed Vichy militia (in the south).

This meant that once the war ended there were large, well-organised, well-armed communist groupings on the ground that were in many cases exercising de facto control over large areas, including many towns and cities. For some time there was a very real fear, particularly in Washington, that many European countries might 'go communist', perhaps even asking to join the Soviet bloc. Greece, Italy and France were felt to be at particular risk.

Before his replacement by Attlee, Churchill in an unguarded moment negotiated with Stalin what he called 'a naughty list' of different countries that might or might not fall into the Russian zone of influence. Stalin was given a free hand in Poland, for example (though this was simply recognising the inevitable), in return for staying out of Greece. Remarkably, Stalin largely stuck to this deal even after Churchill left office, though he did thoughtfully tuck the incriminating document away in his pocket, much as Moshe Dayan would later do when the Eden administration foolishly signed a letter authorising Israel's invasion of Egypt.

Before turning to how Washington chose to counter this particular threat, it might be worth considering just how communism had come to be regarded as a serious alternative to capitalism in terms of both economic theory and practical reality and for that we have to travel back briefly to the nineteenth century, for in order to understand communism it is necessary to look into how the concept of 'value' evolved.

Those who followed Adam Smith, the classical economists whose ideas Keynes would debunk, believed that you could value something by adding up the cost of everything that had gone into producing it, including of course the cost of labour. In due course this idea would be replaced by what is known as the concept of marginal utility.

'Utility' was a concept that was borrowed, or rather developed, from the social philosophy of Jeremy Bentham (one of the academic pioneers at, though not a founder of, University College London) and John Stuart Mill. The Utilitarians became famous for preaching that everyone was free to do whatever they liked in life as long as in so doing they did not cause actual harm to anyone else. Actually their philosophy was rather more complex than this, but their basic approach was to look at the 'utility' of an act, that is its potential for causing good as opposed to harm, and advocate those acts that seemed to offer the greatest utility for the greatest number of people. So, far from being the sort of libertarian creed much quoted by male under-graduates in urgent need of a female bed-partner, it could better be summed up by Mr Spock's celebrated phrase from *Star Trek*; 'the needs of the many outweigh the needs of the few'.

Economists such as Jevons took the idea of utility and turned it around, viewing it from the perspective of the individual. If acts had a utility, then surely so did goods. If we buy something we buy it not for itself but for what it offers us, whether that be survival, sustenance, pleasure or even the sort of pride that comes from having a more expensive car or a more up-to-date mobile phone than our neighbour. Whatever value the individual ascribes to that utility is the price that they are prepared to pay for it. Jevons did not though abandon the idea of cost of production entirely, saying that it would still play a part in assessing value (not least because presumably no rational producer would be prepared to sell an item for less than it had cost him to manufacture it).

As this idea was developed by the likes of Carl Menger, the founder of the Austrian School of economic thought, two further aspects of it became apparent. First, it must follow that no two individuals would value the utility of a product in the same way, since no two would have identical circumstances. To repeat an example we have used before, a man who is dying of thirst will pay more for a glass of water than one who is not.

Second, it must follow that the utility of each successive item decreases. Even a man dying of thirst will not pay as much for the second glass of water as for the first, nor as much for the third as for the second. The idea of each successive item having its own utility value is known as the concept of marginal utility, since this technique of looking totally in isolation at the individual item currently being sold at the moment, rather than the whole series of items being sold through time, is what economists mean when they talk about dealing 'at the margin'. The idea that each successive item will have a lower utility is actually elevated by economists into a law (always a dangerous practice), the law of diminishing marginal utility.

It was left to two of Menger's successors in the Austrian School, Ludwig von Mises and Friedrich von Wieser, respectively, to add the two final pieces of the jigsaw. First, money only has any relevance or validity in terms of the utility of the goods it can buy (Mises). Second, what a person is really doing when they put a price on utility is to decide what *not* to spend on something else (Wieser). Since nobody has infinite resources, every time we buy something we are making a choice. If I can afford to move house or buy a new car, but not both, then the price I am prepared to pay to move house is the 'opportunity cost' of not buying the car, and vice versa.

However, at the time that Karl Marx was thinking through his view of the world in the mid-nineteenth century none of this had come about. Menger had published his *Principles of Economics* in 1871, setting out his theories in print for the first time, but the classical theory of value was still in use and this was unfortunate because it pushed Marx into a profound analytical flaw.

The value of an item, says Marx, is the sum total of all its costs of production. These are, he says, the cost of providing the manufacturing machines and the factories within which they are situated, which he assumed to be a constant cost, and the cost of the labour to operate the machines, which he assumed to be variable. Thus the value of an item must be the sum of the constant capital and the variable capital that go into its production.

Yet manufacturers sell the item not at its real value but at a premium, thus making a profit. Since no rational customer will pay more for something than it is actually worth, then that must mean that it is the sale price that is the real value after all. In other words, the 'value' calculated by adding together the costs of production is incorrect.

The only variable element is the cost of labour. Therefore it must follow that the manufacturer is not paying the workers the full value of their labour. He is paying too little for it, and the profit he is making is exactly the same as the value of the labour that he is effectively stealing from the workers.

Of course to a modern audience this view appears rigid and unworkable. We now recognise that the concept of 'value' is much more complex than Marx appreciated it to be, and much more along the lines proposed by Menger, Mises (who was a fierce critic of Marx's ideas) and Wieser. Yet even without this error in the nature of value, Marx goes hopelessly awry, for he overlooks two essential elements in the cost of capital.

First, when an entrepreneur invests capital into a business he is giving up the present use of that money. Money that he injects as working capital is money he is effectively choosing not to spend on his children's school fees, or on buying a new car, or on making some alternative investment. As we have just seen, there is a cost to this, an opportunity cost, a cost that the entrepreneur is entitled to expect to recoup, or he would not make the investment in the first place. In the case of being kept out of your money for some years there is a further cost represented by things such as inflation eroding the value of your money. Thus on any view it would be irrational for an entrepreneur, a capitalist in Marx's terms, to invest money to set up a business and provide employment to workers unless he could earn back some monetary approximation of both his opportunity cost and the cost of being kept out of his money.

Yet even this does not suffice, for the entrepreneur is taking a risk, both the risk that in any one year he may not be able to recover any money from the business, either because it is unprofitable that year or because it needs to retain earnings for planned capital expenditure, but also the risk that he may actually lose some or all of his capital should the venture fail. So in addition to the cost of his capital, the capitalist is also entitled to recover what the world of finance calls a risk premium, and these two things together must also be factored into the true costs of production. Any business that ignored its cost of capital, the need to pay interest on bank loans and dividends on shares or stocks, would quickly go bust.

He also overlooks the cost of intellectual property, what we might call human capital. An inventor is entitled to earn some reward for his endeavours. If a factory uses his invention, he is entitled to be paid a royalty on every item produced. In modern corporate terms, an equivalent is usually the cost of the annual R&D budget, which is spent on keeping the business competitive in technological terms.

So, even if we ignore the later revelations that value is driven predominantly by demand rather than by supply, Marx's basic theoretical model simply does not work. A pity, since his explanation and analysis of human history is both entertaining and thought-provoking.

Marx envisaged an inexorable quest for operational efficiencies leading to bigger and bigger businesses, able to employ fewer workers to achieve the same production. These large, efficient, monster businesses would gradually drive smaller, less efficient competitors out of business, absorbing and taking over their customers. Actually, this was not a bad prediction since this is exactly what will tend to happen if the capitalist system is left to its own devices, but at this stage prediction and reality part company.

As it becomes more and more difficult to squeeze yet more efficiency out of the system, Marx says, employers will press ever downwards on workers' wages until they reach a point where the workers are simply unable to support themselves and their families. By this time a vicious downward spiral will have developed anyway as bigger and more efficient companies employ fewer and fewer people, which means that there are fewer and fewer customers to buy the goods which firms produce. The firms will react to this by squeezing labour yet more, and so on. At some point, a spontaneous uprising would occur that would sweep away the capitalist system. There is some dispute among communist thinkers about what would happen from this point onwards, but that is not really important for our purposes.

Even by the time of Marx's death it was apparent that he had got it wrong. For example, there was ample evidence that in most industrialised societies, certainly in Germany, the UK and America, the working classes were becoming not poorer but richer. He reacted to people pointing this out by arguing that they were poorer relative to the capitalists, since the latter had become richer still, but this could not mask the fact that exactly the opposite of what he had predicted was actually taking place.

Yet as we know, communism went on to develop into an alternative global religion and different versions of it to form the system of government of various countries. How could this be, if the basic theory was so fundamentally flawed?

The truth probably was that Marxism seemed to provide a ready prop for anyone who felt, understandably, that capitalist society of the early twentieth century was indeed deeply unfair, or at least unequal, with huge discrepancies between the very rich and the very poor. In both Britain and America, for example, the provision of such basics as healthcare, housing and education for the lower socioeconomic groups remained deeply unsatisfactory until after the Second World War (in Germany, by contrast, secondary schooling and welfare provision had been almost universal over half a century earlier). To many of an egalitarian disposition, the prospect of overthrowing the hated privileged class enjoying the fruits of others' labour through inherited wealth, often exhibited ostentatiously, which Marxism seemed to offer, was all they were looking for, and most did not choose to examine matters further. It remains a truism that most Marxists have never read Marx.

After the Second World War it was in the cafes and universities of Europe that earnest people sat around and discussed the dictatorship of the proletariat and what might happen next while, ironically, all around them the conditions that Marx had laid down for the great revolution drifted further and further away. Workers continued to grow more prosperous in both real and nominal terms. The downtrodden masses suddenly had washing machines, colour televisions and foreign holidays, while spending on healthcare, welfare and education spiralled.

Yet in the grim, forbidding days after the skies went dark over first Hiroshima and then Nagasaki, none of this was at all clear. A vast communist bloc had taken shape across Eastern Europe, and to make matters worse a different form of communism was threatening to defeat the West's ally Chiang Kai-shek in China. Communist shop stewards were busy disrupting production in British factories. Communist bands across Europe were refusing to give up their weapons or stop taking orders from Moscow. Even in America, though the administration did not know it, communist agents were active and highly placed.

It was against this backdrop that one of the most remarkable altruistic economic measures ever undertaken was launched by the United States. For four years, beginning in 1948, a vast programme of economic, material and financial aid was pumped into Europe. The Marshall Plan, as it came to be known after Secretary of State George Marshall although it was almost certainly an initiative of President Harry Truman, was also pointedly offered to the Soviet Union and its allies, and equally pointedly refused.

It is difficult to overestimate the impact of the Marshall Plan, whether economic or political. Much of Europe was devastated, its factories, homes and offices widely destroyed. Yet it has been estimated that by 1951 the production of Marshall Plan recipients was roughly a third as much again as it had been during the last year of peacetime production. By then it had become clear that government in each country, though in many cases heavily left-leaning, would at least remain within the Western democratic model. This may seem a slight achievement, but it was not, given the very real threat of autocratic single-party communism which had loomed in many places in 1945.

Not just money was on offer, but also know-how. US industrial experts gave advice to the businessmen setting up new factories in Germany, but the British thought themselves generally above the need for such counselling. After all, had they not been the pioneers of the industrial revolution?

Yet, even with the immediate threat to democracy in Western Europe averted, there was still the rest of the world to worry about. Understandably shying away from direct confrontation, given the ability of rapidly growing nuclear arsenals to obliterate their opponents many times over, the two new superpowers sought advantage through promoting satellite states around the world, though in 1961 one would threaten to morph into the other when a Russian attempt to install missiles in Cuba, America's backyard, would bring the world to the very brink of nuclear war.

This obsession with 'the communist menace', and wondering 'which would be the next domino to fall' would, perhaps understandably, come to dominate American foreign policy for nearly the first half century of the post-war years. It would lead to them repeatedly backing corrupt and unpopular regimes simply on the basis that they seemed to be the lesser of two available evils. In Vietnam, the struggle begun by Ho Chi Minh, the waiter spurned by President Wilson, would prove too much for the US puppet administration, proving that popular sentiment will sooner or later always triumph over superior firepower, as the French had already found to their cost when their colonial subjects defeated them at Dien Bien Phu in 1954.

The final irony was that, when it came, the collapse of Soviet power was due to economic rather than ideological factors. The strain of devoting such a huge proportion of their national budget to military spending became too great when it became clear from the American 'star wars' initiative that it was due to increase by another order of magnitude. The world was fortunate that when that moment arrived it was Mikhail Gorbachev who was in power, rather than one of his rivals or predecessors, any of whom might have panicked and pressed the button in a final, desperate gamble. Seeing the writing on the wall, Gorbachev had already launched programmes of internal reform such as perestroika and glasnost, and had begun to cosy up to the West, earning the respect both of Margaret Thatcher and Ronald Reagan in personal meetings. Thus when the system crashed, with Gorbachev withdrawing support from the likes of Poland and East Germany, it happened both quickly and largely peacefully, though the Romanian people could not resist the chance of killing their own particular communist dictator.

Yet the real shock was still to come. As historians, journalists and intelligence agencies started to rummage through the communist archives, many of which were simply opened up and abandoned, it would emerge that the McCarthy witch-hunt in 1950s America had not been quite so hare-brained as had at first appeared. The senator from Wisconsin had claimed that there were highly placed Soviet agents within the Federal Administration and had originally enjoyed the support of the future president, Richard Nixon, though the opportunist 'Tricky Dicky' was careful to distance himself quickly when McCarthy proved unable to come up with any hard evidence.

Lo and behold, when the Soviet era archives were opened very compromising material indeed was found in respect of two very senior civil servants, Harry White and Lauchlin Currie, both of whom we will meet again in the next chapter.

White was a senior Treasury official, who was suspected even at the time of passing state secrets to the Russians, and was questioned by a committee in 1948. He dramatically collapsed and died of a heart attack a few days later.

Lauchlin Currie was a senior economic adviser to President Roosevelt and may well have been courted by communist elements while attending the London School of Economics in London, long a hotbed of left-wing thought and student sit-ins, but now ironically turning out financial whizz-kids to staff the world's investment banks and hedge funds. Although there was no direct evidence that he was ever an active Soviet agent, as opposed to sympathiser, suspicion was enough. Since he was Canadian-born the US could and did take his passport away and he ended up in Colombia, where he died in 1993.

Lest any Brits be tempted at this point to indulge in *Schadenfreude*, it should be pointed out that the UK had a still worse problem, with even its security service having been deeply penetrated. Guy Burgess, Donald Maclean and Anthony Blunt (the latter having allegedly retrieved compromising documents relating to the Duke of Windsor from Germany during the closing days of the war in Europe) would subsequently be unmasked as long-term Soviet agents, as would George Blake, for whom the Russians organised an audacious escape from Wormwood Scrubs prison in 1966.

There was felt to be at least one safe pair of hands, though. There was a very able and frightfully nice chap who at the end of the war was head of MI6's Middle East section and was being widely tipped as a future Head of Service. His name was Kim Philby, and he already had a senior rank – in the KGB.

# EIGHT

# Building a New Jerusalem

John Maynard Keynes was already in poor health in the summer of 1945 but maintained his hectic schedule, much against the wishes of his wife, the Russian ballerina Lydia Lopokova, who had been a member of Diaghilev's celebrated ballet company. She was known to be a woman of decided views and was disliked by Keynes's Bloomsbury friends such as Virginia Woolf, the Bells and E.M. Forster, who thought her unintelligent, though Forster would later admit shamefacedly that they had all underestimated her. Not quite decided enough evidently, for Keynes would go on working at advising the government, negotiating international agreements, writing, lecturing, teaching, broadcasting, investing and running a theatre on the side as his anguished wife watched him suffer a series of heart attacks, the last of which would kill him in April 1946 at the age of just 62.

As the war in Europe ended, the two party leaders, Churchill and Attlee, wished to extend the wartime coalition government until Japan too had been defeated, but Labour heavyweight Herbert Morrison disagreed, telling Attlee that their party wanted an early election, whereupon Churchill resigned, was reappointed as caretaker prime minister, and called an election. The result was a landslide victory for Labour that took everybody by surprise, not least Attlee.

Summoned to Buckingham Palace to meet King George VI, an embarrassing scene ensued. The King was a very shy man, not least because he had suffered from a severe speech impediment as a young man and still hated speaking in public. Major Attlee, as he liked to be known, was himself famously laconic, well known for lengthy pauses when questions were addressed to him and terse, rather halting responses when at last he replied. After he bowed to the King, the two men simply stood and looked at each other while what seemed an eternity passed.

Finally Attlee plucked up courage, cleared his throat and announced hesitantly, 'I've won the election.'

'I know,' the King replied distantly. 'I heard it on the six o'clock news.'[1]

There were two immediate areas that Keynes was required to address for the new administration, many of whose members had never been in government before. They were both immense, Herculean tasks to which even the great man himself would prove unequal, though in fairness largely because nobody would take his advice.

First, Britain had to play a part in putting in place an agreed financial system that would both facilitate international trade, the potential for which was now recognised as vast and global, and guarantee the financial stability of the post-war world. Second, Britain had to address the parlous state of her own finances, having effectively been bankrupted by the costs of the war. She had been able to continue fighting since 1941 only as a credit client of the United States under Lend-Lease, and, which is much less well known, of Canada, receiving from her both soft loans (which would not be repaid until 2006) and outright gift aid.

That Canada's contribution to Britain's wartime finances should have gone for so long unacknowledged is both unfair and ungracious. Canadian loans totalled $1.2 billion and outright gifts $3.5 billion.[2] To put this in context, the first phase of Lend-Lease was only $1 billion, and even this proved controversial in the US. Writing shortly before his death, Keynes made it clear that in his view Britain would not have been able to continue the war but for Canada's generosity.[3]

Yet it was to address the first point that Keynes attended an international conference held at Bretton Woods, a small New Hampshire town that would give its name to the system that would be agreed by the delegates. These were drawn from no less than forty-four countries, since many had hastened opportunistically to join the Allies in the final weeks of the war, including such exotic additions as Chile, Argentina, Syria and Saudi Arabia. However, the main business of the

---

[1] Peter Hennessey, *Never Again: Britain 1945–51*, 2nd rev. edn, London, Penguin, 2006.
[2] The Canadian Encyclopedia and J.L. Granatstein, *Canada's War: The Politics of the Mackenzie King Government, 1939–1945*, Toronto, University of Toronto Press, 1990.
[3] Correlli Barnett, *The Lost Victory: British Dreams, British Realities, 1945–50*, London, Macmillan, 1995.

conference came down to the United States and Great Britain. For America, former Secretary of State Cordell Hull was nominally in charge but he was still suffering from the ill health which had forced his resignation, and so a lot of the negotiations ended up being conducted by those fine upstanding American patriots Harry White and Lauchlin Currie, whom we met in the previous chapter.

Incidentally, the fact that a former foreign affairs supremo was placed notionally in charge of the US efforts is significant. The American government was coming increasingly to believe that economic stability and prosperity was a necessary condition for political stability around the world (for 'economic stability' read 'a low probability of going communist'), a view that would lead to the Marshall Plan, and this desire for orderly international finances may well have been their primary motivation for Bretton Woods. Certainly it was this same conference that set up the International Monetary Fund and one of the two bodies that would come together as the World Bank,[4] both clear signals of America's vision for a new world order whose activities would be regulated and supported by these two august international bodies, governed by Europeans and Americans, respectively. One Bretton Woods US attendee, economic adviser Bernard Baruch, remembers that the touchingly naive objective of preventing future spending on armaments was also a stated US aim.[5]

It is also interesting to observe that Bretton Woods marked a significant departure from previous government policy in both the United States and Great Britain, which had been largely laissez-faire in both economic and financial matters (Roosevelt's New Deal notwithstanding). There seemed now to be growing acceptance that governments could and should intervene where necessary, either alone or through the medium of international agreements and organisations, to maintain and preserve financial stability. Sadly, similar hopes for another of

---

[4] The World Bank Group, as distinct from the World Bank, comprises five agencies. The International Bank for Reconstruction and Development (established by Bretton Woods) and the International Development Agency together make up the World Bank. The remaining three are the International Finance Corporation, the Multilateral Investment Guarantee Agency, and the International Centre for Settlement of Investment Disputes.
[5] Bernard Baruch Papers, Princeton University Library, quoted online.

Cordell Hull's creations, the United Nations, in the sphere of geopolitics would never be realised.

The post-war period would see this new, interventionist mindset leading to governments on both sides of the Atlantic increasingly looking directly to influence economic factors, as Keynes had advocated before the war, with what mixed fortunes we will shortly examine but let us not get ahead of ourselves.

There was a common element running through just about everybody's ideas at Bretton Woods, literally an 'element', for it was gold. It is interesting that the first thoughts of an uncertain, fragile post-war world should turn to gold, that traditional repository of intrinsic value, and they had history on their side. Whenever paper currency had been used successfully back in the far-off golden days before the First World War, it had been based on the notion of convertibility into gold, whether direct or indirect.

Whenever that convertibility had been abandoned as those in charge of the presses grew intoxicated by the prospect of being able literally to print money, disaster had ensued, most recently of course in the Weimar Republic, but before that in many examples stretching back through human history such as the Confederate States of America in the nineteenth century, France in the eighteenth, Sweden in the seventeenth, Ming dynasty in China in the fifteenth, and Persia in the thirteenth. In France the after-shock lingered so long that for almost two centuries no financial institution dared to use the word 'bank' in their name (though, interestingly, 'credit' which most used instead, would probably today be regarded as an even dirtier word).

So, whether for emotional or practical reasons, and most likely a mixture of both, the Bretton Woods delegates seem instinctively to have reached for the comfort and security of a system based on the solid foundations of gold. Only the details of their proposed systems were different.

Keynes envisaged a global central bank, perhaps to be established alongside the World Bank, or even to form part of its responsibilities, which would be charged with administering a global reserve currency, to which he gave the working title of the bancor. The bancor would be made up of a basket of the world's major currencies. His differences with his American colleagues went much further than this, however. Keynes envisaged a system where countries with a balance of trade surplus (an excess of exports over imports) would be encouraged to target their import orders so far as possible at countries with trade deficits, thus giving them a helping hand to bring their international trade back into balance.

For once, one has to feel that Keynes had lost touch with reality here. Such a hopelessly altruistic system would have required not only huge and enduring international goodwill, but would also presumably have meant governments taking powers to direct where domestic firms should do business and effectively on what terms. For someone who believed in free markets, as Keynes fundamentally did despite his interventionist views, to suggest something that was the very negation of a market economy seems strange, to say the least. Certainly the United States, which already enjoyed a huge trade surplus with just about all the rest of the world, was never likely to agree to anything like it.

It raises an interesting point, however, which was to assume a tragic significance as the next couple of decades unfolded. The discussions seem to have opened up a fundamental difference of opinion between White and Keynes. White believed that a trade deficit was a problem only for the country which was running it, and that a combination of domestic inflationary pressures and money flowing out of the country would force any responsible government to deal with the situation quickly and effectively, even if this involved some short-term pain and suffering. Keynes saw it as a potential problem for everybody. Did he perhaps (ironically in view of what we know about his general mind-set) guess at the possibility that nobody on the American side seems ever to have envisaged, namely that a particular government might *not* behave responsibly? That they may in fact behave so irresponsibly that they would be prepared to destroy the Bretton Woods system itself, on which the financial stability of the whole world rested, rather than face up to the political consequences of economic reality?

Inevitably, it was the American proposals that were adopted. Every currency was linked to the dollar at a fixed exchange rate, while the dollar was linked to gold at a fixed rate of $35 an ounce. All international trade obligations had to be settled either in dollars or in gold. It escaped nobody that this arrangement made the dollar the world's unofficial reserve currency and gave America a stranglehold on the global financial system.

The British now repeated the same mistake that they had made with the re-imposition of the Gold Standard between 1925 and 1931 by pricing the pound much too highly. Given that Britain had effectively gone bust in 1941 and that nobody had come up with any compelling way of repairing this situation, pricing the pound to purchase more than three dollars can only be explained by some sort of perverse air of superiority. This would be revised downwards by agreement in 1949, but even this was still too strong, making life very difficult indeed for British exporters, while encouraging imports of things like electrical products that could undercut British competition on both price and quality. This would exacerbate what would in any event have been a dramatically difficult two decades even with a weaker pound. Remember that the whole rationale of Bretton Woods was that a responsible government would not allow such a situation to run out of control; like many pious hopes, this one was destined to be cruelly dashed.

Returning to the UK, Keynes gloomily surveyed the UK's financial and economic situation, and despaired at what he saw. Britain had gone into the war in a bad position that had rapidly got worse, hence national bankruptcy in 1941 which had been disguised by handouts from abroad. In the trough of the Great Depression national debt had stood at about 170% of GDP. It had only just dipped back below 100% when the war came along and now, in 1946, it was nearly 250%. The abrupt end of Lend-Lease again threatened national bankruptcy. Keynes negotiated an American loan to plug the holes.

Things were just about as bad as they could be. British industry had been unproductive before the war, partly because of restrictive trade practices going back to its roots in craft unions and batch production, partly due to ageing and unmodernised plant, partly because of second-rate management and partly because of confrontational industrial relations. The future prime minister, Harold Wilson, writing of his experiences during the war, admitted that strikes were widespread, even while the Battle of the Atlantic held a knife to Britain's throat, so that production never reached anywhere near its full potential.[6] In fact, more days were lost to strikes each year between 1941 and 1945 than in the last year of peacetime. If unions were not prepared to cooperate with management even at a time of national crisis, when the country's very survival was at stake, what hope was there of them doing so once victory had been achieved and they were supposed to be reaping the benefits of living in a New Jerusalem, as Labour ambitiously dubbed their social model?

American advisers in the UK for the purposes of administering the Marshall Plan reported back in some bewilderment that the British did not seem remotely interested in planning to drive down unit production costs or boost production volumes, and they also noted the lack of skilled engineers in British factories (the observations were probably closely related). Throughout the war British production in all areas was significantly lower than in Germany, even though German factories and their suppliers were being heavily bombed while British factories were not. The historian Correlli Barnett notes that in 1944 it took three times as long to construct a Spitfire as it did its Messerschmitt Bf 109 equivalent. A Ministry of Production inspection team at one aircraft factory were unable to identify a production line and found that the production manager's assistant was indeed qualified – but as a lawyer. In 1945 a factory making Gloster Meteor jet fighters was labelled 'chaotic'; again, no assembly line at all could be discerned.[7]

So Britain headed into the post-war period needing desperately to boost manufacturing and exports in order to grow the economy and tax revenues, but with a desperately inefficient and uncompetitive manufacturing sector, poisonous relations between management and workers, and an artificially strong currency. Hardly a recipe to lend encouragement to Attlee's Labour administration or its advisers, such as Keynes.

---

[6] Harold Wilson, *New Deal for Coal*, London, Contact, 1945.

[7] *The Lost Victory*, op. cit.

Into this already unpromising brew the politicians chose to mix two further toxic ingredients: defence, and Labour's plans for New Jerusalem.

At the heart of what might be called the defence dilemma was the magic phrase 'Britain's place in the world', which would be parroted by just about every prime minister and foreign secretary for the next several decades. The phrase was (and is) a delusion wrapped in bombast. The delusion was that Britain was still somehow the 'workshop of the world', a great naval power and a great military power, with a great global empire to boot. It followed from this that Britain was strategically obliged to play her part on the world stage and it followed in turn that the only way in which she could do this was to project her military power around the globe.

The reality was of course sadly different. Britain had not been the workshop of the world since the nineteenth century, nor a great naval power since the Treaty of Washington in 1922. She had never been a great military power, preferring to leave others to do her fighting for her on land. In both world wars British strategy had been based around allowing the French army to bear the brunt of the German onslaught, and her own military build-up had been long, slow, painful and inefficient. Britain was now a small, bankrupt island in the Atlantic Ocean, her industrial base outdated, uncompetitive and riven with internecine conflict. Her way ahead was clear: batten down the hatches for short-term survival, while paying off debt and planning and building feverishly for long-term industrial health and consequent national prosperity. In such a dire situation as Britain now found herself, no distractions from the job in hand could be permitted. Sadly, however, distractions there were aplenty and delusions of grandeur took a long time to die. They would still be a factor in British policy-making in the subsequent century.

Tantalisingly, the new prime minister saw some of this quite clearly. Clement Attlee prepared a memorandum for his Cabinet colleagues in which he queried whether Britain still needed military bases around the world. Such a maverick view quickly vanished under the combined weight of a strategic appreciation by the chiefs of staff, and the foreign secretary's trumpeting of 'our place in the world'.

Thus Attlee, memorably described by Churchill as a sheep in sheep's clothing, stands exposed as a perceptive thinker but a weak leader; had he wished to, he could have made a stand and insisted on dramatic reductions in the defence budget, but he did not. In any event, it is questionable just how radical any such cuts might have been. He had previously spoken of the need 'to carry our full weight in the post-war world with the US and the USSR'.

In the event Britain would elect to devote no less than 69% of total public spending to defence in 1946, nearly as much in a year of peacetime, with no expenditure on munitions, as in 1945, the last year of war. The amount, nearly £4.5 billion, was fifteen times greater than the amount spent on education and thirty times greater than the amount spent on healthcare. The amount set aside for industrial regeneration? Zero.

To be fair, defence expenditure did begin to decline steadily from the following year onwards, but even by 1951, the end of the Marshall Plan period, it was still, at nearly £1.5 billion, about 26% of total government spending. That it declined at all is almost certainly due not to some belated recognition that Attlee was right, but that, as we will see, the monster that was New Jerusalem began quickly to run amok, trampling anything that got in its way.

Attlee's government would decide in 1946 to build Britain's own atom bomb even though both Hugh Dalton and Stafford Cripps, the finance and trade ministers, respectively, stated categorically that Britain could not afford it. The cost of the nuclear deterrent would acquire a massive upward momentum of its own, encompassing various generations of V-Bombers and submarines as well as an ill-fated British delivery rocket project, Blue Streak, which would finally be abandoned in 1960, by which time its projected cost had risen to about £23 billion in present-day money.

The 1946 budget alone represented an enormous betrayal of British interests. The defence allocation for that year represented about £130 billion in present-day money. If even half of that had been devoted to re-equipping British factories and training production engineers, and similar amounts for each of the next five years, the results must surely have been hugely beneficial in the long term. In the struggle between defence expenditure which, once spent, disappeared for ever, and investment in Britain's future that would possibly have sown the seeds of future prosperity, the fantasy mantra of 'Britain's place in the world' won out over the bleak reality of Britain's parlous state, and would continue to do so. Britain was like an ageing bankrupt socialite spending her last few pounds to attend a fashionable dinner for the sake of appearances, only to go home afterwards and commit suicide in her unheated, over-mortgaged mansion while her frustrated creditors banged at the front door.

Even when the military weakness of Britain, despite years of bloated defence spending, became obvious the self-delusion continued. America would commit more than 300,000 troops to the Korean War between 1950 and 1953, and Britain a standing commitment of 27,000 (including non-combatants), but still no politician would admit that Britain was just a doddery old has-been waiting to be put out of her misery. Yet if the fantasy of Britain's place in the world made it likely even in 1946 that the country would never properly recover from wartime bankruptcy, New Jerusalem made it certain.

William Henry Beveridge, or at any rate his ideas as implemented by Attlee's government, would do to the British economy what Richard Beeching would later do to its railways. He was a brilliant, determined idealist, passionate about his beliefs and cunningly proficient in his use of the media. In short, he was a highly dangerous man, a fact recognised by Ernest Bevin, later foreign secretary under Attlee, when he was Beveridge's boss during the war at the Ministry of Labour. Finding him both highly opinionated and highly conceited, Bevin was casting around for a way in which to be rid of him and found it in appointing him chairman of a commission enquiring into social insurance (Beveridge was a supposed expert on unemployment – 'supposed' since even after the Great Depression he still believed in full employment). It was to prove a fateful decision.

The Beveridge Report, when it was published in wartime Britain in 1942, was a document that nobody could attack, at least in principle, since it espoused causes with which nobody could possibly disagree.

Everyone wanted an end to poverty and disease, a decent quality of life for retired people, decent housing, decent healthcare and decent education. In the same way, everyone wants peace on earth, democracy, justice, free beer and everlasting sunshine. Beveridge seemed to promise that not only were all these things attainable, but at little overall cost.

For his system was based on a contributions system. Everybody would pay National Insurance and this money would then be used by the government to look after them when they were sick (by funding the National Health Service), old (old age pension) or out of work (unemployment benefit). Other benefits would be available to those who were unable to work through sickness or disability. It seemed churlish to object that this might not work. Even Conservative MPs, while they were still in office, were keen to implement the proposals right away.

With the benefit of hindsight it is easy to see the flaws in Beveridge's rose-tinted world view.

In 1942 life expectancy was only just over 60, so the projected cost of providing old age pensions would hardly have been significant. In the event, life expectancy rose steadily after the war, though the full effect of this would not be seen for some time.

Remember that Beveridge believed in full employment, even though Keynes and the Great Depression had shown that, at the very least, this was not always the case. Accordingly he envisaged that unemployment benefit would be payable only for short periods, as people first came into the workforce and as they moved between jobs. He also did not believe in voluntary unemployment. He believed that it was shameful not to work and as a young man had advocated that the unemployed should be stripped of their rights to vote and to have children. He was adamant that nothing in his proposals should in any way discourage the natural sense of duty and responsibility of his fellow citizens to provide for their families. Sadly, few of these assumptions would in fact hold true in the future. Even by 1950 Britain would be spending a staggering £920 million on social security, nearly 20% of total public spending and more even than that earmarked for defence.

Similarly, the cost and usage assumptions on which he built his National Health Service proved hopelessly wide of the mark. By 1950 spending on the NHS was already in excess of £350 million, over twice what had been estimated for the 1950 budget four years earlier. The sham of Beveridge's contributory system had been laid bare. Far from being self-funding, it was already after just four years draining the lifeblood out of the British economy. While its objectives might be socially laudable they were, contrary to what Beveridge had promised, coming at a cost the country simply could not afford.

All of which raises two obvious questions. First, why did Britain launch such an ambitious programme as a full-blown welfare state at the very moment when she could least afford it? Second, once it became apparent that the financial cost, contrary to initial expectations, was likely to prove crippling, why did she persist with it, not even attempting to scale it back, let alone abandoning it?

There are three answers to these questions.

First, there was the very real sense among Labour politicians that British society before the war had been deeply unfair, with wealth divided very unevenly, and the working class forced to bear the brunt of the suffering imposed by the Great Depression. There was thus a feeling that the British people deserved to live in the better world promised by New Jerusalem and that politicians were therefore under a moral duty to provide it, no matter what the cost.

Second, there was the matter of popular expectation. In setting up the welfare state Labour had opened Pandora's box. A host of problems, most of them budgetary, had promptly flown out, yet they had at the same time raised people's expectations, creating a new norm under which people were to be looked after 'from cradle to grave'. The supposedly contributory nature of the system, though in reality a sham, exacerbated this. It encouraged people to see things such as unemployment benefit as a right rather than a privilege, and made it all but impossible for any government to turn back the clock. Even by 1950 the welfare state had become the white elephant that it has always remained, seemingly immune from any radical reform.

Third, and following on from this, any attempt to reign back the scale of benefits and services provided would surely have spelled electoral disaster even had Attlee's administration wanted to do something about it, which there is no evidence that they did. It would become a leitmotif of governments of both parties as the post-war period progressed, that important policy decisions would be made not according to the long-term interests of the country, but to maximise the chance of re-election. In other words, extremely short-term (on any economic scale) tactical considerations, heavily weighted towards the interests of those in power, would always triumph over the long-term strategic interests of the country as a whole.

Despite its acts of reckless generosity, Labour's majority was dramatically reduced at the next election in 1950 by voters whom the Queen (later the Queen Mother) had described in a letter as 'half-educated and bemused' for having rejected Churchill in 1945. The advent of the Korean War then led to the new Chancellor Hugh Gaitskell proposing what was referred to as an austerity budget, though all this really meant was that defence spending went up to 26% of the total, facilitated by the introduction of contributions towards the cost of some things such as spectacles and dental services that had previously been provided completely free. This was opposed by some Cabinet members, such as Aneurin Bevan and Wilson, who resigned in protest. This made a further election inevitable in 1951, which Labour lost.

In passing, it is worth asking how and why Britain came to get mixed up in the Korean War at all. It had been apparent even by the time that the United Nations had been set up that with the advent of the Cold War it was stillborn. Nobody other than the United States, which was the major driver of its policy towards Korea, and the UK made any significant contribution. France, for example, sent no troops at all and it is difficult to see what Britain could have lost by following a similar line.

Yet Britain's 'place in the world' demanded that she be seen to be playing her part, the military chiefs were determined to be involved so as to justify the swollen defence budget and the British government fell victim to the perpetuation of the myth that there was somehow a sort of special relationship that governed Anglo–US foreign policy. Stanley Baldwin, not noted for his statesmanlike qualities, nonetheless saw the reality of this clearly even during the 1930s. 'All you will ever get from America,' he pronounced prophetically, 'will be words. Fine words, but just words.'

So Churchill returned to power with the country committed to an expensive war from which it could never possibly derive any personal benefit, newly swollen levels of defence spending to support this, a broken industrial base that nobody had made any serious efforts to repair, a strong currency that discouraged export and encouraged imports, high levels of debt (now 175% of GDP), and the vampire bat of the welfare state sucking the patient's very lifeblood. Surely things could not get any worse?

# NINE

## 'A little local difficulty'

The answer, sadly, was that they could and did, not least because the onset of the Korean War made it doubly impossible to make any significant inroads into the defence budget, even had the government wanted to do so. However, before moving on we should note two further points.

The first is that, in the full flush of socialist zeal, Attlee's administration decided to nationalise whole industries. Iron and steel, coal and the railways all passed into public ownership. This was little short of a disaster. These were all industries in urgent need of massive investment, rationalisation and modernisation, both as regards plant and working practices. This might just have been forthcoming in the private sector if experienced industrial managers and engineers could have been recruited from America and international equity markets tapped for capital. Unlikely, certainly, but just faintly possible. As it was, the dead hand of public ownership simply hurried them into obsolescence. Despite the clear and fairly immediate evidence that having large amounts of GDP under the control of government did not work, either for the individual companies or for the economy as a whole, the same 'remedy' would later be extended to large parts of the motor industry, shipbuilding and power generation. Telecommunications was already under government control, and would remain so. As the postwar period progressed, these industries would become a huge drain on public resources and any attempt at rationalisation the focus for bitter and prolonged union unrest.

The second is the answer to the obvious question 'whatever happened to Marshall aid?'

The applications submitted by France and Germany under the European Recovery Programme (ERP), to give it its proper name, were models of clarity. They were remarkable in their vision of long-term strategic planning and in their emphasis on industrial development, particularly in new, modern industries such as electrical appliances, motor vehicles and synthetic materials, for example rayon and nylon. The British proposals were by contrast a masterpiece of obfuscation, designed to baffle and confuse rather than inform. Where reference to industry does appear it is significant that it is to the old primary industries such as coal and iron and steel that Britain should have been looking to run down and transition away from, rather than encourage and build up.

There were two main reasons why Britain wanted to fudge their ERP plans. The first was that they wanted to fund an ambitious programme of house-building, which was a pet project along with the National Health Service and the welfare state of the forceful Nye Bevan, who represented the left wing of the Labour Party, and dominated Attlee's Cabinet. While clearly socially desirable, this would not have found favour with the Americans, as it would produce little direct economic benefit, and they had made the early achievement of economic viability by European countries the specific aim of ERP applications.

The second was that, quite remarkably, having signed up to Bretton Woods, Britain was proposing also to sit outside it. Before the war she had maintained something called the Sterling Area, which encompassed all the Empire and Commonwealth. This was at that time a very large part of the world, including the whole of the Indian subcontinent, Burma, Malaya, Singapore and significant parts of Africa, particularly in the south and east. Of all of these, by the way, the only net contributor was resource-rich Malaya. This is a hugely important point. Successive British governments seem to have seen the Empire, and later the Commonwealth, countries as assets providing significant benefit to the UK, whereas in fact they were never anything other than a cumbersome liability, both financial and strategic, and a continuous drain on British resources.

The Sterling Area was partly for exchange control purposes, but it was also much more, effectively an alternative global financial system with Britain sitting at its hub as central banker and lender of last resort, the ultimate source of dollars and gold reserves upon which any member country could call. Having now signed up to Bretton Woods, which required that all international commitments had to be settled in either gold or dollars, to enter into such an open-ended commitment over which ultimately she had no direct control, was thus hugely dangerous and gratuitously stupid. Nonetheless, this was exactly what Britain did.

It is impossible to offer any rational explanation as to why Britain, with every reason and excuse now to discontinue the arrangement, chose instead to continue it. Particularly so since during the war Britain had built up huge debts to various Sterling Area countries. For example, she had promised to pay India for the privilege of basing troops there, partly because of concerns that many Indians might actually welcome the Japanese as liberators from their imperial masters. Britain would attempt to pay these debts off by exporting large amounts of goods completely free of charge to India, thus reducing export revenues at a time of course when the British government's main strategic objectives included building them up.

So, the main reason that Britain wanted to fudge the issue of their ERP plans is that they wanted to use the Marshall Plan as a general monetary reserve fund for the Sterling Area, something on which the Americans were likely to be none too keen, first because it was not what it was intended for and second because the Sterling Area had been rendered unnecessary by Bretton Woods. If individual countries had problems paying for their imports, they could apply for advice and assistance from the IMF, whose role Britain was usurping within the Sterling Area. British ministers and officials would even try to persuade America to continue supporting the Sterling Area after the Marshall Plan came to an end, complaining plaintively that the Americans did not understand Britain's wish to maintain these reserves. Unfortunately for Britain, the Americans understood all too well.

In addition to the Marshall Plan itself there was also the money it generated within the national economy by means of the economic multiplier effect, starting with the purchasing of materials for industrial renewal. These became known as counterpart funds, and countries such as Germany, France and Italy reinvested all of theirs into industrial development, thus leveraging even further the effect of the Marshall Plan. Britain, by contrast, devoted all of hers to reducing the national debt.

Yet the amount of Britain's national debt at the end of the Marshall Plan period was almost exactly the same as it had been at the beginning. In other words, the government had failed utterly in both the strategic imperatives for national recovery (revitalising industry and paying down debt), effectively running a budget deficit but hiding this fact by purloining counterpart funds, just as they had purloined Marshall funds for house-building and Sterling Area reserves. Thus it was that the Marshall Plan period would in due course lead, in France, to new factories, nuclear power stations, high-speed railways and government-funded industrial research centres, but in Britain to new houses, the welfare state, a National Health Service and unsustainable commitments to a deeply flawed and highly dangerous financial system of her own deluded devising.

In the event the Conservatives would prove no more equal to the challenge than their Labour counterparts. However it should be clearly stated that the Attlee government has enjoyed, most unfairly, a generally good press that is quite unjustified by the facts. If we once remove the rose-tinted spectacles of social idealism and look instead simply at actions and consequences, challenges shirked and national interests betrayed, then the only possible conclusion, sad though it may be, is that Attlee and his colleagues wilfully threw away Britain's first and probably only real chance of national recovery. They failed either to reduce debt, restructure industry or boost exports; even by 1950 Britain's exports were only 27% in real terms[1] of what they had been back in 1913 and more than half of these were to the Sterling Area, many of which were not being paid for. Most damaging of all, they passed on to their successors the notion that it was acceptable to live beyond one's means, and that whenever spending plans outstripped projected income the shortfall could simply be made good by running a budget deficit and borrowing more money.

---

[1] Author's own calculations using the GDP deflator, a good measure of industrial inflation. Original facts from *The Lost Victory*, op. cit.

This 'abnormal expenditure' would now become the norm in the politicians' warped view of the world, which was in fact totally at variance with Keynes's original ideas. Remember that he had proposed increased spending funded by a budget deficit only in bad times, when there was considerable slack in the labour market. Yet he had in mind spending that had a direct economic impact, such as building infrastructure, rather than increasing the budget to things such as defence, welfare and health. He also suggested that in good times policy should move in the other direction, raising taxes and cutting spending in order to try to regulate economic growth before it sparked high inflation and also to build a contingency fund against future deficits or, presumably, reduce the national debt. In the event, none of this was ever done.

For politicians in search of electoral popularity and thus a quick fix, running a deficit and using increased borrowing to spend money they did not have was to prove a siren call that they were unable to resist. The irresponsibility of such an approach did not take long to manifest itself. So inept was the handling of the economy that wartime rationing could not finally be ended until 1954 because of lack of government action to create a new export base (even bread would be rationed at one stage, something which the government had not dared to attempt during the war), while reckless budget deficits helped contribute to inflation moving above 9% in both 1951 and 1952.

The tragic futility of Britain's defence spending was brought home by the Suez Crisis of 1956 when President Nasser's Egypt nationalised the Suez Canal and Britain, for all her much-vaunted military might, proved unable to respond except after a lengthy planning and preparation period. Rather like Austria's action against Serbia in 1914, the delay proved fatal, with any diplomatic support which Britain and France (who between them owned the canal company) might have initially enjoyed, most crucially from the United States, having ebbed away, with the USSR deciding to use the crisis as a distraction while they used force to crush a nascent pro-democracy movement in Hungary.

Britain and France were then lured down the path of dishonour, agreeing that Israel would invade Egypt and then themselves invading in the guise of peacekeepers. Prime Minister Anthony Eden, who had resigned in protest at the appeasement of dictators in the 1930s, lied to the House of Commons, suffered a nervous collapse and resigned. So much for Britain's place in the world, yet the delusion would remain in place. So would the accompanying delusion of the 'special relationship' with the US. Increasingly, this would become a self-serving delusion, as the only real opportunity for many future British prime ministers to take what they saw as their rightful place on the world stage would be as a sycophantic glove puppet of the US president of the day.

Economic mismanagement reached new heights of irresponsibility under Eden's successor, Harold Macmillan, who pursued populist high-spending policies under the guise of seeking full employment, even though his own treasury team warned him this could only lead to high inflation. When he rejected their advice in 1958 (the next year was an election year, and the last thing he wanted was a responsible and thus potentially unpopular budget) the entire team, from the Chancellor of the Exchequer downwards, resigned in protest. Macmillan famously brushed aside the self-sacrifice of these honourable men as 'a little local difficulty' and went on to win a landslide majority the next year. It was effectively the end of their careers for the three ministers involved, Peter Thorneycroft, Nigel Birch and Enoch Powell.

It was during the 1950s that intellectual opposition to Keynesian thought began to be heard for the first time, though it would not gain widespread support until the 1970s and even then would prove controversial. This was the monetarist movement, led initially and most influentially by Milton Friedman, yet another major economist to teach at the University of Chicago and later a recipient of the Nobel Prize.

Friedman saw the flaw in Keynes's approach. Rather than the economy tending naturally to full employment, and requiring stimulation if it did not, there was in fact a natural rate of unemployment and governments could only seek to reduce this at the cost of generating high inflation. To be fair, later, revised versions of Keynesian thought did acknowledge this concept of NAIRU: the non-inflation accelerating level of unemployment.

However, specifically in the UK there was another flaw in the Keynesian model which no politician ever admitted and certainly no politician ever had the courage to do anything about until later, under first Heath and then Thatcher. The British labour market did not behave perfectly if left to its own devices in a normal economic situation. On the contrary, its workings were severely distorted by trade union activity. Thus, unless this defect could first be fixed, the market could never reach its proper equilibrium point because there would always be artificial supply and demand, and thus no 'natural' level of unemployment. To take but one example, when diesel trains replaced steam on Britain's railways, management readily agreed with the unions that the now-redundant firemen should continue to be employed and travel on the footplate even though they no longer had anything to do but hand the driver his thermos flask and admire the view.

So it was that with this issue ignored there was always rampant wage inflation at work within the system. Between 1946 and 1984, the year of the great coal strike, retail prices increased about thirteen times (itself a staggering fact), yet average wages increased more than twenty-four times. The fact that industrial relations continued to be allowed by all concerned to poison output, exports and competitiveness is shown by the fact that the worst year ever for stoppages, with 29.5 million working days lost, came as late as 1979. The unions had been formed in the days of mass exploitation of labour to campaign for humane working hours, safe working conditions and reasonable wages. That struggle had been long and bitter, and perhaps that experience had unduly coloured the view of trade union members, particularly the older ones. Yet it was difficult to escape the conclusion that in the post-war period many trade union officials were hardcore communists determined to bring down any democratically elected government that tried to curb their powers, as did the Heath government of 1970–74, or which did not accede to their demands, even when constituted by their own union-funded Labour Party, such as the Callaghan administration at the end of the notorious 'Winter of Discontent' of 1978–79, which saw even firefighters, refuse collectors and gravediggers withdrawing their services.

The coming of Thatcherism would be as much as anything a reaction against what many had by now come to see as the unacceptable face of unbridled union power. Yet the damage done by weak management and militant shop stewards was already incalculable. For instance, the port of London was the busiest port in the world at the beginning of the 1960s but a decade later the London docks no longer existed at all, victim of many strikes led by the active communist Jack Dash, culminating in one particularly lengthy one that saw cargo shippers and shipowners alike finally lose patience and abandon London for foreign ports such as Rotterdam.

The combination of trade union activity and the nationalised industries was particularly damaging, with higher and higher wage claims at the likes of British Leyland (the collective ownership entity for the motor industry) driving them ever further into losses that could be made good only by even more public expenditure, which in turn fuelled more deficits and national debt.

Monetarism, while building on the work of Keynes, recognised that his model was no longer valid, even if it had once been (and that even this was arguable). It was the amount of money in circulation, monetarists argued, which drives both production and inflation, coupled with the rate at which that available money gets spent. The former they called the money supply, and the latter they called velocity. By increasing the money supply you can stimulate growth, though only at the expense of also stimulating inflation, while by reducing the money supply you can clamp down on excessive inflation, but only at the expense of also holding back growth.

Let us look at both these concepts in a little more detail.

Money supply proves a rather slippery customer if one attempts to consider it in detail, and even governments, economists and central bankers have changed their views of it over time. Briefly, a 'narrow' measure such as M0 looks only at physical money (coins and notes in circulation) but such measures were to prove inadequate when used for monetary policy purposes. It was therefore found necessary to adopt instead increasingly 'broad' measures, starting with M1 and moving onwards from there. The currently accepted measure is M4, which has grown to accommodate first deposit accounts, then current (checking) accounts and finally all sorts of specialist institutional funding devices.

Suppose we were to receive a cash gift and place it in our bank account, then write a cheque to someone else. Money would be transferred first from the donor to us, then from us to our bank and then from our bank to another bank for the account of a third party. None of this would have any effect on any broad measure of money supply, such as is commonly used today. All that would have happened is that money would have moved around within the system. The total amount of money supply within the system would be unchanged.

This is where the idea of velocity comes into play. This measures the rate at which that money changes hands and is typically measured by reference to a year. Suppose that our cash gift was £100. We write a cheque to a restaurant a few months later for £100 that we spend on a meal. Some weeks later the restaurant pays out £40 of that to its suppliers. They then pay out £30 to their workers. The year then ends. If we were to make the very artificial assumption that the initial £100 was the only money in the economy, then during the course of the year it would have transferred £270 of value around the system, and thus during the course of the year velocity would be 270/100 = 2.7.

There is an important limitation here. Velocity is measured only on domestic spending. It is actually formally measured by GDP divided by whichever measure of money supply you choose to adopt. So, huge amounts of money could be flowing out of the country being spent on imports and this would not show up in velocity calculations at all.

At first sight this may seem similar to the idea of the Keynesian multiplier that we have already considered. Remember, Keynes believed that increased government spending would have an effect on the economy far beyond its original amount as firms hired more workers who in turn spent some of their wages on goods produced by other firms, who could then hire more workers, and so on, though this multiplier effect would be eroded steadily at each stage by saving and taxes. For the monetarists, however, at least if they are using a broad measure of the money supply, velocity applies to all the money currently in the system, so distinguishing between spending and saving (as Keynes did) becomes irrelevant.

This is a much more important difference than it may at first appear, because it points to a totally different conceptual framework underlying each of the two approaches. Let us go back for a moment to the relationship between velocity and GDP.

The quantity theory of money had been recognised for some time even before Keynes started writing. It originates with John Stuart Mill and was stated by Irving Fisher of Yale before the First World War in the classic formula MV = PQ. This is the economic equivalent of Einstein's $e = mc^2$ and by coincidence the two were unveiled within a decade of each other. The formula may seem forbidding at first sight, but simply restates what we have already seen in the text. If velocity equals GDP divided by money supply, then velocity times money supply must equal GDP. PQ is simply a fancy way of stating GDP since GDP equals the quantity of all domestic goods (which includes services) times their price.

So, MV = PQ (which is shorthand for $M \times V = P \times Q$)

Where
M = money supply
V = velocity
P = price (of domestic goods) and
Q = quantity (of domestic goods).

Let us now consider the implications of all this. The crux of the great Keynesian/monetarist debate can be summed up in a single question: is velocity constant, or is it liable to change? Constant, said the monetarists,[2] and so must be the quantity of goods available for sale and purchase in the short term, assuming economic conditions are

---

[2] This statement is made in the interests of simplicity for explanation purposes. I fully recognise that any professional economist would see this as simplistic, or even misleading, though they would hopefully agree that this was the standpoint of the original monetarists and that even today most economists would hold that velocity is constant, or at least very sticky, in the short term. Certainly it would be difficult to imagine anyone launching QE if they did not have this belief.

stable and firms are producing at close to maximum output. Thus if both V and Q are constant and governments (or, strictly speaking, central banks) increase the supply of money, then prices must go up, and vice versa.

The Weimar hyperinflation that we met in an earlier chapter is usually quoted as a perfect example of this. Money supply spiralled out of control, as did inflation. Even Keynes, who in his youth was an avowed monetarist, advocated bringing money under control to solve the problem, and this is of course exactly what Schacht ended up doing.

In fact, the monetarists go further and insist that even if there is some slack in the economy so that in the short term Q can increase, leading to an increase in GDP, in the long run money supply changes can only act on inflation. They also exhibit another important point of difference with the Keynesian approach. Increased government spending, they say, has no effect on the economy as such, but only if it also represents an increase in the money supply. Thus rather than interest-rate policy and fiscal policy (government budgeting for income and expenditure), it is control of the money supply by the central banks that is the only effective economic lever. In a monetarist world, central banks buy back government bonds to push cash out into the system to stimulate growth, though necessarily at the same time boosting inflation, particularly in the long run, or issue government bonds to pull cash out of the system, thus reigning in inflation, but at the cost of also suppressing economic activity, particularly in the short term.

There is a crucially important point here that is worth noting before passing on, as it will occupy the centre stage of later chapters. Most economic policies that are likely to confer a long-term benefit are also likely to cause short-term pain, while those that confer a short-term advantage (often no more than a brief alleviation of a long-term or naturally occurring condition) almost always cause long-term damage. Having read this far, it will already have become apparent which one politicians tend to choose.

Keynes disagreed with the monetarist approach. Remember, he started out as a believer in the quantity theory of money but for him the Great Depression showed that velocity was not constant at all but could change significantly as people switched between spending and saving. So, interest rates were a crucial weapon in making it more or less attractive for people to save and firms to borrow for invest- ment. Even so these measures might not work, as humans do not make rational financial decisions. In Japan, the United States and the United Kingdom in recent years people have continued to save even when a combination of inflation, tax and interest rates make it inevitable and obvious that they can only lose money in real terms.

These days economists tend to be not two-handed but two-footed as most tend to have a foot in both camps. While both interest rates and government budgeting are still seen as useful levers, some passing attention is also paid to the money supply, though there was a time, as we will see, when full-blown monetarist policies were tried out in the UK but, some would argue, in an inconsistent and ineffective manner. However, if money supply is admitted to have even a partial effect, then this raises the obvious question of why various central banks have in recent years been so eager to trot out programmes of quantitative easing (QE), which is relatively new technobabble for buying bonds, effectively printing money and pushing it out into the system. It will be argued in a later chapter that in fact it is difficult to see QE as serv- ing anything other than the short-term interests of central bankers' political masters.

As the British economy lurched into the 1960s, however, televised monetarist debate by high-profile pundits still lay in the future. The story of the two decades since the war was coming full circle. The skies over Downing Street were heavy with the flapping wings of chickens coming home to roost and attention turned once again to something that was supposed to have ensured the health of the global financial system for all time: Bretton Woods.

# TEN

# The Chickens Come Home to Roost

The 1960s would prove the high point of Keynesian economics and, as we have seen, the idea that the government could and should intervene to regulate levels of economic activity had already set up a conflict between short-term political pressures and long-term national economic interests that would prove impossible to resolve. We saw an extreme example of this in the last chapter which proved too much even for some politicians to stomach, with Macmillan's Treasury team resigning en bloc.

Thorneycroft and his fellow members of the awkward squad believed that irresponsible use of the Keynesian stimulus by the government must lead inevitably to artificially exaggerated short cycles of boom and bust, with the government first overstimulating the economy and then, as inflation threatened to run out of control, slamming on the brakes. It was this pattern of boom and bust that Gordon Brown would later claim famously to have eliminated from the British economy (he may in fact have eliminated many things from the British economy, including the national gold reserves, but the cycle of boom and bust was not among them).

Remember that Keynes had argued for increased government spending only on a temporary and 'abnormal' basis in recessionary times, during which substantial slack could open up in the labour market, and that even so the government should try to compensate for this in good times. What happened during the post-war period was that the government started routinely running a budget deficit every year, good or bad, and using this to increase public spending. Remember too that Keynes had advocated spending on things wherever possible that would have a real and lasting economic advantage, such as building new railways or roads, whereas almost all of the increased spending in fact was going on defence, health and welfare.

Obviously this ongoing deficit from year to year resulted in the size of the national debt getting bigger with each successive year, exactly as it would for a household of people who were spending beyond their means every year and living on their credit cards. The effect of this was masked by the fact that, although the *amount* of debt was getting bigger each year, its *proportion* relative to GDP was gradually getting smaller as GDP grew. If debt was getting smaller relative to the size of the economy, politicians would doubtless have argued, what could possibly be wrong with that?

Well, quite a lot, actually. It is in fact a well-known politician's trick called a *non sequitur* (literally 'it does not follow'). Tack two statements together that sound as though they belong together, draw a conclusion from them and hope nobody notices that actually you are pulling the wool over people's eyes. You see, GDP and the economy are not necessarily the same thing and certainly not if you are after some sort of measure that represents the long-term health of the economy.

First, GDP stands for gross *domestic* product, and it is important to understand what this means. It means for example that it would include money made by a Japanese company in the UK, but not money made by a UK company in Japan. To reverse this state of affairs we would have to look at gross *national* product (GNP). This is important since, assuming both repatriate their profits and reinvest at least part of them in their respective businesses, the Japanese company will appear to have boosted the UK economy while bringing little lasting long-term benefit at all, and vice versa. To be fair, this issue is addressed in part by offsetting imports, but this is a complex area and in any event does not fully compensate for the discrepancy. For a country such as the UK, which runs a permanent trade deficit, this is a point of some significance (recognised by Margaret Thatcher, who encouraged Japanese car manufacturers to establish factories in the UK).

Second, GDP only measures *activity* that takes place within a single year, how much money is being spent, not how efficiently that money is being spent. If a business school student wishes to analyse a company they do not do so by looking at its sales revenues in isolation, yet this is exactly what GDP expects us to do. What our student needs to do is to look at what proportion of those sales ends up as profit. By looking at the proportion, and different elements within it, we can assess how efficiently a company is operating.

This highlights two very important truths that are well recognised by financial commentators who look at companies, but not by their economic counterparts. First, it is possible for a company to have high sales and yet still be making a loss. Second, it is often possible to *increase* the profits of a company while *decreasing* its sales (for example, by discontinuing an unsuccessful product line). Only in economics do we find the belief that more production and consumption must always be a good thing, regardless of the surrounding circumstances.

Having examined the company's profitability, our student would then turn their attentions to the balance sheet, the statement of the company's assets and liabilities, and analyse its solvency (ability to pay off its debts by selling off assets if necessary) and its liquidity (ability to pay off its more pressing debts with cash, or assets that might quickly be turned into cash). GDP shows us nothing of this.

The third thing to understand about GDP is that all sorts of unexpected things turn up within it, including the cost of new homes as they are sold to the public, or the costs of their construction if they are to be used as social housing. There is also, more fundamentally, the matter of (directly or indirectly depending on which measure you are using) government expenditure such as defence spending, and, as they get spent within the economy, salaries paid to public-sector employees and benefits paid to welfare claimants. Think back to the Attlee administration, which spent hugely on house-building and defence as well as hiring new civil servants to administer New Jerusalem, and it becomes clear that it is quite easy for government to boost GDP simply by spending more money.

If the government spends more money, then GDP must increase compared to what would have happened had it not spent that extra money. Small wonder, then, that it has been for so long accepted unquestioningly that the government can boost the economy by increased spending. It is a classic case of accepting what is being presented to you without bothering to question the methodology. Even this grim fact does not tell the whole story, however.

If we think of the economy as being separated into the private sector (businesses being operated with a view to profit) and the public sector (government), then very crudely the private sector may be seen as creating wealth and the public sector as consuming it. In order to run the whole machinery of myriad departments and public bodies, the government needs to raise taxes, and ultimately the existence of wealth to be taxed relies on the private sector, which produces it. Thus, the larger the public sector is relative to the private sector, the worse it is for the economy, the greater the proportion of the nation's wealth that the government is destroying.

Armed with this knowledge we can fully appreciate the magnificent irony of the situation. The government can boost GDP any time it likes by creating a larger public sector and thus look like a hero with the electorate. Yet, if one looks beyond the annual GDP figures, they are actually damaging the economy, not helping it. Nor of course are they under any imperative to make the public sector more cost-efficient. On the contrary, they have an incentive to spend more money rather than less, since the more money they spend, the higher GDP will be.

There is yet another angle to all this. Some economists believe that increased government spending simply 'crowds out' private-sector money that would be spent more efficiently. Increased public spending requires more taxation, which leaves less capital available for investment in private-sector hands. Conversely, any public-sector employee who becomes redundant will logically ultimately find work in the private sector, thus becoming a wealth producer rather than a wealth consumer.

All of which raises the obvious question: why is GDP not calculated as the total profits before tax of the private sector, less the total costs of the public sector? The answer to this question is a closely guarded secret; 'guarded' needless to say by politicians. One could perhaps hazard a guess at one possibility. GDP data is produced and presented by civil servants who of course just happen to be part of the public sector...

Following on from this distinction between the private and public sectors, a further principle may be advanced. If a business in the private sector is incapable of producing wealth then it will sooner or later go bankrupt, allowing the capital and labour it has been using to be redeployed into other, more profitable ventures. Just as successive governments, particularly those of the Labour Party, seemed incapable of grasping that growing the public sector was actually a bad thing rather than a good thing, so they proved unwilling, subject to trade union pressure and fear of short-term electoral unpopularity, of allowing this normal economic process to operate. Rather than allow businesses to fail, they took them into public ownership, thus creating the worst of both worlds, an unprofitable business that could only be propped up with public money, yet which had none of the normal incentives to become profitable or cease to exist. For example, the Wilson administration of 1964–70 would nationalise the steel industry in a final, forlorn throw of the dice. This commitment to nationalisation of industry was in fact enshrined in a special clause (Clause Four) in the constitution of the Labour Party, despite a spirited fight to remove it by Hugh Gaitskell after he lost the 1959 election.

Harold Wilson had the misfortune to be in office when things finally and demonstrably started to fall apart, Gaitskell having died suddenly in 1963, following which Wilson scored a very narrow general election victory over Alec Douglas-Home, who had sportingly relinquished his peerage on a temporary basis to take over as prime minister from Macmillan. Home had the misfortune to both look and sound like a relic from an earlier age. He once complained to the BBC that their TV cameras made him look odd, whereupon they replied with surprising candour that this was because he did indeed look odd.

Wilson and his colleagues actually inherited an economy that appeared to be in pretty good shape, having been going through one of its periodic boom cycles. However, the operative word here is 'appeared' since, as we have just seen, GDP presents at best an incomplete view of the economy and at worst a transitory and misleading one. In the event, his government, like those before it, would be rocked at regular intervals and ever-increasing frequency by a 'sterling crisis' or a 'run on sterling', though almost certainly the public, when they saw these phrases in the newspaper headlines, did not really understand what they entailed.

In fact they were rather misleading in any event since it was not really sterling that was 'running' but gold and foreign currency reserves, mostly dollars.

Britain had since the war run a constant trade deficit, an excess of imports over exports. This was because British exports were often uncompetitive on grounds of quality (because British industrial plants and processes had not been retooled) and price (partly because of the strong pound). Imported goods, however, were attractive in terms of quality and variety as well as relatively cheap (again, partly because of the strong pound). Demand for these imports was fuelled by a huge bubble in consumer credit, with hire purchase becoming both widely available and massively popular for the first time. The effect on British industry, incidentally, was catastrophic. To take just two examples from the areas most affected (motorcycles and electrical appliances), just about every UK manufacturer eventually went out of business.

Needless to say, there were those both at the time and since who argued that this was all part of some sinister Korean/Japanese/German/American (delete whichever do not apply) plot to destroy the UK's industrial base by flooding Britain with unfairly cheap imports, but the truth was sadder and more prosaic. Thanks largely to Attlee's squandering of Marshall Plan funds and continuing failure by successive governments to address the issue of industrial relations, most British companies were no longer capable of competing effectively in an increasingly global market. In a final sad footnote, Tony Benn, an unrepentant Clause Four man, would actually set up a workers' cooperative in an attempt to save the final British motorbike manufacturer while Secretary of State for Industry in 1974. He was very shortly afterwards moved to Energy, perhaps because Wilson (who was decidedly lukewarm on Clause Four) thought he had been showing rather too much of it recently.

Wilson was a highly intelligent man who had been one of Oxford's most brilliant graduates, staying on to become a don at the age of just twenty-one. He was a trimmer, a manipulator and a chameleon, a man who never let his principles get in the way of his own interests and whose instinctive reaction when presented with any crisis was to urge the person concerned to go away and think about it for a few days. He had, in short, exactly the characteristics required for a successful political career. He was hugely popular when first elected, and remained so until it became impossible to hide the truth any longer, after which he experienced corresponding lows, at one time polling a lower approval rating than any premier since Neville Chamberlain. Fortunately for him the electorate's memory proved so short that none of this prevented them from electing him again in 1974.

Any country suffering from a trade deficit will experience a flow of money out of the country as domestic companies pay foreign companies for their goods as they are imported into the country. Logically, this money can come only (ultimately) from three possible sources: (1) borrowing, (2) being substituted for corresponding amounts that would otherwise have been invested back into domestic industry (including being paid to domestic suppliers) or (3) the sale of assets. It will be readily appreciated that viewed from the position of the domestic economy (in this case the British one), none of these options can be regarded as a good thing.

However, all this supposes that the foreign seller is prepared to accept your currency. Remember that under Bretton Woods this was not usually an option. International obligations had to be settled either in gold or dollars. In addition, knowing it to be effectively overvalued, investors and bankers (dubbed 'speculators' in government circles) were quite naturally selling sterling heavily whenever they could get their hands on it. Thus, every month Britain's gold and foreign currency reserves were being depleted. Whenever they reached danger levels, this was what was referred to as a sterling crisis.

Bretton Woods assumed that all of this would operate as a check on irresponsible government behaviour. No rational government would want to bankrupt its own country or risk destroying its own industrial base. Therefore they would take steps to bring the trade deficit under control and move back into surplus. This was a problem with which various successive British governments had grappled. They could, for example, have imposed strict limits on the amount of consumer credit available. They could have tried, even belatedly, to encourage investment into the industrial base, perhaps by way of tax incentives. Most importantly of all, they could have asked for a formal devaluation of the pound against the dollar. They could have presented all this to the IMF as a package and asked for a US dollar loan to tide them over until their measures took effect. They could even, in an extreme situation, have thought about erecting trade tariffs to make imports much more expensive in British shops.

Yet there were always strong countervailing arguments. Limiting consumer credit would have been hugely unpopular with an electorate that was enjoying a spending spree after the long austerity of rationing. Thanks to hire purchase agreements they were enjoying a dramatic jump in their standard of living. Taxes could not be reduced without also reducing the amounts spent on defence and New Jerusalem, which was likewise considered unthinkable. Devaluation would inevitably lead to inflation and would, it was believed, do incalculable damage to Britain's international prestige. Going to the IMF would similarly be seen as a sign of weakness and might involve some foreign oversight of how British politicians ran the economy (this was naturally seen as undesirable). Import tariffs tended to lead to retaliation and would thus risk damaging British exports still further.

Inevitably, politicians of all persuasions sought to evade the issue, sacrificing the long-term economic health of the country to their own short-term political interests. It just so happened that it was Wilson's government that was left holding the baby when the whole pack of cards finally collapsed. Perhaps he felt himself unfortunate to be in Downing Street at the wrong time, but the fact that he was a former assistant to William Beveridge carries a certain dramatic irony. So too does the fact that he was in office when the government first debated whether sterling should be devalued in 1949 (it was, but not enough). It was at this time that he first showed his true political mettle, telling some people that he was for it and other people that he was against such a move. In much the same way he first backed and then opposed Hugh Gaitskell as party leader. Wilson was a man who pursued keeping his options open with messianic fervour. Others saw this as simply being two-faced, or worse; Cabinet colleague Dick Crossman referred to him as a crook.

In the summer of 1966, just a few months after having called and won an election, Wilson was forced into a massive deflationary package by a string of sterling crises that found the government, despite the fact they had been warned to prepare for precisely this eventuality ever since taking office in 1964, totally unprepared, with policies being supported or opposed purely on the basis of personal rivalries within the Cabinet, most notably between James Callaghan (Chancellor of the Exchequer), Roy Jenkins (Home Secretary) and George Brown (Foreign Secretary, but also deputy leader and originally in charge of Labour's central planning initiative). Wilson seems to have seen his main challenge as being playing these political heavyweights off against each other to avoid a decision as long as possible, rather than actually taking steps to deal with the situation.

Labour announced higher taxes, both direct and indirect, reduced public spending, long overdue curbs on consumer credit and a wage freeze. Thus people would have to pay higher prices with less money and, with interest rates also being increased, have to cope with much more expensive and less freely available credit. Needless to say, though, there was no suggestion of eliminating the budget deficit. On the contrary, rates of welfare payments, including pensions, had just been increased to record levels. By 1970 welfare would be, at 19% of public spending, by far the biggest item in the budget, nearly twice the size of health and much bigger even than defence.

Had Wilson really been the consummate politician he liked to think he was, he would surely have spent time preparing the nation for all this, perhaps blaming as many other people as possible (speculators, foreigners, etc.) and declaring that these were unpleasant but necessary steps that he felt forced to take in the national interest. As it was, when they came it was obvious to everyone that he had been rushed into them, very much against his will and with no coherent plan of action. From this time onwards the press turned heavily negative and many of the electorate must surely have decided they could not trust him again – at least until the next time they elected him prime minister.

Many, too, wondered why on earth the government had not taken this opportunity also to ask for a devaluation of the pound in 1966. It would surely have been readily granted on the back of the deflationary package, which was widely praised in America, while the IMF had already granted Britain a supplementary loan. The main reason (apart from not wanting to be associated personally with such a step) seems to have been that Wilson did not want to lose face with the Americans, precisely the same reason that Bevin had given for Britain getting nuclear weapons, and one that would caper sardonically down the corridors of British policy-making for decades yet to come.

In the event, Britain would be forced to devalue, hurriedly, ignominiously and, importantly, unilaterally in November 1967. The actual catalysts were another round of heavy selling of sterling and the national dock strike referred to earlier, which cut off much of Britain's export revenue, leading to a rapidly deepening trade deficit. The IMF loan was by now almost completely spent. Callaghan resigned, though in reality simply exchanged jobs with Jenkins.

Even now the pound was still almost certainly too strong against the dollar. In response to the obvious question of why the government did not simply allow the pound to float instead of fixing a new exchange rate, the answer is partly that Wilson believed this would be seen as a sign of yet greater weakness (apparently on the simplistic assumption that a strong currency must always be a good thing) and partly that he feared how far it might fall on the open market if there was no floor in place. To its natural level, perhaps?

Incidentally, the Bretton Woods system would finally formally collapse in 1971, an event that passed largely unnoticed at the time but in retrospect has assumed huge significance. It had already been fatally wounded by the unilateral British devaluation, but would probably have failed anyway since its creators had failed to allow for inflation. As the purchasing power of the dollar declined, heightened by extra inflation caused by the Vietnam War, its official value in gold remained the same. This created a growing 'grey' market in gold, which the US was increasingly unable to control. It is interesting to conjecture what might have happened if a simple inflation-adjusting mechanism had been built into the system at the outset. As it was, America was reluctant to allow the price of gold to rise since one of the major beneficiaries of this would have been the Soviet Union, one of the world's major producers.

, Even after devaluation, the pain was not over for the UK. Secret Cabinet documents show that Wilson was preparing emergency plans in 1968 for something called Operation Brutus, which would effectively have been a total lock-down of capital within the UK, involving a ban on foreign travel, a ban on money being moved out of the country in even the smallest quantity, the seizure of sterling deposits held abroad and the closure of the London gold market. In a memo dated 16 March, Wilson's economic adviser, Thomas Balogh, advised that the measures, which remarkably Wilson was thinking of implementing the very next day (17 March), 'imply a drastic and permanent abandonment of the sterling system as it has been known. They are certainly irreversible.'[1]

The British financial system was, however, saved from this dire fate not by any sudden reconsideration of the economic consequences, but by Wilson's highly developed political instincts. Happily this coincided with George Brown's resignation and Wilson, fearing that his administration could survive one shock but not two, shelved Operation Brutus. It was never implemented and many senior Labour politicians remained ignorant of its very existence.

As we have seen, Wilson was so lacking in backbone throughout his career as almost to qualify as an invertebrate, though on this occasion his cowardice seems to have saved Britain, albeit largely by accident. It is almost impossible to imagine what the consequences of Operation Brutus might have been. Almost certainly they must have included the end of the City of London as one of the world's two leading international financial centres.

---

[1] Quoted on BBC News, 1 January 1999.

Brown had defeated Wilson in the contest for deputy leader in 1962 and on Gaitskell's death he and Wilson challenged each other for the party leadership, leading to Richard Crossman's famous aside to his diary that he felt the Labour Party was being offered a choice between a crook and a drunk. The latter was a reference to Brown, who by the 1960s was an alcoholic.

Beginning drinking in the morning, Brown's already colourful speech and behaviour would become increasingly bizarre as the afternoon and evening progressed. He appeared drunk on live TV, indulged in fisticuffs in a TV studio 'green room' with a fellow guest, publicly harangued newspaper editors, journalists and various religions impartially, gratuitously insulted total strangers when there was nobody else immediately available and had a tendency to be photographed staring intently at nearby female cleavage. It was said of him that he spent most of his mornings in the office heavily hungover and writing wretched letters of apology for his behaviour the previous evening.

The potential for such a personality causing upset in so sensitive a role as foreign secretary is obvious and, from a narrative point of view, exciting. Public insults to the Belgian army and the president of France, and telling a British ambassador's wife that she was too old and ugly properly to represent her country pale into insignificance compared to the most dramatic of the many apocryphal George Brown stories that became (and happily remain) part of Foreign Office folklore.

Attending a state function in South America, which started quite late in the evening, by which time, as the travelling Foreign Office officials knew to their despair, Brown would already be well-lit, he arrived to find a band playing a jaunty little tune. He promptly picked out a lady clad in a rather gorgeous coloured gown, approached her somewhat unsteadily and, in appropriately debonair manner, asked her to dance.

'I will not dance with you, Foreign Secretary, for three reasons,' she explained politely. 'First, you are clearly very drunk. Second, that is not a dance that the band is playing but my country's national anthem, for which you should be standing to attention. Third, I am the Cardinal Archbishop of Lima.'

As Wilson's government lurched towards defeat by Edward Heath's Conservatives in 1970, the central problem of Britain's uncompetitive industrial base remained unresolved. In 1970, more than 10 million days were lost to strike action. Wilson had Cabinet colleague Barbara Castle prepare a document called 'In Place of Strife' setting out proposals to regulate industrial action, but characteristically abandoned it as soon as it became clear that it would be opposed by the unions. Equally characteristically, he bemused his ministers by telling some of them that he was for it and others that he was against it. Ironically, very similar proposals would finally be implemented by Margaret Thatcher.

The next two governments, Conservative (Edward Heath, 1970–74) and Labour (Harold Wilson, 1974–76, and James Callaghan, 1976–79), marked the high water mark of trade union power, both administrations being brought down by strike action. Initially, nobody seemed to mind very much. Heath fought the 1974 election using the slogan 'Who governs Britain?' That the people voted twice within a few months (the first election of 1974 produced no workable majority) both for the unions and the man they had reviled and rejected four years earlier suggests that Heath and his colleagues were widely seen as having been inept and naive. They had sought to impose legislation on the unions, which they must have known would be bitterly opposed, yet made no contingency plans to deal with the trouble when it came. Two miners' strikes, a state of emergency and a three-day week with rolling electricity blackouts were the result. Heath's Education Minister, Margaret Thatcher, watched and learned. In 1975, after Heath had lost two elections in one year she challenged him for the Conservative leadership and won.

The 1979 election saw the biggest swing to the Conservatives since the war, Thatcher being given an absolute majority of forty-three seats. This was almost certainly driven by the strikes of the Winter of Discontent in 1978–79. It was perhaps the most politically polarised election ever, with Labour promising 'real socialism' if re-elected and decrying the possibility of allowing inefficient firms to go bankrupt, presumably seeing this as akin to taking your ageing parents into the back garden and shooting them. The Conservatives were equally scathing about the role of the public sector and saw controlling inflation and trade union power as the key requirements.

Even Thatcher, probably the one politician since the war prepared to be unpopular if she believed that what she was trying to do was genuinely for the long-term national good, could not resist some electioneering, though. Standing for a photo opportunity alongside protesting nurses, she publicly pledged herself to honour the recommendations of the Clegg Commission, which was considering the pay of key public-sector workers, which in cases such as the nurses had been badly eroded by inflation. She would pay a heavy price for this cheap and easy popularity, since these new pay levels would prove a major stumbling block in the subsequent fight to restrain public spending and bring inflation under control.

Heath and his Chancellor of the Exchequer, Anthony Barber, had tried reflating the economy ('the Barber Boom') as a last desperate bid for electoral support. Yet again, political short-termism had triumphed over long-term economic interests. The British economy could not take any more. Inflation, already running at 7% in September 1970, spiralled rapidly out of control and stayed there. The oil crisis of 1973, when the OPEC countries led by the Saudis flexed their muscles for the first time, saw motorists queuing overnight for petrol and drove industry's costs, and therefore also prices, up still further. In 1975, annual inflation reached 25%.

During the subsequent Wilson/Callaghan government, the old Keynesian certainties were shown to be deeply flawed. It was supposed to be impossible to have high inflation, high unemployment and no growth, all at the same time, but that is exactly what happened. Denis Healey, Labour's Chancellor, raised income tax to 83% (98% on income from savings) but needless to say took no steps to eliminate the budget deficit or reduce national debt. On the contrary, it grew from £46 billion to £87 billion as welfare spending was boosted. Perhaps one proudly espousing 'real socialism' (as Healey did on television) could afford to ignore oppressive capitalistic devices such as debt and interest, but sadly the markets did not share such views and Britain went officially bust in 1976, receiving yet another loan from the IMF and this time finally agreeing to submit the British economy to nominal IMF supervision.

All of this had little effect on inflation, however. So Margaret Thatcher took office in 1979 in the nightmare situation of being prime minister of a country which was officially bankrupt, ravaged by strikes, many of them politically motivated, with an uncompetitive industrial base, high inflation and high unemployment.

Yet as well as marking sharply different political ideologies, the 1979 election also offered voters a choice of economic schools, though they would not have understood this at the time. Labour was thoroughly Keynesian, at least in the sense of the corrupted Keynesian principles that politicians had adopted, with a public commitment to full employment, for example. The Conservatives, on the other hand, were heavily influenced by the likes of Milton Friedman and the UK was about to witness a revolution in economic ideology. Like any revolution, however, it would not be accomplished without a great deal of pain, anguish and ill-will.

# ELEVEN

# The Thatcher Revolution

It is difficult for a modern reader to grasp just how deep were the senses of despair and frustration felt by many people in Britain in the 1970s, so quickly and significantly have things changed since then, and the greatest single architect of this change was undeniably Margaret Thatcher. On so much would most observers agree. Regardless of whether they thought her approach laudable or tragically misguided, her influence in shaping the course of history cannot seriously be contested.

Perhaps never had British politics been so polarised as by 1979. True, socialists and fascists had fought each other on the streets of London in the 1930s, but they had been relatively small proportions of the population, which had by and large stayed loyal to the major established parties and to the electoral system. Four decades later, two large groups were heavily represented, with the rest of the country dispersed somewhat apathetically elsewhere along the political continuum.

On the one hand, there were those who believed that the left-wing ideals that had promised a collectivist utopia, with New Jerusalem as its glorious harbinger, had been betrayed by successive Labour governments, who had allowed American influence and financial considerations to get the better of their socialist dream. Like those of a fundamentalist religious persuasion, they believed that whatever problems had arisen were the result of doctrinal backsliding by middle-class champagne socialists and that full public ownership, central planning and a command economy would have long since answered all society's needs if firmly implemented. It was to this group that the likes of Denis Healey were appealing with their promise of 'real socialism' if re-elected.

Most publicly prominent were the extreme left-wing 'ginger group', Militant Tendency, which had efficiently infiltrated not just the Labour Party itself but also, deeply and comprehensively, local government and the trade unions. The party's youth branch was similarly deeply compromised. As the party leadership grew increasingly embarrassed by media coverage of Militant's activities, such as when they took control of Liverpool City Council, party members were officially banned from also being members of Militant in 1983. However, only about 400 expulsions had taken place by 1986, whereas Militant themselves claimed up to 8,000 members at this time, and the influence of the hard left would remain a thorn in the side of successive Labour leaders.

On the other hand, there were those who felt angry and frustrated that successive governments had seemed powerless in the face of trade union action, that the nationalisation of various industries had not been a success and that the nation's finances had been mismanaged; witness inflation, which between 1970 and 1979 had averaged 13.2% a year, meaning that retail prices more than tripled during the decade. Anyone who had spent £25 on a basket of groceries in 1970 would have required £115 to do so by 1983. Charities such as the Distressed Gentlefolks' Association tried to help those who had saved diligently for their retirement, only to see the purchasing power of their carefully preserved nest egg destroyed in the course of a few years.

Part of the frustration of this group, for whom Margaret Thatcher seemed to articulate everything they felt, was that while the forces of the left had an ardent faith in Marxist doctrine, often well expressed, they themselves had no comparable sexy belief system to flourish. Despite the basic theory of Marxism being fundamentally flawed, this had not prevented socialism gaining the status effectively of a religion for its adherents and, as demonstrated repeatedly by events through the ages, you cannot argue with a religion. What would become known as Thatcherism would fill that void, and Thatcher herself, an able and gifted orator, would give as good as she got in the business of trading words.

While it is understandable that the body of policies that would be employed by her governments until her departure from office in late 1990 would come to bear her name, they were in fact an amalgam of ideas culled from various sources, all of which she openly acknowledged.

From Thomas Paine she took a belief in the democratic system and the rights of the individual. From Adam Smith, a basic faith in capitalism and free markets. However, there were two other important influences on her thinking of which even today many people may be unaware: Milton Friedman and Friedrich Hayek.

As we have already seen, in the post-war period governments on both sides of the Atlantic became increasingly interventionist (using Keynesian economics as both a justification and a tool) and paternalistic. This in turn somehow morphed into a belief that government intervention in any situation must always be both justified and beneficial. It was Milton Friedman of the University of Chicago who challenged this view most vociferously. As he memorably said, most people believed that it was necessary for the government to protect the consumer, whereas what was really much more important was to protect the consumer from the government.

A similar view had already been espoused by Hayek in *The Road to Serfdom*, a book adapted for the general reader from an earlier academic work and published towards the end of the war. It was a work that flatly contradicted the approach that would be taken by the post-war governments of Attlee, Truman and their successors. Government intervention in economic activity, whether by central planning or interference with decisions that should be taken on purely commercial grounds or otherwise, is bad not good, he said. It tends to acquire a momentum of its own and concentrate more and more power in the hands of the government, power that can only be created by taking away individual freedom. The eventual logical outcome is complete control by the state over every aspect of the life of its citizens.

Many were outraged that Hayek failed to draw a distinction between socialism and fascism. For him they were both just manifestations of a totalitarian approach dressed up in different clothes. Despite the fact that his view was historically valid (Mussolini began as a socialist and Hitler attempted at various times to draw socialist factions into the Nazis, the proper name for which was the National Socialist Party), it enabled those who found his views inconvenient to suggest that they may actually be politically suspect.

As we will see, there was much more to Hayek than this (just as there was to Friedman) but it is perhaps his view of the respective roles of the state and the individual that condemned him to decades of being seen as at best unfashionable and at worst unacceptable. It is both richly ironic and a sad comment on post-war society that one whose guiding principle was individual freedom should have come to be seen in some quarters as a dangerous right-wing reactionary.

Hayek himself recognised this, saying 'economists very largely treat me as an outsider, somebody who has discredited himself by writing a book like *The Road to Serfdom.*'

Those who have read George Orwell's *1984* will remember with a shiver the Ministry of Truth and its slogan 'who controls the past controls the future', as it creates heroic pasts for present members of the administration while simply erasing those who have fallen from favour. It is indeed almost as though by some tacit agreement among economists and politicians that the Austrian School, of which Hayek is probably the most famous member, has been airbrushed from history. It is possible to read well-known books on economics and economists in which they are entirely ignored. In *The Worldly Philosophers,*[1] for example, whose subtitle tells us it is about 'the great economic thinkers', Hayek receives just a single, brief, passing reference, while in *New Ideas from Dead Economists*[2] it is as if he and his predecessors never existed at all.

Thatcher was a believer, however. It is said that she once actually produced a copy of *The Road to Serfdom* during a meeting with a civil servant and said simply 'this is what we believe in' (the royal 'we' crept into her speech pattern as her rule progressed). For the electorate she kept it simple, talking about rolling back the boundaries of the state. For her, this meant essentially keeping the state out of commerce and industry, leading in time to a programme of re-privatising most of the nationalised industries. Her subsidiary objective of wholesale revocation of regulations would remain sadly unfulfilled.

---

[1] Robert Heilbroner, *The Worldly Philosophers*, 7th edn, London, Penguin, 1998.
[2] Todd Buchholz, *New Ideas from Dead Economists*, London, Penguin, 1989.

She well recognised the dangers of deficit funding, drawing comparisons with households that lived beyond their means, but the economy was by this time in such a total mess that initially she had to accept this as an unpleasant fact of life though she would strive to reduce it, finally succeeding in eliminating it altogether. It is a sad fact that she remains the only prime minister since the war to make balancing the books a government objective.

In fact national debt would roughly triple during her time in office to about £150 billion, but one needs to take into account both a decade or more of relatively high inflation (a condition that she inherited) and the economic growth that her policies helped to stimulate. While not wishing to detract from what was said earlier about its limitations as an economic measure, relative to GDP debt fell sharply towards the end of the period as recovery kicked in.

In part this was because her perceived freedom of action was not great in 1979. She had decided on a 'softly softly' approach to the unions, hoping to persuade them to accept some limitations on industrial action voluntarily. She had already committed to honouring the Clegg awards on public-sector pay, which placed additional burdens on public spending as well as providing further upward pressure on inflation. She cut rates of income tax, hoping to stimulate the economy, but this could only be done at the expense of tax revenues in the short term. Most damaging of all, welfare spending was pushed ever upwards by unemployment, which rose remorselessly as firms went out of business.

It was this aspect of her policies that was perhaps most damaging to her short-term political interests as well as to her long-term legacy in certain quarters. People had grown accustomed to the state intervening to throw a lifeline to a failing business rather than allowing it to go to the wall. Thatcher believed that the market should be allowed to operate freely and that sooner or later workers laid off by an inefficient business closing down would be re-employed by an efficient one as it expanded. While theoretically sound, this was not what people wanted to hear when the main employer in a town, say a coal pit or a steel mill, closed down, throwing hundreds or thousands of people out of work at the same time. It was all too easy for the unions and Labour to represent unemployment as something that was somehow a deliberate objective of government policy and Thatcher rapidly became a figure of hate in many areas of south Wales, northern England and Scotland.

In fact nothing could have been further from the truth. Thatcher was acutely aware of the human misery of unemployment, having witnessed the Great Depression while growing up in Grantham, and did everything she could to alleviate the problem. However, she saw the answer not as creating phoney jobs at public expense, as had happened so often in the past for the sake of short-term political popularity, but in creating real, sustainable jobs for the future by encouraging businesses that could be efficient and competitive in the long term. She did what she could to help, taking the brakes off arms sales to countries like Chile and Iraq to assist British defence manufacturers and encouraging Asian motor and electronics companies to set up manufacturing plants in particularly hard-hit areas of Britain.

The scale and success of urban renewal, the results of which can so easily be seen today, were to vindicate her approach over time, but time was something Margaret Thatcher did not have. Even many of her own party began to oppose her views, with ministers regularly leaking Cabinet disagreements to the press and MPs in constituencies suffering high unemployment openly querying whether such seemingly radical measures should be taken. In truth, there had always been a wing of the Conservative Party, the 'One Nation' faction, which espoused the view of reconciliation and cooperation between all parts of society based on community of interest. These would now come to be labelled the 'Wets', with their Thatcherite colleagues, who believed this was an impossibly idealistic view and an approach that had anyway already demonstrably failed under Edward Heath, inevitably dubbed the 'Dries'.

By the end of 1981, two Cabinet reshuffles had replaced many of the Wets with Dries, people such as Keith Joseph who shared her determination to push through new policies. However, by this time there had been riots on the streets and Thatcher's approval ratings in the polls had fallen even below the previous lows of Harold Wilson.

There was no doubt that, regardless of how effective it may prove in the long term, the people of Britain were not prepared to swallow her bitter-tasting medicine and were intending to vote her out of office at the next election, which would have to be held by 1984.

The course of British history, and almost certainly of the British economy, would now, however, be irrevocably changed by events many thousands of miles away.

The military junta that ruled Argentina had been facing civil unrest of its own, prompted at least in part by economic woes. In December 1981 there was a fresh round of musical chairs, bringing General Galtieri to prominence.

Shakespeare, ever an astute observer of public policy, has Henry IV advise his son 'be it thy course to busy giddy minds with foreign quarrels', noting that frequently when a government is in trouble at home it seeks out some foreign adventure with which to divert popular attention away from its domestic woes. This is what Galtieri did, invading the Falkland Islands in 1982.

As it was, he very nearly got away with it. It was only after a meeting at which Thatcher was being briefed by her defence ministers and civil servants that no military response was feasible was literally gatecrashed by the imposing figure of the First Sea Lord in full uniform to argue robustly to the contrary, that it was announced that a task force would be sent to retake the Islands.

In fact, any military historian would be forced to sympathise with the opposing view. Britain had no air base anywhere near the Falklands and no longer had any conventional aircraft carriers. While the Fleet Air Arm's Harrier Jump Jets performed valiantly, the British anti-aircraft batteries to which so many hopes had been pinned were to prove completely ineffective and the British were never at any time able to achieve air superiority over the Islands. Several ships were sunk by air attack in consequence, some with tragic loss of life such as was suffered by the Welsh Guards at Bluff Cove, and one of which was carrying most of the heavy lift helicopters. That victory on land was achieved was due to the outstanding courage and dedication of a relatively small professional force opposed by a large, badly-led conscript army with poor morale. Yet victory inevitably came at a cost, with 255 British servicemen losing their lives, including the Paratroops' commanding officer after his battalion went into action against a much larger force at Goose Green on direct orders from the UK as a result of political pressure and faulty intelligence, an attack moreover that was tragically announced by mistake by the BBC before it had actually taken place.

About 650 Argentinians also lost their lives, including more than 30 of their fast jet pilots, who performed well and bravely throughout. The scale of the total casualties was much greater, though. Nearly 800 British servicemen were wounded, some of whom were disabled or disfigured (the Welsh Guards had many bad burns victims at Bluff Cove) for life.

Rather than calling a snap election, which many might understandably have questioned, Thatcher waited until June 1983, but the afterglow of the Falklands War still ensured her a massive majority of 144. So, ironically, it was the albatross of 'Britain's place in the world', which had hung damagingly and expensively around the neck of every prime minister since 1945 and was something which had unquestionably done irreparable damage to Britain's economy, which now saved it from being thrust straight back into the irresponsible hands of lesser politicians. She would win another election victory in 1987, but never again would her very political survival be in doubt. In fact, with only one exception, until she left office in November 1990 her sureness of touch would never be in question again.

That one exception was the notorious poll tax, which she introduced in 1990. While impeccable in principle (matching the liability for local taxes with the extent to which families actually used them), this was badly bungled in its execution. Thatcher had failed properly to cap the ways in which local authorities could spend money and this enabled them (many of them Labour-controlled) to increase their budgets and then present the subsequent rises in the bills dropping through front doors as somehow due to the poll tax. Perhaps understandably, this led to mass protest, and even rioting in Central London. Abolished by John Major almost as soon as he took office, the idea of a poll tax has remained so sensitive that no British politician has ever dared mention it again.

By the time Thatcher departed the scene in 1990 she had finally eliminated the budget deficit and was starting to make small repayments of the national debt. Along the way, she had finally brought inflation under control (though this was not fully apparent at the time), privatised almost all of Britain's nationalised industries, presided over 'Big Bang', successfully seen off a major coal strike, broken the power of the trade unions and created a society in which people were encouraged to set up their own businesses.

Incidentally, Big Bang is often described as the deregulation of the City, but this is not correct. If anything, there were more regulations afterwards than there were before. Lawyers and bankers alike joked that Big Bang should really have been called 'Big Thud' because that was the noise the new rule book made as it landed on your desk (few lawyers or bankers have ever become successful comedians). It should more properly be described as the re-regulation of the City, creating a new environment with new regulatory bodies. Most important of all, it swept away old-fashioned distinctions such as jobbers and brokers in equity markets and allowed firms in different areas of financial services to come together for the first time. For those interested in social equality, it also opened up senior positions in the City to working-class people for the first time, as huge new dealing rooms were set up and proved in desperate need of streetwise young people (the so-called 'barrow boys').

Yet it would be futile to pretend that there were not losers too under Thatcherism. Chiefly there were those who were unable or unwilling to fend for themselves and were left behind by the new-found prosperity of many of their fellow citizens. There were those too who sincerely believed that the state had a responsibility to guarantee full employment even at the cost of keeping open loss-making pits, mills and shipyards. Even today many of these people, now mostly in old age, maintain that Thatcher was morally wrong to do what she did. The socialist dream, though it collapsed officially with the Berlin Wall, continues to cast a long shadow.

There were those also who said that the education system had suffered unduly from government spending cuts. Thatcher was memorably refused the customary honorary doctorate by her alma mater, Oxford, after an academic revolt. In truth, though, it could have been much worse.

For it was a well-kept secret of the Thatcher years that a swingeing tax on North Sea oil production was bankrolling public finances. Without these windfall revenues there would have had to be truly savage spending cuts and, given the discontent that even relatively mild ones had occasioned, it is difficult to see that anything other than a wholesale breakdown of law and order might have resulted. Yet without them, Britain would also finally and comprehensively gone bankrupt, defaulting on its foreign debts and leaving the IMF to pick up the pieces. So, in a marvellously random and unlikely sequence of events that would gladden the heart of any proponent of chaos theory, the British economy had been saved from total collapse first by the resignation of a drunkard Cabinet minister, then by an Argentinian foreign adventure and finally by North Sea oil production peaking in the mid-1980s.

From an economic point of view, the Thatcher era had showed up some limitations in the monetarist approach, an issue to which we will return. Despite raising interest rates in an attempt to encourage saving and discourage borrowing, thus reducing velocity and with it the money supply, inflation remained stubbornly high for a long time. Interest rates, it seemed, were something of a blunt instrument where inflation was concerned. At the very least, they took much longer to work than anyone had anticipated. This in turn prompts two further thoughts.

First, inflation is partly a monetary phenomenon, and perhaps also partly a natural product of economic growth (though some would dispute this, at least as a general statement). However, it is also partly a psychological phenomenon. As long as people believe that prices will rise inexorably, then those who provide their labour will continue to demand more money. Similarly, those who supply goods will expect their own costs to rise, not least the cost of labour, and will seek to increase their prices, and preferably at once, so they can stay one step ahead. It would seem logical to suggest that the longer an inflationary period lasts, the stronger these impulses will grow and that thus after a certain time inflation becomes a self-sustaining upwards spiral that is extremely difficult to control.

Second, the figures seem to suggest that such a spiral may begin to develop at much lower levels of inflation than many people currently seem to think. If the evidence of the 1970s and 1980s is to be believed, the tipping point for retail price inflation (RPI) may be at about 6%. UK inflation went above 6% in 1970 and did not fall again to this point until 1983, and even then rose again to peak at 9.5% in 1990, though this final flurry was probably largely due to large wage increases in the financial services sector following Big Bang. Thus, if the past is any sort of guide to the future British politicians should be gravely worried whenever inflation approaches this figure, but then, as we have just seen, inflation is always viewed as a long-term problem that is likely to come back to haunt the next government rather than something that should trouble the present one.

Given the apparent failure of monetarism to control inflation, at least in the short term, Thatcher came under increasing pressure formally to abandon it, which she did calmly in 1986, announcing during a television interview that she had never really been a devotee of it in the first place. It should, however, be noted that it had been tried in the United States by President Reagan where it *did* seem to keep inflation under control, but similarly at the price (its critics argued) of deepening or at least prolonging a recession. Nonetheless the Federal Reserve, which is believed to have been fairly lukewarm on the idea all along, abandoned these tactics in 1982, choosing instead to increase the money supply, which resulted (the same critics would say) in the great boom of the Reagan era.

Many seized on this as evidence that they had been right all along in arguing that the medicine Thatcher had applied had actually made things worse rather than better, that by stamping on the monetary brake she had made the downturn more severe than it need have been and that more businesses had gone bust and more people had been thrown out of work, in consequence.

It is impossible to answer any of these points definitively and nobody claims to be able to do so. Economics is not a precise science, if indeed it is a proper 'science' at all. However, it is possible to identify some issues that should be borne in mind and which may be explored in later chapters.

First, the Keynesian approach was seen by many people to have been discredited. As we have seen, this criticism may itself have been unfair, since the 'Keynesian' measures adopted by politicians were actually a rather bastardised version of his work. However, there were sincere concerns that even the idea of the Keynesian multiplier itself, which lay at the core of his thinking, might be flawed. There is in fact more modern research that suggests that this may indeed be the case, at least given the current environment. In the circumstances, then, it is understandable that some may have felt a need to take a different tin down from the shelf and sample its contents.

Second, there is much more to Friedman's work than monetarism, though this does admittedly play a key role. Central to his thinking, for example, is the idea of limiting the role of government and greatly reducing public spending in the process. Neither Reagan nor Thatcher was able to implement any such proposals. Friedman himself says, 'they were able to curb Leviathan, but not to cut it down'.[3] In fact, until towards the end, neither Reagan nor Thatcher were able even to eliminate the budget deficit, and many would argue that running a deficit is of itself inflationary since it pumps into the system money that would not otherwise be there. It is even possible that running a deficit may act directly against attempting to control the money supply, since there will always be leakage into the system.

Third, it is questionable just how effective interest rates can be as a monetary weapon. Modern monetarist thinking favours the use of government bonds (debt) instead. By buying existing bonds in the market a government can increase the money supply, effectively printing more money and pumping it out into the system ('quantitative easing'). By selling new bonds a government can decrease the money supply, effectively replacing cash (which counts as 'money') with bonds

[3] See his 2002 preface to *Capitalism and Freedom*, Chicago and London, University of Chicago Press, first published forty years earlier, in 1962.

(which do not). Note this is a subtly different approach. Remember the equation MV = PQ. Here, the tactics work upon money, not velocity. Given the pure monetarist view that velocity tends to be constant, at least in the short term, this is perhaps a more sensible approach. Again, though, anytime the government is running a deficit, then money is going to be leaking straight back into the system, either as wages for public-sector workers or payments to public-sector suppliers or contractors. Once again, we circle back to Keynes's belief that running a deficit must of itself be inflationary.

So perhaps the fairest verdict on monetarism is 'not proven'. It seems difficult to believe that running high interest rates will not reduce inflation in the medium to long term, though the required period may be longer than either politicians or economists would like, and it seems logical to assume that the longer inflation has been running for, and the higher the level, the longer the adjustment will take.

A common problem wherever this has been tried has been the difficulty of actually measuring and keeping under control the 'M' part of the equation. Friedman was originally talking about a very narrow measure of money but was forced, as were Thatcher's finance ministers in practice, steadily to broaden this. It is probable that one reason why this proved so difficult is that it is now remarkably easy for people to manufacture money. Not to go out and print their own *Notgeld*, admittedly, but every time a bank grants a new loan they are effectively creating money, since they do not do so by handing over banknotes but by creating account money. Similarly, every time a central bank indulges in quantitative easing it is creating account money. It is a little understood fact, for example, that the amount of money in circulation has been dramatically increased in recent years by means of QE, an issue to which we shall return. Thus, it could be argued that so long as a government does not control bank lending (although it may seek to limit this indirectly through capital adequacy rules) and is not prepared to forego QE, then it is effectively impossible to control the amount of money in the system and certainly impossible to reduce it.

In America, the equivalent of Thatcherism was dubbed Reaganomics. Its broad thrust was very similar. Reagan did not have to worry about nationalised industries, because they did not exist in the USA. He did, however, take a tough line with trade unions, once memorably parading striking air traffic controllers in leg irons on television. Like Thatcher, he sought to control inflation through the money supply, though the Federal Reserve had a much more independent role than the Bank of England, at least officially, and it was the Fed, not Reagan, that formally abandoned a strictly monetarist approach in 1982.

The main plank of his approach was dubbed 'supply side economics' and was based on something called the Laffer curve. This worked on the premise that once tax rates reached a certain level both GDP and tax revenues could actually level off and even start to decline. Clearly, for example, if tax rates were zero then tax revenues would be zero. However, if tax rates were 100%, then nobody would have any incentive to work and tax revenues would also be zero. Logically, then, if both ends of the curve were anchored at zero, there must be some point along the curve where tax revenues would be maximised.

However, the argument ran, tax rates also had an effect on GDP. High tax rates deterred firms from initiating new projects and deterred people from working more. The self-employed, for example, might choose to work fewer hours a week because the added net benefit to them would be too small to justify giving up the extra leisure time. Accordingly, Reagan based his approach on cutting taxes. There is hard research, incidentally, that supports the view that cutting taxes is a more effective way of boosting the economy than increasing spending, something that governments around the world have for the most part studiously ignored.

As things turned out, the Laffer curve did take effect, but not to nearly the extent that the economist Arthur Laffer (yes, you've guessed it, University of Chicago) had predicted. To be fair, Laffer himself never claimed original authorship of the concept, citing variously Keynes and the fourteenth-century Arab scholar Ibn Khaldun. It is said that he drew the curve on a scrap of paper to illustrate a point for Dick Cheney and Donald Rumsfeld, one of them then showed it to a journalist and the rest is history. America's taxpayers did not seem to mind. They gratefully pocketed their tax breaks and re-elected Reagan.

# TWELVE

## A Last Chance Squandered

When Thatcher left office towards the end of 1990 the British economy was dipping back into the next 'bust' period of its perpetual cycle of boom and bust. Despite this, John Major would win an unexpected victory in the 1992 general election, which would keep the Conservatives in power until New Labour's electoral triumph in 1997.

As we have seen, Thatcher had finally managed to eliminate the budget deficit right at the end of her premiership, but she would be the last politician to attempt to do so. The short period of surplus a decade later was almost certainly the result of increased tax revenues at the height of what would become known as the dotcom boom and would actually be presented as an opportunity to increase spending, rather than pay down debt, by that trusted custodian of the national finances, Gordon Brown.

Shortly after winning the 1992 election, Major's government was rocked by 'Black Wednesday', an event from which it would never recover. This was the culmination of a short-lived flirtation with partial monetary union, which saw Britain join the Exchange Rate Mechanism (ERM), under which European currencies effectively traded at fixed exchange rates, albeit 'fixed' within bands rather than at a single specific level for each. It became apparent that sterling had joined this at too high a rate, a depressingly familiar echo of Britain's last period of fixed exchange rates. Proving that there is nothing new in history, investors (again inevitably dubbed 'speculators' by the politicians) led by George Soros sold the pound hard while they could and the phrase 'sterling crisis' was once again banded about. Only briefly this time, though. So powerful had financial markets become, chiefly because of greatly increased use of both leverage and derivatives, that Britain was driven out of the ERM almost immediately when it became impossible for the Bank of England to hold it at the required level, despite having spent most of its foreign currency reserves and announced increases in interest rates to 15% in the process. That evening, presumably on the assumption that this was where many of the City's investment bankers spent their spare time, sterling's fate was announced in the interval at the Royal Opera House (*Tosca*, starring Pavarotti), to be greeted by ironic cheers.

Perversely, Prime Minister John Major had been one of the champions of ERM but like a good rugby player he had deftly passed the ball in time, thus avoiding the killer tackle. It was the unfortunate Norman Lamont, who had already gained a certain level of humorous interest in the City by regularly claiming to have spotted the 'green shoots of recovery' more or less ever since the recession had begun, who would be stretchered off at half-time.

Black Wednesday was a disaster for the Conservatives in electoral terms and also economically, at least in the short term. Had Britain kept her foreign reserves intact, then she could have sold them for a great deal of sterling at the pound's new, devalued price. Instead, they had been spent at a loss to no result. Yet again, short-term political self-interest had triumphed over long-term economic logic. It had been obvious for some time that the ERM had been unsustainable. Britain was in the bust period of the economic cycle and trying to keep interest rates low in order to stimulate growth. Germany, by contrast, was doing very nicely, thank you, and most unsportingly wanted to keep interest rates high to choke off inflation.

As would later prove the case with the eurozone, this unsustainability seemed glaringly obvious to everyone except politicians. As befitting a proud tradition of offering political problems to financial problems, when the French franc came under similar attack shortly afterwards the French simply changed the rules without warning, widening the band within which the franc was allowed to move to such an extent as to make it meaningless. At this point the 'speculators' folded their tents and went home, thus sparing the Italian lira, which was widely rumoured to have been the next item on their shopping list.

In the longer term Britain would, of course, reap the benefit of a weaker pound in the export markets and this undoubtedly did speed the end of the recession, though sadly for Norman Lamont once the first green shoots really did start to emerge he was no longer around to be able to claim responsibility for them.

So it was that by the time New Labour came to power in 1997 the economy was now in a buoyant mood, partly because of the natural turn of the cycle, partly because of a more realistic value for sterling and partly because of the euphoria and massive investment interest generated by the so-called New Economy, with internet and telecom start-ups blossoming in every coffee shop. This led to a happy combination of lower unemployment and higher tax revenues, with the result that the budget actually balanced in 1998 and then went into a small surplus for each of the next three years.

The cycle then reversed itself once more, chiefly as a result of the bursting of the dotcom bubble with attendant large falls in equity values. The most extreme example of this was the Neuer Markt in Germany, which lost about 90% of its value and was closed down by the German Stock Exchange. A severe yet brief contraction then occurred. Brief (at least in the UK), because while all this excitement had been going on in the New Economy, with lots of paper fortunes being made and lots of real money being lost, the old economy had actually remained quite strong in its boring old way and in Britain the period from the middle of 2003 to the middle of 2007 was one of strong economic growth, fuelled at least in part by cheap and plentiful credit, with consequences we shall shortly consider.

It therefore looks very odd that whereas a budget surplus had been achieved before this occurred, it never was again, not even during this very favourable period of about four years, which represented, as we can now see all too clearly, positively Britain's last chance to bring its public finances under some sort of control and start paying off at least some of the national debt. In the event what actually happened was rather like a family on the verge of bankruptcy suddenly being saved by its major breadwinner getting a fantastic and well-paid job and, instead of starting to pay off its credit cards, buying a new house, a new car and going on several expensive holidays, applying for an increase in its credit rating along the way.

In his Budget statement issued in 1999, Gordon Brown spoke of his fiscal policy being designed 'to ensure economic stability through prudent management of the public finances'. Marx memorably said that history repeats itself, first as tragedy and then as farce. Perhaps sooner or later there comes a time when both occur together.

As we have seen, by this time monetarism, or at least attempts to put it into practice, had been largely discredited. It had proved very difficult even to define money, let alone control it, while interest rates had proved a very blunt instrument in respect of either money or velocity, seeming to operate less effectively and with a much longer time lag than anyone had anticipated, and at some clear cost to the economy and society as a whole.

The government had therefore fallen back on a more traditional Keynesian approach, though there remained a lingering belief that interest rates could and should be used to control inflation. So in effect there were now not one but two brakes and accelerator pedals, one pair taking the form of government spending and the other interest rates, an approach that remains to this day.

Once again it seems a little unfair to link Keynes's name with selected highlights of his theory applied in a world very different to the one that he modelled. Remember that he regarded budget deficits as 'abnormal spending' and assumed that the budget would normally be balanced, and that while one might allow a deficit in recessionary times, so as to facilitate additional government spending that might reduce unemployment, you could only do so if you were also prepared to run a corresponding surplus in good times to make up the difference. By the time Brown became Chancellor (in 1997), the government had run a deficit in all but six years since the end of the Marshall Plan (in 1951).

By the 2003 Budget, Brown was already talking of borrowing more money but, he insisted, only to fund investment, not normal expenditure. He also spoke of balancing the budget over the economic cycle, pointing out that he had a surplus built up from the three good years that had just passed. Of course both these assurances would turn out to be totally worthless.

Keynes had never envisaged a situation in which a government would run a budget deficit more or less continually for more than half a century. Brown did not just have one economic cycle to worry about, but the accumulated deficits from all the ones that had gone before. He could not simply shrug his shoulders and pretend they had never happened.

Furthermore, he had enjoyed a dream situation where a downturn in economic activity had nonetheless resulted in budget surpluses. This appears an illogical outcome according to any sort of economic theory and can perhaps be explained in part by the underlying resilience of the old economy and in part by the fact that many taxes are effectively assessed and collected in arrears. Yet, while the economic outlook had indeed been characterised by uncertainty (the price of oil, for example, had been highly volatile and stock markets had fallen heavily), the Treasury's own projections showed the UK economy picking up strongly from 2004 onwards.[1] Using his own avowed logic, this should have been seen as an obvious opportunity to continue thinking in terms of a surplus, not a deficit.

By the 2004 Budget, Brown was acknowledging openly that Britain's position since 2000 had not in fact been nearly as bad as had been believed at the time and that the economy had recovered strongly, experiencing 'the longest sustained expansion on record'.[2] Yet still the inconsistency between practice and expressed theory continued. Far from budgeting for a surplus, Brown did the opposite, though assuring the nation that the budget was planned to return to balance in 2007.

This was deeply illogical on a number of grounds. First, if Brown really believed in balancing the budget over an economic cycle, then surely a period of projected growth was the time to run a surplus, not a deficit. Second, Brown claimed repeatedly that government policy was to eliminate the cycles of boom and bust that had characterised Britain's situation since the war, yet if this was indeed so, then a period

[1] HM Treasury Budget Report, 2003.
[2] HM Treasury Budget Report, 2004.

of economic growth was the time to be trying to keep a damper on the economy by restricting public spending and increasing taxation, not turning up the gas. Third, there has been much discussion over the years that Britain's financial and economic affairs seem to run in cycles of roughly seven years. If so, then 2007 could be expected to mark the exact point when it fell back into bad times, in which case there would be a possible need to run a deficit, not 'return to balance'.

Nor, despite Brown's brave words to the contrary, is there much evidence of his much-vaunted capital investment. Between 2003 and 2007 public spending would rise from £415 billion to £543 billion (when arguably it should have been falling instead), yet the big winners seem to have been pensions, healthcare and welfare, none of which would be able to claim to have made any contribution to the country's long-term economic wellbeing. Yet again a depressing impression emerges of politicians having been more concerned with short-term electoral popularity than with the long-term financial health of the nation. Far from using this almost-unprecedented period of prosperity to pay down the national debt, it rose between 2003 and 2007 from £347 billion to £500 billion, heading steadily towards £10,000 for every man, woman and child in the country.

In retrospect it seems clear that the period from 2003 to 2007 represented Britain's last chance to bring the public finances into any sort of order and that this opportunity was squandered. Along the way, Brown sold off Britain's gold reserves at an historically low price, having first considerately informed the market of what he was planning to do. The reason given for this apparently quixotic act was 'to diversify away from gold'. Given that the pound has now lost over 93% of its purchasing power against gold since 1971, this did not turn out to have been the most brilliant decision of all time. After all, though admittedly highly volatile in the short term, gold is the ultimate symbol of value, not paper currency.

Various other things occurred during this period that would subsequently prove to have had a significant impact on subsequent events. In no particular order these included a dramatic growth in financial transactions that were highly geared with debt, such as leveraged buyouts, a similar growth in the amount of capital managed by hedge funds and a major shift in regulatory approach.

Leveraged buyouts were an American invention – only as recently as the late 1980s did they start to be seen in any great number, but they rapidly gained ground on both sides of the Atlantic. The most well known is almost certainly the acquisition of RJR Nabisco by the private equity house KKR in 1988, which became the subject of the book *Barbarians at the Gate* and the film of the same name starring James Garner. It serves as a useful model for the genre as a whole. A private equity firm raises a fund (usually structured as a limited partnership) from institutional investors such as pension funds and insurance companies, and then uses this money as equity with which to buy businesses, mixing it in each case with debt supplied by the banks. The analogy of buying a house with a mortgage facility given in the film is a good one; this is exactly what happens, although with much larger numbers involved (nearly $50 billion in current value for RJR Nabisco, adjusted on a retail price basis).

Between 2003 and 2007, private equity funds raised so much money that this amounted to roughly half the capital ever raised. Mixed with a greatly increased availability of cheap debt on generous terms, buyout activity mushroomed, with even large public companies falling into private equity hands. High profile examples in the UK included Debenhams, Boots and the music business EMI, the owners of the famous Abbey Road recording studios.

At the same time, greatly increased amounts of real-estate debt were also being made available for property deals. We will examine shortly exactly how and why this came about, but the net result was to leave far greater amounts of debt on bank balance sheets in mid-2007 than had existed in mid-2003. Incidentally, in the wake of the first buyout boom, which had ended in about 1990 shortly after the RJR Nabisco deal, and reacting to the consequent credit crisis which followed, the Federal Reserve had for a while insisted on separate accounting for leveraged transactions on a regular and rigorous basis in the hopes that banks would be deterred in the future from advancing money on such a basis again. Yet by 2007 the amounts involved would be vastly greater.

Reliable hedge fund statistics can be rather hard to come by, but at least one respectable source[3] shows an increase in funds under management from \$600 billion to \$2 trillion between 2002 and the high water mark in 2007; an increase of more than three times in just five years. This, however, tells only part of the story since, as with the investments made by private equity funds, hedge funds tended at this time to be very highly geared up with debt; just how highly we will see shortly.

Hedge funds have been blamed as a generic group by the likes of the European Union for causing the events of 2007 and 2008 and this is almost certainly unfair. Indeed, it shows a basic ignorance of what hedge funds are and what they do. Many are marketed to the likes of pension funds on the basis of reducing investment risk rather than increasing it. The EU would later betray the depths of its ignorance by issuing draft regulations to control hedge funds that seemed incapable of distinguishing between a large hedge fund dealing in public markets and things that were demonstrably not hedge funds at all, such as a small venture capital fund dealing with start-up entrepreneurs. Hardly encouraging and certainly not reassuring.

Hedge funds certainly had a part to play, though. For one thing, this vastly increased hedge-fund activity required significantly more product and the investment banks were only too happy to oblige by issuing new derivative instruments, as we will see in the next chapter. This enabled, for example, many hedge funds to make a lot of money in 2007 by shorting various credit markets. It remains a matter of some mystery why banks did not do the same, as they would thereby have been hedging their own by now considerable credit risk.

What this meant, though, and it was felt that this certainly *did* add to market uncertainty and nervousness in 2007 and 2008, was that hedge funds had large amounts of capital with which to go long or short the market on any particular day, so that this added to market volatility, the extent to which prices went up and down. However, even this is a contentious issue with the benefit of hindsight. A research study by

---

[3] The City, UK.

a team of academics at Cass Business School[4] seems to show that, when short selling was banned during the crisis, then far from reducing volatility it actually increased it. If true, this would be yet another example of the principle that governments should be very slow to interfere in the operation of free markets.

Probably of far more consequence was the much greater volume of credit derivatives that had been created and were now washing around the system. Many of these were what is called over the counter (OTC), which is a confusing term since it was originally applied in a very different context. Simply put, it applies to a derivative instrument that is a private arrangement between two contracting parties. The opposite would be an 'exchange cleared' instrument.

In the case of the former, something arose in late 2007 and came to full shocking prominence during 2008, the significance of which had not been fully grasped. Since an OTC derivative was a private contractual arrangement, then its efficacy depended entirely upon the party who stood liable to pay, rather than receive, money on its expiry being both able and willing to do so. This is called counterparty risk. It is the risk that one contractual party will default. For example, the counterparty risk on a British government bond is that the British government will default on its debts. Traditionally the risk of this has been regarded as zero so that British government bonds are treated as being risk-free. Whether this is still a safe assumption to make is left to the reader to decide.

In the case of an exchange cleared instrument, that default risk is replaced by the risk of the exchange itself defaulting, since it guarantees due performance of the instrument and this risk is very small indeed by comparison.

Yet just as the risk of the British government defaulting was regarded as non-existent, so the risk of a major bank or insurance company was felt to be so negligible that it could safely be disregarded. Lehman Brothers, for example, had very significant liability as a counterparty to credit derivatives. When it fell, it sent shockwaves through

---

[4] Led by Dr Richard Payne.

the entire global financial system. The corporate bond market, in particular, effectively curled up and died for several weeks. Most worrying of all, it was rumoured that the failure of various rescue efforts was largely due to Lehman not being able precisely to quantify its counterparty liability, and that similar levels of uncertainty might hang over the balance sheets of other banks. In America, the Fed had been known to be nervous about the delay in recording and settling credit default swap (CDS) positions since 2005, but it is unclear how much had been done actually to address this within the banks.

All of which makes it rather surprising that CDS instruments, which we will consider further in the next chapter when we look at the way in which the banking industry developed over time, should not have been regulated. On the contrary, in the US at least, a decision was made specifically to exempt them from any regulation on the grounds that they were neither securities such as shares or bonds, nor futures.

Yet this decision was taken with the best of motives, the reason being that instruments such as swaps were seen as filling a very beneficial role. Institutions such as pension funds can use them to hedge out interest rate and inflation risk. Government bond holders can use them effectively as credit insurance. So too can banks, though they appear not to and certainly did not when they most needed to, heading into 2007.

However, while this view may have been correct in 2000, when the decision was taken, it only told part of the story and as time progressed that part of the story became smaller and smaller in relative terms. Even by 2000 many of these instruments were being used not for hedging but for speculation, typically by hedge funds, and by 2007 the overwhelming majority of them were in fact being used in this way. As we will see, the practice also grew up of writing 'naked' swaps that did not relate to any specific underlying debt but were effectively just a means of making a bet.

So, if CDS instruments were not regulated but were flooding the market and being used by hedge funds in a highly speculative manner, then surely the hedge funds themselves were regulated? Well, no, actually. A few were, but many were not. In the US there were major exemptions, such as where the fund run by the manager was itself domiciled overseas, or where there was a long 'lock-up' preventing investors from recovering their capital except on two years' notice. This latter exception has always seemed a curious one. Surely there was more argument for regulating these funds and exempting the others, rather than vice versa?

In the UK the Financial Services Authority (FSA) produced a report on the hedge-fund industry in the wake of the well-publicised failure of Amaranth and concluded, with excruciatingly bad timing literally a few months before the crisis began, that the industry as a whole did not seem to pose any significant risk to financial systems and that no further regulation was required.

A further important event had happened in 1997. Responsibility for the supervision of the banking sector was taken away from the Bank of England, who had always exercised it, and passed to the FSA. This was to prove doubly unfortunate.

First, it meant that the FSA was now being asked effectively to perform two very different tasks at once. On the one hand it was being asked to create and ensure compliance with a vast mass of financial regulation over firms as diverse as venture capitalists and commodity managers, though strangely not pension consultants who, for reasons which the FSA is reluctant to divulge, were exempted from supervision despite the key role they play.

On the other hand, they were being asked to exercise an effective oversight role in respect of a specific industry with increasingly sophisticated and specialist daily practices, some of which, as the Fed feared in 2005, were probably not operating as efficiently as they should have been. These are two very different tasks and the FSA would itself subsequently point to this bifurcation of its activities as an excuse for its failure to spot or take action in respect of the gathering storm.[5]

Second, it took the task of banking supervision away from those who were best qualified to perform it. Not only did many of the

---

[5] Adair Turner, TV interview.

Bank's staff have actual experience of commercial and investment banking, but the Bank itself was in constant contact with the commercial banks because of its role as a stabiliser of inter-bank lending and, should it ever be called upon, as a lender of last resort. If the Bank had been left in charge, might it perhaps have been suggesting, in the early part of 2007, that banks should be considering hedging their loan books? Or asking difficult questions about derivative settlement practices? Probably not, but at least there might have been some small chance of this happening.

With the FSA in charge, there was no chance of this happening at all. Indeed, even after the event the ineptness remained. The FSA would subsequently produce its report into the failure of the Royal Bank of Scotland (RBS) only about three years later and even then it would be heavily criticised for how much it had appeared not to understand.

So Britain headed into the middle of 2007 heavily drunk on a toxic cocktail of reckless public spending, unnecessarily swollen national debt, an asset-price bubble (particularly in equity and property markets), a huge explosion of bank lending (particularly to highly leveraged and therefore highly risky transactions) and clouds of credit derivatives swirling around whose true ownership, value and underlying liabilities were not always known with any exactitude.

These different elements had come together like an explosive mixture of gases in a bell jar, a bell jar moreover that was not fitted, as it should have been, with a proper regulator valve to allow them to bleed away safely into the atmosphere, but rather with an ill-fitting general purpose stopper that would sooner or later inevitably allow the introduction of a fatal spark.

The spark, when it came, would take the form of liquidity, the short-term availability of cash, drying up in the banking industry.

# THIRTEEN

# 'Certificates of Dubious Odour'

The banking industry may be said to have evolved through three different stages, rather like a butterfly having to be first a caterpillar and then a pupa. However, unlike a butterfly (some species of which, contrary to popular belief, can live for several months), the third and final stage has been very short compared to the first two. In fact, in the case of banks the caterpillar stage lasted for several centuries.

The basic principle is very simple. Banks offer a rate of interest to attract people to deposit their savings with them. They then lend that money out to other people at a higher rate of interest and the 'spread' between the two rates represents their gross profit, before they deduct all the costs of doing business to arrive at their net profit. The practice of fractional reserve banking, whereby they can lend out many times their own capital on the assumption that they will never have all their depositors turning up on the same day to withdraw their money, multiplies the potential for profit.

Of course a run on the bank can and does happen. The scene in the film *It's A Wonderful Life* in which Jimmy Stewart and Donna Reed heroically give up both their honeymoon and their own money to keep the struggling local building and loans institution open has a happy ending which is often not available in real life, bereft of the assistance of Hollywood screenwriters. In the immediate aftermath of the Wall Street Crash more than 4,000 banks failed in the United States alone. Nor are they solely the stuff of history. Northern Rock famously suffered a run in 2007, with depositors queuing outside its branches for many hours, desperate to reclaim their savings in cash.

Despite such occasional difficulties, the basic model survived for hundreds of years, largely driven, at least in Europe, by the Reformation. The Catholic Church banned the taking of interest on loans as 'usury', though the Jewish moneylenders to be found in every large town were of course exempt from this. It was left to the commercially motivated burghers of northern Europe, as the various Protestant creeds spread through the Low Countries, to invent what rapidly became the traditional banking model; this made the jump across the North Sea to England in the most unexpected of circumstances when Henry VIII's desperation for a solution to his marital problems led him to repudiate the Pope as his spiritual overlord. Thereafter the word 'usury' gradually gained its modern meaning, as the charging of interest at an excessive rate. The charging of any interest at all remains forbidden however (as 'riba') under Islamic law.

As the nineteenth century progressed, other, rather more exciting activities started to be carried out in the banking halls of European and American banks. Banks began the practice of accepting loan notes, usually known as bills, from their customers at a discount. For example, a business that wanted to borrow £500 might be allowed to sell a £550 bill payable in a year's time to their bank for £500. In the same way, banks might in turn issue their own bills as a way of raising money from other banks, or persuade them to accept at a discount bills which they had taken from their customers. Ultimately, the central bank, such as the Bank of England, would accept bills from banks as a means of preserving financial stability. These various practices led to many banks in London becoming known as accepting houses and forming their own association under the aegis of the Bank of England, one of whose purposes was to provide support operations (often referred to for some reason as an 'armchair') in a suitably discreet and gentlemanly way for any one of their members who might find themself temporarily embarrassed.

Other similar instruments, known as bills of exchange, were used to facilitate payment, often across national borders, under contracts for the supply of goods, and both banks and other merchants might sometimes be persuaded to accept these bills at a discount before their payment date. Bonds issued by various governments around the world might similarly be discounted. Banks that carried on this subtle game of juggling risk, interest rates and compound returns employed the financial whizz-kids of their day and were often referred to as discount houses.

In time some banks, particularly in America, also became involved in company share issues. They could do this, for example, by underwriting an issue. Underwriting is the equivalent of issuing insurance or a guarantee. The bank agrees to pay to the company the full amount of capital it seeks to raise from the market, less a fee for its troubles. Should the issue fail for any reason to be fully taken up by new and existing shareholders, then the bank is forced to make good the shortfall, taking the remaining unsold shares onto its own books.

Clearly all these sorts of activities entail both different risks and higher levels of risk than those associated with basic caterpillar banking. This was felt, rightly or wrongly, to have played a part in the mass demise of banks in the United States following the events of September 1929, and in 1933 Washington passed a Banking Act that is widely known as the Glass–Steagall Act after its two champions: Senator Carter Glass of Virginia and Congressman Henry Steagall of Alabama.[1]

The Glass–Steagall Act effectively separated the caterpillar banks from what we might call the pupa banks, banning any business organisation from owning at the same time both a traditional bank that took deposits and lent out money, which were becoming known as commercial banks, and one of the newer, flashier variants that were increasingly becoming known as investment banks.

This legal separation never occurred in Britain, though there was for the most part a practical separation. As investment banking widened to include advisory work, for instance on mergers and acquisitions, these activities were carried out by a small elite group of institutions working behind tasteful brass nameplates in the City of London, which would for some time continue to call themselves merchant banks in deference to their origins in financing international trade, the latter in which they sometimes even participated. A merchant banker was someone whom every British mother aspired for her daughter to marry, while for every British schoolboy it was simply rhyming slang for someone of whom they did not have a very high opinion.

---

[1] In fact, there were two Glass–Steagall Acts. The other, a year earlier, had widened the powers of the Federal Reserve to discount bank and government bills.

So, while caterpillar banking was motivated by the taking of interest on loans, pupa banking was motivated by the charging of fees for facilitating or advising on hugely complex financial transactions, often involving the issuing of securities such as bonds or shares. For a long time these two models, the old and the new, coexisted quite happily, being carried on by different types of banks staffed by different sorts of people. The separation would be ended, and the caterpillar model effectively killed off after a useful life of several centuries, by different events occurring about a decade apart in Britain and America, respectively.

In Britain in October 1986, Big Bang changed forever the way in which the financial practitioners of the City of London would operate. A change from face-to-face trading on the floor of the stock exchange to a modern, screen-based system made possible the abolition of a legal separation that had existed in the UK between stockbrokers and jobbers. Brokers might be thought of as retailers, dealing with members of the public who wanted to buy or sell stocks and dealing on their behalf with the jobbers, who held their own portfolios ('books') of stocks and acted as wholesalers, buying and selling through the brokers. The brokers made their money by way of commission on the trades that they executed for their clients. The jobbers made their money by buying and selling on their own account.

The practical effect of Big Bang was to spawn a craze for massive financial services conglomerates, usually built around a commercial bank buying both a broking and a jobbing firm and putting them together with a merchant bank, which they either bought or started from scratch. The fee-driven mentality of the former merchant bankers, now often supplemented by imports from American investment banks, rapidly killed off the caterpillar model of the hapless commercial bankers who had initiated these mergers often only to find that they had a tiger by the tail (a number of these high-profile mergers were not successful). From now on new loans would be granted only in return for an arrangement fee and individual bankers would be judged not on the repayment record of their borrowers, as had previously been the case, but on the level of arrangement fees that they were able to generate during the year. One of the most important seeds of the present crisis had just been sown.

Change came to America in 1999 with the repeal by the Clinton administration of the Glass–Steagall Act. With commercial banks moving into the issuing and trading of securities, caterpillar banking had now finally passed away on both sides of the Atlantic.

Pupa banking emphasised the earning of fees rather than financial prudence. The riskier the loan appeared to the bank, the more likely a higher requested arrangement fee rather than rejection by the credit committee. This state of affairs would reach its peak in the so-called 'Cov-Lite' period between about 2005 and the early part of 2007 when banks poured loans into private equity and real-estate deals at much higher rates of leverage than before, but with much less legal protection (fewer borrowers' covenants in the loan agreement, hence Cov-Lite).

Such transactions were entered into in the good times, when levels of corporate profitability were high and banks were eager to lend money at high multiples of cash flow. The need to refinance these deals in bad times, with profitability under threat and banks lending only grudgingly and at low multiples, forms one strand of the present situation whose potential for causing grave damage to the banking system as well as to the shareholders and employees of the companies concerned is only now becoming widely recognised, though there have already been a number of high-profile casualties, including the international music business EMI.

Banking now entered the final stage of its evolution, though a bluebottle rather than a butterfly may be a more apt way to symbolise it, since the former vomits over its own food before eating it.

Not content with earning both interest on loans and fees for lending money, issuing securities and advising on transactions, banks looked around for further sources of income. They found them in three areas of activity: securitisation, credit derivatives and proprietary trading. These had already existed, but the first two were now dramatically ramped up and linked directly with the third in what would become an unholy triangle, each creating more and more demand that could only be satisfied by yet further expansion of the other two. The fatal catalyst, which would ignite the undergrowth and smoulder for a while before bursting out into a full-blown forest fire, was intermediation.

Securitisation simply involves bundling things together into a parcel and then selling financial instruments that represent a share of the ownership of the parcel. A REIT (real estate investment trust) would be a good example. An ordinary investor cannot afford an office block in Tokyo, but they can afford to buy some shares in a REIT that in turn owns an office block in Tokyo. So there is nothing intrinsically wrong or undesirable about securitisation. On the contrary, it can enable investors' access to areas they would not otherwise be able to afford, as in the example just given, or businesses to get rid of liabilities from their balance sheet, thus freeing up capital for new expansion.

For example, a bank (or in the case of America, a government-related mortgage corporation) may have lent money to many people with which to buy homes. Those loans will sit on the balance sheet of the bank as assets, since they represent the right to receive money in the future. However, if those loans can all be bundled up into a parcel by an investment bank and sold to institutional investors around the world, then everyone can be happy. The bank receives money now rather than in the future, the investment bank makes a big fee and the investors who wanted to swap present cash for future cash flows have also got what they wanted. Incidentally, such instruments are known as collateralised debt obligations, or CDOs, though in 2008 there were some who began referring to them as certificates of dubious odour.

The theory behind a CDO is that the risk of any one of the individual loans defaulting is diversified away by holding instead a small piece of many different loans. Like all theories, however, it depends on what assumptions are being made. If all the loans are of good quality, so that one is subject simply to the usual probability of occasional default, fine. What happens, though, where a great many of the individual loans are not of good quality and never were?

The problem here is intermediation. Even though banks had been making riskier and riskier loans to their business customers in return for higher and higher fees, they were still lending their own money.

Mortgage brokers were not. Furthermore their remuneration was tied directly to the amount of money they were able to direct from lenders to borrowers. The result was inevitable. Mortgage borrowers were encouraged to borrow large amounts of money that were beyond their ability to repay, and to self-certify their financial affairs in order to do so. These loans became known as subprime mortgages, though such terminology hardly does them justice. It would be akin to describing Jack the Ripper as someone with whom a woman should not necessarily be eager to go out on a date.

There is a deliberately misleading statement in the last paragraph. Banks were indeed at least lending out their own money, but the custom rapidly grew up of making the loan but then immediately looking to syndicate it among a number of other banks, thus keeping only a small part of it on your own books. When it came to things such as leveraged buyouts (LBOs), banks could even go one better than this. They could underwrite all the financing requirements of a deal in advance in return for a fee and then syndicate these in the weeks leading up to completion. Ideally a bank could end up with none of the debt at all on its own balance sheet, but still retain a large chunk of the underwriting fee.

Embarrassingly, when the music stopped in 2007 some banks were left with underwritten exposures that nobody wanted to take. Some tried to wriggle out of them, claiming a 'material adverse change'. So did some private equity buyers, though not Terra Firma in the case of EMI, which their investors must have regretted when they found themselves £1.75 billion the poorer.[2]

Like securitisation, there is nothing intrinsically wrong with derivatives. Indeed, they can serve a very useful purpose for businesses that wish to reduce their levels of risk, such as when a coffee producer sells their next crop in advance at a fixed price, or when an importer buys a foreign currency in advance to lock in a certain exchange rate. Derivatives take the form of futures, which confer the obligation to buy or sell a fixed quantity of a certain thing at an agreed price on an

---

[2] *Financial Times*, 1 February 2011.

agreed future date, and options, which confer a similar right, but no obligation. However, there had been an early warning of how dangerous derivatives could be if used purely for speculative purposes when Barings went spectacularly bust as a result of the unauthorised trading activities of Nick Leeson in Singapore. The Accepting Houses Committee duly convened in London overnight, but found to their dismay that the old way of doing things did not work anymore. Barings had various open futures positions that were incurring bigger losses by the minute.

What occurred to drive banking beyond the pupa stage was that there was a desire for greater and greater bank profits, beyond even those which could be earned by syndications and the like. The combined profits of Britain's banks would actually peak at over £40 billion in 2006.[3] To place such a figure in context, it was more than the UK's defence budget for that year and only just below total welfare spending.

Investment bankers are renowned for their inventiveness in creating new financial products and this went into overdrive during the pupa stage and the transition from it. Chief among these new innovations were credit default swaps, which we met in the last chapter. Again, CDS instruments had been around for a long time and could serve a useful purpose since they could be regarded as insurance for a debt, though there are important legal differences. If you are owed money by a company payable on a certain date, you can buy a CDS under which you effectively pay somebody else to assume the risk of the company going bust in the meantime.

So far, so good. However, one of the 'important legal differences' is that you generally cannot insure something which you do not own. If you attempt to insure something in which you have no legal interest, the law will regard that as a gambling contract, not a commercial one, and will refuse to enforce it. Not so CDS transactions, which can be 'naked'. All this means is that you can buy or sell a CDS that relates to a loan in which you have no interest. If you buy a CDS in respect of Deutsche Bank but are not owed any money by Deutsche Bank,

---

[3] *Guardian*, 19 February 2007.

you will nonetheless be allowed to enforce the contract against your counterparty should Deutsche Bank in fact default on its debts.

Banks therefore found that they could create CDS and other exotic instruments (currency swaps, interest-rate swaps, etc.), take a fee or a 'spread' for doing so and also trade them through their dealing desks, including proprietary trading (trading on their own account), which is what Nick Leeson was doing at Barings.

Swaps were tailor-made for hedge funds to use in setting up speculative positions and a seemingly insatiable demand for them sprang up. According to an ISDA[4] survey, the total CDS market had grown by the time of the first signs of trouble in 2007 to somewhere in excess of $60 trillion. The fact that this was very nearly equivalent to the total GDP of the whole world did not seem to alarm financial regulators or central bankers unduly.

Indeed, Mervyn King (the Governor of the Bank of England) would memorably say at a press conference in August 2007, literally days before the full awfulness of the situation began to become apparent: 'Our banking system is much more resilient than in the past ... Precisely because many of these risks are no longer on their balance sheets but have been sold off to people willing and probably more able to bear it.'

Not only did many of these CDS positions greatly exceed the actual total debt of the companies or governments in respect of which they were issued, but many of them had themselves been bought with debt. When Carlyle Capital Corporation went bust in 2008, it was reported to have borrowed between 19 and 33 dollars for every dollar of investors' capital. Others, such as Amaranth which went bust in 2006 losing its investors more than $5 billion, were thought to have borrowed even more heavily. So original debts were geared up many times by derivative exposure and those derivatives were then geared up again by more debt. Such an unstable edifice was bound to topple over under its own weight sooner or later and it duly did during the course of 2007 and 2008.

---

[4] International Swaps and Derivatives Association.

As events began to unfold quickly and disastrously, banks found their traditional sources of short-term liquidity drying up and the government was faced with a choice between intervening to recapitalise them at public expense or allowing them to fail. It was felt that a total failure of the UK banking sector and, in particular a sudden rupture of the payments system, could lead to unimaginable and long-lasting damage both to the economy and to society as a whole and so taxpayers' money was used to rescue them, merging them into two groups and taking them effectively into public ownership (a majority in the case of RBS/NatWest and a significant minority in the case of Lloyds/TSB/ HBOS). Northern Rock and Bradford & Bingley were also taken into public ownership, though in much more controversial circumstances. Barclays alone stayed out of the clutches of state ownership, rejecting the terms on offer from the government and managing instead to get a capital issue away towards the end of 2008 largely from big Middle Eastern investors, though on much less generous terms.

It is difficult to criticise decisions effectively taken in the heat of battle, at short notice and under intense pressure (often overnight) and they were undoubtedly prompted by the belief that all these financial institutions were too big to be allowed to fail, but it should be noted that all of these mergers would have been rejected both at national and European level on competition grounds had they been attempted in normal times by the banks themselves. It is also difficult to see how these injections of share capital would not fall foul of the European rules against illegal state aid since this includes 'investments in share capital on terms that would not be acceptable to a private investor'[5] and we know that Barclays did in fact have to pay substantially more to entice investment from the private sector. So, far from allowing markets to function freely, the government in fact moved the goalposts a great distance, creating a completely different playing field in the process.

More troubling is the case of the shareholders in both Northern Rock and Bradford & Bingley, whose shares were nationalised without

---

[5] EFTA Surveillance Authority.

compensation. These were both businesses that were essentially illiquid (having problems finding cash to pay their debts in the short term) rather than insolvent (having insufficient assets to pay their debts in the long term), though admittedly under English law this distinction is not made explicit. However, it must be the case that on any normal accounting view there would in fact have been some value left for shareholders once the businesses had been wound up and it therefore seems difficult to justify the government's action on either legal or ethical grounds. On the contrary, it was perhaps an arbitrary exercise of executive power about which any society that values the rule of law and the rights of the individual should feel distinctly uneasy.

So the main result of the first wave of the crisis, the failure of the banking sector in 2007 and 2008, was that the cost of intervention by the government turned a banking liquidity crisis into a sovereign debt solvency crisis. Figures released by HM Treasury early in 2012[6] show that, for the financial year ending in 2011, public debt excluding the cost of 'financial intervention' (the rescue of the banks) was 60.5% of GDP, but if the cost of financial intervention had been included then the comparable figure would have been 150% of GDP. That is nearly as high as Greece, and even so does not include either the government's contingent liabilities under public–sector pension schemes (which could easily be another 100% of GDP) or their contingent liabilities under partnerships with the private sector for various infrastructure projects.

So one interpretation of the Brown administration's actions, which were naturally presented by the government spin doctors at the time as having heroically snatched the British banking industry, not to mention the global financial system, from the jaws of imminent disaster, is that it saddled Britain with an enormous level of debt that it may never be able to repay. There is, however, a serious debate about whether it was actually the right thing to do at all rather than letting the normal mechanics of financial markets and the legal insolvency system, if appropriate, play themselves out to a natural conclusion.

---

[6] HM Treasury Statement, January 2012.

We shall explore these issues in due course. However, one thing must be clear to everybody. Whether the financial intervention was right or wrong, Britain could not possibly afford to attempt anything similar ever again. It would be pleasant to report therefore that since 2008 the government has been working hard to put a system in place that would ensure that no such further intervention would ever be necessary, that the issue of 'too big to fail' would never again have to be faced.

Pleasant, but untrue. In fact, perversely, it is almost as though the government has been working to exactly the opposite end. They do seem to have got the message that a systemic failure of the banking sector has the power to paralyse the country, bankrupt the government and spread contagion rapidly across all financial markets, but the measures they have proposed seem to make this more, rather than less, likely to happen. They also raise serious questions about whether the government has properly thought through the nature of financial crises, what causes them and what form they are likely to take.

Incidentally, the European Union, the financial woes of whose members are well known, did eventually move to ban naked credit default swaps, but only in respect of sovereign debt. The words 'self' and 'interest' come irresistibly to mind.

# FOURTEEN

# Planning to Fight the Last War

In 2008 the government felt obliged to use large amounts of taxpayers' money to rescue many parts of the British banking system from imminent collapse. As we have already seen, this crippled the public finances, perhaps beyond any prospect of eventual rescue, increasing national obligations, even ignoring pension and infrastructure commitments, from just over 60% of GDP to somewhere around 150%, a two and a half times increase. Of the traditional major high street banks, only Barclays remained in private ownership, having got a capital raising away on the Stock Exchange in the nick of time, but heavily disadvantaging their existing shareholders in the process, denying them their traditional right of pre-emption.

Since then we have been bombarded with media comment about banking reform, Parliamentary committees, capital adequacy, solvency requirements and ring-fencing. It is understandable that, faced with this flood of jargon and political soundbites, few have any idea at all about what is going on. The history of the banking system, and how it progressed towards and stumbled into the present financial crisis, has already been described. Yet what is of much greater importance, for it will affect us all fundamentally, is its future, and it is this that the government has been supposed to be planning.

The scale of the increase in public debt outlined above makes it clear that, whether the last rescue was justified or not, any further one would be out of the question. One would have hoped, therefore, that since 2008 the government would have been hard at work creating a set of circumstances that would make such an eventuality as unlikely to occur as might be humanly possible. It is sad to have to report, however, that such a need may have been obvious to the anxious taxpayer, but clearly was not so to the government. They have been much more interested in distancing themselves in advance from the potential fallout from future events than in taking any firm and constructive action.

While they have pulled all the usual political levers, such as passing the buck to a committee (the Vickers Commission) to discuss and report on the situation, and producing firm, manly utterances on the need for responsible banking, they have actually done nothing to remove the nation from its present danger. 'Danger' is an emotive word, so let me justify it. Two facts are indisputable.

First, as the Vickers members noted themselves, the balance-sheet liabilities of British banks are about four times GDP, a much larger proportion than just about any other country. Only Switzerland, the Netherlands and Sweden have similar exposure, while in the US it is about a quarter of the UK level. For example, at the time of its bailout Citibank represented 16% of US GDP, while at the time of its bailout RBS represented 99% of UK GDP.[1] Second, any further attempt to rescue the British banks on anything like the scale of the financial intervention of 2008 would inevitably bankrupt Britain.

So, it must be accepted both that Britain cannot possibly afford any further major turmoil to occur within the banking sector and that as a nation we are massively exposed to the risk of any such turmoil. Hardly a happy situation.

Of course, banking turmoil does not occur in isolation, but as part of some wider financial crisis. It would therefore have been logical for the Vickers Commission to have begun by studying the history of financial crises and considering what lessons might be learned as to how and why they occur. Bafflingly, since a great deal of research on the subject is readily available, in particular from US academics Carmen Reinhart and Kenneth Rogoff, they chose not to do so, moving straightaway to discussing bank failure, which is often actually a symptom, rather than a cause, of financial crises, as the research makes clear.

Had they done so, they would have learned that financial crises arise from a number of possible causes. Yes, the crisis that began in 2007 was caused by a lack of liquidity in credit markets but it also had its origins, as we have seen, in the abuse of securitisation and intermediation as well as in fundamental changes to the banking model itself.

---

[1] World Bank figures, quoted in the Vickers interim report.

The Asian crisis that began in 1997 was caused initially by difficulties of foreign currency. The Great Depression is said by some to have been caused by a rapid and unsustainable rise in asset prices. The crisis in Germany and Central Europe in the 1920s was caused by inflation. More importantly still, some point the finger of blame in many cases at central bank policy.

So, assuming blithely, as Vickers and the government seem to have done, that the next financial crisis would also revolve around banks' balance sheets or even that it would revolve around banking at all, might be argued to be akin to planning to fight the last war rather than the next one. As we are currently observing, it may well be triggered by fundamental concerns about sovereign solvency, not bank liquidity, and even then transfigured by political issues such as election-driven short-termism in various countries and efforts to prop up a single currency that may prove economically unsustainable.

Assuming that the enemy will obligingly attack exactly where you wish them to has been the undoing of many an unwary general in the past and Vickers unfortunately falls straight into this trap. However, this first glaring mistake pales into comparative insignificance compared to the second, even more incomprehensible, one.

Anyone sitting down to frame banking regulation comes face to face at once with a dilemma. Are financial crises naturally and inevitably recurring events, or are they the equivalent of traffic accidents, which arise through human error, and thus can theoretically be prevented? The need to resolve this dilemma is clear. In the first case, you need to plan how to alleviate the effect of the disaster should it occur, while in the second, you need to plan how to prevent it from happening. Vickers confronts this dilemma boldly and decisively, by ignoring it completely.

Instead of choosing which path to follow, Vickers simply assumes that one of them is the right one and takes it. Unfortunately it is almost certainly the wrong one and the consequences of following it may yet prove disastrous. It is unclear whether this failure to confront the one vital issue with which they were faced arose through political pressure or intellectual cowardice, but neither explanation feels reassuring.

The situation may perhaps be better understood if one imagines the situation of a young army officer who is called upon unexpectedly to deal urgently with a very large unexploded bomb in a residential neighbourhood. Straightaway, he is faced with a fundamental choice between two different courses of action, and once he has embarked on one it will be extremely difficult and hugely dangerous to change his mind and pursue the other one instead. Should he sit down and attempt to defuse the bomb? Or should he pile sandbags around it, evacuate the area and then conduct a controlled explosion?

This is exactly the choice faced by the government and the one that was fudged by the Commission. Let us be clear about this. If you choose the approach of defusing the bomb, then if you get it wrong you lose everything. Yet this is the path that Vickers and the government have chosen.

What is even more remarkable is that, in choosing it, they did not even bother to enquire into the nature of financial crises first. Let us go back to our young officer. Suppose we now put him in possession of one key piece of new information. Despite his best efforts, the bomb is likely to explode anyway sooner or later. Would this not strengthen him in his resolve efficiently to conduct a controlled explosion, even if he had not already decided to do so? Yet that is the equivalent of what Vickers would have been told had they bothered to ask any of the experts.

There are two different schools of thought here, but both point to the same conclusion, namely that financial crises are naturally occurring events and if this is so, then clearly the only sensible approach is to attempt to alleviate their effect when they occur, not to try to create an environment in which it is impossible for them to occur. Remember, if you try this and get it wrong, then you lose everything.

The first line of thought is that since crises occur from a wide variety of causes it is impossible to predict in advance what will cause the next one, or when and where it will occur. Suppose, for example, that you focus your efforts on making the banking industry safe only to discover that the next crisis breaks out within the insurance industry? Or, you concentrate on capital adequacy only to find that the next crisis is caused by something totally unrelated to liquidity, such as a stock-market crash? Or even something not really related to finance at all, such as a war, a major nuclear accident, a terrorist incident (such as a poisoning of the nation's water supply) or a horrific epidemic?

Or even that you do by chance happen upon the right cause, but fail to deal with it properly? After all, there were capital adequacy rules in place in 2007 that were supposed to make a banking crisis of the kind that ensued impossible. Or suppose that the government or central bank policy (effectively the same thing in many countries) itself triggers the next crisis, as the Bank of England may already have done with QE?

The second line of thought is based on the work of an American economist called Hyman Minsky, who had been dead for some years by the time the present crisis arose, but whose success in predicting it is therefore all the more striking. He believed that the world of finance moves in ever-recurring cycles based upon the lending practices of banks. His work has acquired almost cult status, with many observers claiming to be able to detect 'Minsky moments' when one cycle alleg- edly gives way to another. The truth is probably more prosaic and, as Hegel said, Minerva's owl takes flight only in the gathering gloom, which is a smart way of saying in philosophical German that by the time you notice that an era is beginning or ending then it already has.

It was Minsky who coined the term 'merchants of debt' to describe banks, and showed how they advanced money against the expectation of future capital flows: future rental income from a building, or future profits from a business. He agreed with Keynes that the key building blocks of any capitalist economy (capital assets, labour force and finan- cial relations) were thus linked by time-based flows of funding stretch- ing into the future. Present borrowing was based upon the expectation of future cash flows.

For Minsky, the first cycle was what he called hedged lending, where the projected cash flows of the project or investment would be sufficient both to repay the loan and service the interest on it during its lifetime. A good example of this would be a repayment mortgage, where both interest and capital are paid every month.

The second cycle is speculative lending. Here, the projected income should prove sufficient to service the interest but the capital amount of the loan (what bankers call the principal) can only be generated by selling the asset at the end of the term of the loan. A good example of this might be an interest-only mortgage such as is used by many buy-to-let landlords. Although the word can be used in different ways, this is often called a bullet loan in banking circles, with all the principal being repaid at the end in a single, 'bullet' payment.

The third stage is graphically described by Minsky as Ponzi lend-ing, after the Italian-born American fraudster who sprang to promi-nence in 1920 and after whom any investment swindle has been named that relies upon paying back investors with other investors' money. During the Ponzi stage, banks are prepared to lend money in circumstances where repayment of both the interest and the principal is dependent upon being able to sell the asset at a profit at the end of the loan. This is typically known as a balloon loan, as it is repayable with a single payment that, because of the compounding of inter-est, grows dramatically from the original amount borrowed. Once the Ponzi period is entered, said Minsky, then sooner or later a financial crisis becomes inevitable.

So, it can be argued that the Vickers Commission was deeply mis-guided in attempting to prevent any future crisis from occurring for three reasons: first, they seem to be naturally recurring events, rather like natural disasters; second, it is impossible to predict in advance with which particular problem you will be confronted next time around; third, if financial crises are driven to any extent at all by lending policy, then the only way in which a crisis might be avoided would be by the government taking control of the lending practices of commercial banks and, understandably, there has been no suggestion of that.

So, rather than seeking an environment within which banks can fail safely, the government has sought to create an environment within which the question of safety is irrelevant because no bank will ever fail. They have designed a cruise ship with no lifeboats because they believe that the new radar system they have installed will stop the ship from hitting anything. Needless to say, this not only overlooks any chance of human error, but also the possibility that the ship may hit an underwater obstruction, explode, catch fire or be attacked by terrorists, pirates or enemy submarines.

Yet despite such a nonsensical approach, the government asks us to believe that the banking system is in safe hands (theirs). The reality is very different. They have actually made it much more likely, rather than less, that a further rescue will be required, regardless of the fact that they can no longer afford to mount one. It is rather like Neville Chamberlain's strategic blindness in the 1930s when he was being simultaneously advised by the Treasury that the only war Britain could afford to fight was a very short one and by his defence chiefs that the only war Britain could win was a very long one.

Let us look at what the government is proposing in order to stop another financial crisis from occurring and then at what they *should* be doing to plan for what happens when the next one does in fact occur.

The government's plans, as suggested by Vickers, are a masterly and unoriginal fudge, aiming for a combination of Glass–Steagall and capital adequacy.

The Glass–Steagall element is the separation of banking activities, as happened in America, into investment banking and commercial banking. Many point to the fact that no major bank failed during the time that Glass–Steagall was on the statute book, and to its repeal as a major cause of the present crisis. This is a neat argument, but not wholly convincing.

First, by the time it came into force more than 4,000 banks had already failed in America and therefore arguably those that remained were bigger and stronger as a result of consolidation. Second, it falls into the trap of assuming that all financial crises come in the same form and are prompted by the same causes.

It is true that there was no financial crisis between 1933 and 1999 that precisely mirrored that of 1929 to 1933. There was, however, the savings and loans crisis of the 1980s and 1990s in the US, which saw nearly 750 financial institutions go bust and have to be rescued by a government-backed investment vehicle, Resolution Trust Corporation, at a total cost of about $90 billion (about $160 billion in present purchasing power). This enormous sum contributed to the need for a budget deficit in America in the early 1990s. This was ironic, since most agree that the crisis was sparked by well-intentioned but misguided government policy (financial deregulation coupled with the encouragement of home ownership). Yet again, short-term political issues turned out to be directly contrary to the national long-term economic interest.

There was also the credit crunch beginning in 1989 (surely a clear example of one of Minsky's cycles), which led to the Fed introducing extra reporting requirements for leveraged transactions in an attempt to discourage banks from lending to them, and the collapse of a number of highly leveraged businesses, including Jim Walter Corporation and Seaman's Furniture. Even the biggest of them all, RJR Nabisco, barely survived a major scare with its controversial 'reset' bond financing in 1990. This crisis coincided with, and was partly caused by, Drexel Burnham Lambert being forced into bankruptcy in 1990 following indictment as a party to insider trading.

Then there was the Asian crisis, which began in Thailand in 1997 and spread rapidly. This had ramifications far beyond South East Asia. The Argentinian government later defaulted on its debts, major corporate bankruptcies occurred in Japan and the New York Stock Exchange fell 7% in one day and suspended trading. This, too, was an unforeseen consequence of government policy, in this case encouraging other countries to peg their currency to the dollar. When Thailand was forced to abandon the peg, chaos ensued.

So, while it may be true that Glass–Steagall prevented any recurrence of a financial crisis strictly similar to that which began in 1929, the argument is far from conclusive. For example, Britain also avoided any similar crisis during the same period, but without any equivalent of Glass–Steagall, even after its investment and commercial banks merged in the 1980s. The only real exception to this, Barings, arose through failures of internal oversight, and had no real commercial banking activities anyway.

Strictly speaking, even the first statement in the last paragraph is not true. In 1974, Franklin National Bank failed, amid allegations of fraud and criminal association. At the time it was America's twentieth-biggest bank, and biggest-ever banking failure.

Nor is it clear how it could have saved banks such as Northern Rock or Bradford & Bingley, which carried on no investment banking activities at all and dealt entirely with retail customers.

What is quite clear is that it did not prevent crises occurring from other causes. For example, neither Glass–Steagall nor anything else prevented the conflicts of interest that helped create an overheated IPO[2] market in America in 1999 and 2000, and which would see every leading investment bank pay what were effectively large fines in consequence. Nor did it prevent the turmoil in the American banking system in the hours following the terrorist attacks on the World Trade Center, which saw the Fed intervening directly to help operate various payment systems.

The second string to the government's bow is capital adequacy. Here, the argument is more difficult still to make out, since such rules were in place at the time (as a result of the global agreements known as the Basel Accords) and proved totally useless in preventing bank failures, which was after all exactly what they were designed to do.

Nothing daunted, the government has decided that what is needed are bigger and better capital adequacy rules, following in the footsteps of the canny Swiss, who had already decided that even the latest suggested Basel requirements were too lax. However, such an approach is subject to all sorts of objections and trade-offs, not all of which appear to have been fully appreciated.

First, many have expressed concern that the effect of accounting rules, based on international accounting standards, might be instrumental in causing a bank to fail despite the presence of stringent capital adequacy rules because the balance-sheet values of its assets and liabilities, though technically correct from an accounting point of view, might not mirror reality. For example, a bank is not allowed to write down a loan if it has not yet physically gone into default, no matter what subjective view the bank may take of the borrower.

---

[2] Initial public offering, the first time a company issues shares on a stock exchange.

Yet again short-term political interest seems to rear its head, the Treasury being unwilling to allow an allowance against tax unless and until it is absolutely necessary.

Thus a bank may be carrying various loans as assets on its balance sheet (since they represent the right to be paid this money in the future) and yet the actual commercial value, the value for which they might be able to sell them to another bank for example, may be quite different. So a bank might be insolvent, or at least illiquid, without actually appearing to be.

Second, as we have seen, fractional reserve banking has long been an established fact and is generally accepted as having a benign effect. Yet the precise degree to which the directors are prepared effectively to over-lend their depositors' cash and capital from shareholders has always been a matter for their own business judgment.

It has always been agreed, moreover, that pressure from their shareholders and bondholders will operate to reinforce responsible conduct in this regard. If they believe that the directors are adopting a high-risk strategy, they will demand a higher return and sell their instruments in the market if they are disappointed. Since different directors are likely to adopt different approaches, this leads to investors being able to exercise a choice between different banks with different risk-reward profiles.

Impose the same lending ratio on all banks and only this choice falls away. You may just as well effectively have just one big bank with a government-directed lending policy. In practice, however, a more likely result is that, since directors will seek the highest possible return on capital for their investors, they will start seeking riskier borrowers, from whom they can extract higher fees and rates of interest in return for loans. Yet risky loans are more likely to default, particularly in difficult times, and so government policy designed to make it impossible for a bank to fail has arguably now instead made it very possible indeed.

The last two objections both take us into the realms of interaction with other elements of the crisis.

We examine elsewhere the issue of government intervention in the economy in an attempt to offset the effects of a recession and conclude that the government seems determined to do this, regardless of the arguments for and against. Well, one of the most important weapons at the government's disposal in seeking to boost economic activity (note the choice of words: the government is concerned with short-term economic *activity* levels, not long-term economic health or strength) is the encouragement of bank lending to business, traditionally brought about by keeping interest rates low in order to encourage firms to borrow.

Yet if you limit the multiple of the capital that banks are allowed to lend, then this clearly operates in directly the other direction, *discouraging* banks from lending. This is but one of a distressing number of examples of government policy pointing in both directions at once. It remains a matter of some puzzlement why they are never challenged to explain and resolve it.

Finally, there is the little matter of what banks are allowed to hold against what is called their Tier 1 capital, what might be thought of as their emergency reserve, the locked cabinet in which the last few rounds of ammunition and packs of rations are kept. The Basel Accords seek to regulate what goes into this locked cabinet on a risk-weighted basis. If you put some cash into the box, then you are allowed to count 100% of its value. In the case of some high-risk loans, you may not be allowed to count any of their value at all. So, in order to make the most efficient use of your assets, it makes sense to try to have entirely risk-free assets inside the cabinet, which in turn means that if you do not wish to hold actual cash, which is generally regarded as financially inefficient, then you will hold government bonds, since these are traditionally regarded as risk-free. This raises two main issues.

For our present purposes it is only necessary to understand one thing about bonds. Since they are issued at a fixed face value (the amount of money that the bond issuer must repay to the bond-holder on the expiry of the bond) and a fixed interest rate, then the only way in which the yield payable on it can be changed is by its market price also changing. Suppose that a ten-year bond is issued with a face value of $100 and an interest rate of 5%. This means that assuming it was issued at par it would have a market price also of $100 and pay 5%, or $5 in this case, of interest ('coupon') every year.

Suppose, though, that something occurred to make you feel less confident in the ability of the issuer to repay you $100 on the expiry ('maturity' or 'redemption') of the bond at the end of the ten-year period. You now feel that a yield of 5% is no longer sufficient to compensate you for the extra risk you see yourself taking. Let us say that to hold the same bond now you would require a yield of 7% instead.[3]

The amount of interest payable by the bond is fixed when it is issued at $5 and cannot be changed; it is 5% of the face value of $100. So the only way in which we can obtain a higher yield is by paying less for it in the first place. Instead of $100, we need to find the amount of which $5 is 7%. That amount is $71.43, so that becomes the new market price of the bond. Observe that as the yield on a bond goes up, the price goes down, and vice versa. They always move in opposite directions to each other.

Now imagine that you hold government bonds, as the Basel rules virtually force you to, and something happens to make you less comfortable about the ability of the government in question, say Greece, to be able to repay you. This is a good example, since in the case of Greece private bond-holders (such as banks) do not just suspect, but actually know that they will not receive repayment as originally agreed. As this lack of confidence percolates through the bond market, investors decide that they require a higher, perhaps even a much higher, income yield to justify them buying Greek bonds. The market price of the bonds sinks and therefore so too does the value they represent in the hands of the bank. They now need to open up their emergency cabinet and place still more assets within it.

So capital adequacy only works if there are genuinely risk-free assets in the world and that assumption now clearly no longer holds. Even if the government does not default expressly, it may do so impliedly, for example by issuing so much currency and/or stimulating

---

[3] Anyone familiar with bonds will notice that we are dealing only with the current yield in the interest of simplicity. In practice, we would obviously be thinking in terms of the yield to maturity.

such high levels of inflation that they will be paying you back with greatly devalued money.

There is another angle to this objection as well, which harks back to something we were discussing a little earlier. If the government is really concerned that banks should lend more to firms, then this is hardly the way to go about it. If they are holding eurozone government bonds, for example, and the value of those bonds declines, then clearly they will be prompted to lend less, rather than more, in order to stay within their prescribed capital ratios.

Incidentally, this problem can only get worse for UK banks and other institutions, chiefly insurance companies and pension funds, that hold British bonds. A glance at the financial pages will reveal that British bond yields are at historically low levels, driven there mainly by the artificial contrivance of QE in combination with such regulations as Basel III and Solvency II. By forcing institutions to buy its own bonds while simultaneously going out into the market to buy them itself, the government has created a false market. One, incidentally, of which it is now seeking to take advantage by attempting to issue 100-year bonds. The con trick is complete. The time for the sting, when the con artist takes the victim's money, is at hand.

As time goes by yields can only go up, particularly if and when inflation gathers pace and, as we have just seen, as yields go up, prices (and thus values) go down. So British institutions will be left sitting on large piles of bonds whose value is constantly falling. In the case of institutions that are not actually compelled to buy bonds but which do so eagerly nonetheless, such as pension funds, this raises serious doubts as to the sanity of those currently involved with the decision-making process, particularly since at the time of writing the real yield on British government bonds is already negative.

Finally, there is the most powerful objection of all. British banks will tend to hold British bonds. This makes financial sense given that many of their liabilities are denominated in sterling. Yet it creates an additional risk where none need exist, since it creates a direct link between the solvency of the British government and the solvency of British banks. Once the national debt rises to a sufficiently high level, then government will and must default, either expressly or, much more likely, by printing yet more heavily debauched money that nobody wants. If that happens, the value of British bonds may fall dramatically, perhaps even effectively to zero. Thus the government defaulting would mean also every British bank failing for want of capital. Ironically, of course, the most likely thing to cause the national debt to spiral out of control would be another round of bank rescues.

Having painted a depressing picture of just how disastrous the choices that the government has made (or failed to make) might prove to be, it is only fair that one should suggest just what they should have done instead. That these suggestions may seem bizarre, radical and perhaps even ridiculous may be explained by the fact that, unlike the government's, they are designed to make it easier, not more difficult, for banks to fail.

Most important of these, and the one that should be pursued urgently since much precious time has already been lost, is the removal of the payments system from within the banks. It was the potential collapse of the payment system that seemed to frighten politicians most back in 2008. All sorts of arguments could be advanced about how it is illogical to treat the bond-holders and shareholders of banks differently from those of other commercial enterprises, but the thought of voters not being able to take cash out of ATMs swept all logic aside.

This is such an obvious and fundamental step to take that it is deeply puzzling why it forms no part of the government's plans. It is almost as though they are setting up in advance a situation in which they will have no choice but to step in and rescue not just one bank but all the banks should the need arise, exactly the opposite of what they say they want to achieve.

Incidentally, lest this proposal seem radical or controversial, it should be revealed that both BACS and CHAPS, the two main forms of customer-to-customer bank transfers within the UK, are already outwith the banking system, operating as non-profit subsidiaries of the Bank of England. It would seem inconceivable if both the ATM network and remaining payment systems could not be similarly split out with a little ingenuity from the IT experts, and, of course, more crucially, the political will to do so.

After all, it would be unthinkable for the National Grid, which transmits electricity, to be in the ownership of individual utilities which produce and sell electricity, so why should banking be any different? As long as the payment system remains in the hands of the banks, then, like it or not, they can hold the government to ransom any time they want.

Once implemented, this principle would facilitate another possibility, which is that with the payment system in their hands the Bank could create another non-profit subsidiary that could act as a virtual shadow bank, with every commercial bank being obliged to back up their records to the shadow bank every evening. In the event of a bank failing, this would enable the Bank of England subsidiary, with both the payment systems and the current customer records under its control, to continue to operate customer accounts while it made arrangements (which it could be given power to do by mandatory order) to transfer the accounts of all affected customers to new banks. This sort of transition management is already professionally provided, albeit in a different form and on a smaller scale, in the world of investment management.

These two arrangements are core to allowing banks to fail safely. One is therefore forced to ask why on earth the government had done nothing to move in this direction. There are probably two main reasons.

The first is that retail customers in the UK have got used to what is essentially free banking. It is important to note that this arrangement is not mirrored in many other countries, including many of our European partners, where retail clients are used to a bank charging them fees, whether annual or transaction-based, for the services they supply. Again the example of electricity comes to mind. Voters do not expect free electricity, so why should they expect free banking? It is as if banking, like housing, now falls into the realm of the welfare state, with these things being expected to be supplied by the state, like healthcare, as part of some giveaway society.

So yes, there would be a cost to all of this, and some or all of that cost would have to be passed on to the customers, either in the form of taxes or bank charges, but this seems a small price to pay compared to the total destruction of the public finances that any new rescue attempt would entail.

The second is perhaps more obvious. If these arrangements were put in place, then there would be no need for any bank regulation at all. If banks can fail safely, and in future will be allowed to do so, then both separation and capital adequacy become irrelevant. Banks can function just like any other commercial firm, with the directors being allowed to choose how much risk and reward they wish to target, and which types of each. If anything goes wrong, then the bank can be placed into administration or liquidation and go through exactly the same insolvency process as any other business. No longer would the capital providers of banks be treated differently to the capital providers of oil companies or supermarkets. A level playing field would be restored.

All this is of course anathema to politicians and, more importantly, to the civil servants who advise them. They believe that big government is good government and that more regulation must necessarily be better regulation. The idea of dispensing with bank regulation altogether and being able to dispense likewise with the many civil servants who frame and administer it would surely induce palpitations and fainting fits in the corridors of power. Just as the residents of certain Surrey commuter towns judge themselves against their neighbours on the basis of who has the latest model of BMW, so ministers judge themselves against their peers by how large their departmental headcounts and budgets are. Try assessing them instead on the percentage headcount reduction that they achieve each year, or the number of pages of regulation they annul, and we might have a very different system of government, but such thoughts remain sadly in the realm of fantasy.

The other aspect to this is that modern British politicians seem to have a compulsion for being told what to do by foreigners, even down to what sort of herbal supplements we can buy and what sort of electric light bulbs we have to install. Capital adequacy is a matter of international agreement, as enshrined in the Basel Accords, and to reject it would be akin to suggesting that the City of London might just know more about financial services than a Portuguese olive farmer or a Bavarian factory worker and that clearly cannot be right.

So, unless and until the British people subscribe to fund brain and backbone transplants for their politicians, then the government will only do away with banking regulation in Britain if foreigners say it's OK (or, even better, tell them to do so, for that way they do not have to take any responsibility for the consequences), and the chances of this seem non-existent given that Europe is populated by large numbers of people who sincerely believe that the only reason the current crisis occurred in the first place was that insufficient regulation was in place.

So, in considering the vexed question of the future of the banking industry and its relationship with the public finances, this is one of the many cases where it is perfectly safe to assume that politicians actually mean the exact opposite of what they say. They say that future financial crises can be averted (chiefly by much more regulation), yet we know from the available research that this is not so. They say that they will not have to rescue any bank in future, yet have created an environment in which it seems highly probable. They say that they want banks to be properly capitalised yet more or less force them to hold government bonds that must fall in value in the coming years as bond yields rise, making the banks horribly vulnerable to the inflation that the government and central bank policy must surely create and linking quite unnecessarily the fate of the banking sector to the risk of sovereign default.

Politicians, however, see things rather differently. Banking regulation is a wonderful opportunity to appear on television and say stern things about the banks while fixing the camera with a steely gaze, yet surely nobody actually expects them to *do* something, at least not unless it is something which has been proposed by a commission, or comes as a directive from a foreign body. Doing something, as opposed to saying something, is hideously dangerous and any politician proposing such a thing would instantly suffer the ultimate fate of the prime minister publicly declaring his support for him, while preparing to accept his resignation on health grounds sympathetically the next day. In the old days, of course, he could simply have been transferred to Northern Ireland.

# FIFTEEN

# Drinking Poison Can Be Dangerous

One strand of the current crisis is the recurrent threat of recession. As we have already seen, this has a highly technical meaning for economists, namely two successive quarters of negative GDP growth, when GDP shrinks rather than expands. In more general usage the word simply denotes a period, often quite prolonged, of very difficult economic conditions, often characterised by unusually high unemployment. The Great Depression of the 1930s would be a good example, and, as explained earlier, if this looser, more general description were employed, then the UK can be argued to have been in recession solidly for about two decades following the end of the First World War.

Recessions often follow a financial crisis of some kind, though whether there is always an identifiable causal link between them is another matter. Economists are far from unanimous as to whether the Great Depression was the direct result of the Wall Street Crash. It is possible to argue, for instance, that the real problem was a dramatic rise in asset prices, fuelled by the over-availability of debt (sound familiar?), and that the Crash simply marked the inevitable bursting of this bubble, which had already worked its mischief. However, it is also possible that the two were at least to some extent coincidental, perhaps with the economic woes of other parts of the world finally making themselves felt on what had during the Roaring Twenties been a vibrant US industrial sector.

There again, others argue that it was actually the Federal Reserve that caused, or at least lengthened and worsened, the recession through mistaken central bank policy. This is in fact the stated view of none other than the current chairman of the Fed, Ben Bernanke,[1] as well as, perhaps more predictably, Milton Friedman.[2]

---

[1] WND.com archive, 19 March 2008.
[2] Milton Friedman and Anna J. Schwartz, *A Monetary History of the United States*, Princeton, Princeton University Press, 1971.

Friedman damningly points out that the Fed was set up in the first place (in 1913) to forestall any banking crisis, to avoid a situation in which banks would go bust. Yet we know that between 1929 and 1933 several thousand banks went into liquidation, so clearly not only had the Fed failed in its appointed task, but it also seems to have produced exactly the opposite effect to what had been intended. Why was this?

Recessions come and go as part of the normal business cycle of boom and bust, says Friedman, so what was it that transformed this one into such a deep and lengthy disaster? Two separate but related mistakes by the Fed; the first was their policy towards the money supply, while the second was their attitude towards failing banks.

The governor of the Federal Reserve in New York until 1928 was Benjamin Strong. He is a significant figure in the story of the Great Depression. Unusually for an American of the time, he took an active interest in European affairs and was troubled by what he saw.[3] He was concerned that if America continued to be blinded by its own prosperity to the economic problems of other parts of the world, then sooner or later these would wash over into US markets.

More importantly for our present discussion he also had very strong views about the money supply, derived from the great economist Irving Fisher, the father of monetarist theory, who believed that the supply of money in circulation should be regulated at such a level as would produce stable prices. Sadly the weight of his teaching was greatly diminished by his announcement in 1929 that the stock market would continue to rise inexorably over time. At least he put his money where his mouth was, losing a great deal of it in consequence.

For the monetarists, Strong's death in office in 1928 and Fisher's public relations disaster a year later were major setbacks occurring at exactly the worst possible time. Had Strong still been directing affairs as 1929 gave way to 1930, he would have presumably found ways of boosting the money supply to counteract falling demand and would have continued to do so. As we will discuss later, though, this is a

---

[3] Charles Kindleberger, *The World in Depression 1929–1939*, Berkeley, University of California Press, 1992.

fascinating 'what if' scenario since experience seems to have shown that it is infinitely easier to pump money into the system than to extract it again and the after-effects of such a policy might have been rampant inflation in the late 1930s.

After Strong's passing, however, the Fed, perhaps influenced by what they had seen unfolding in Germany in previous years, moved to a 'strong money' policy, insisting that new money should only be issued against assets of proven value, such as high-quality bonds and bills of exchange, hence its name of the 'real bills doctrine' in the United States. Where Fisher believed in the quantity theory of money (that there is a direct linkage between the amount of the money supply and levels of demand and pricing), the Fed at the time of the Crash disagreed, believing that the amount of money had no effect on such matters, since if money is issued against 'bankable' assets then it has a fixed value.

Obviously, to a monetarist such views are anathema, as for them it is the amount of money in circulation, and the speed with which it does so, which causes prices to rise or fall. Even under the real bills doctrine, they say, there can be inflation. If asset prices rise and money is issued against them, then the amount of money in the system will increase and inflation will occur. Asset values rise still further, and further money is issued, most obviously by banks lending against such assets. Far from containing inflation, it can lead to a self-perpetuating inflationary spiral.

This is a highly partisan debate that has raged over the years and had until recently seemed to have been thoroughly settled in favour of the monetarists, even among economists who did not believe that the quantity theory of money (our old friend $MV = PQ$) necessarily offered a complete theoretical solution in itself. However, repeated bursts of quantitative easing on both sides of the Atlantic might be said recently to have reignited this debate, with both the Fed and the Bank of England apparently believing that they can pump as much new money into the system as they like, but that as long as this is done by purchasing government bonds, then any inflationary consequences can safely be ignored.

Whatever its effect on inflation, a tighter money supply in the aftermath of the Crash was a disaster for economic activity, which would itself seem to confirm the quantity theory of money at least in part (Q). Nor is 'tighter' really an adequate word. Friedman believes that US money supply contracted by a third. Even in a benign economic environment, this would surely have had a dramatically constricting effect on production.

Incidentally, many have said that a desire to keep interest rates high to maintain the dollar's fixed exchange rate against gold was also a factor in the Fed's thinking, at least after October 1931 when Britain went off the Gold Standard again and America was keen to be seen not to be pushed in the same direction. As the recession deepened and continued, many people sold dollars for gold, leading to yet more cash outflows from banks, and more bank failures, a situation that Roosevelt would deal with by banning US citizens from owning gold.

So, the Fed's first mistake, misguided monetary policy, turned what should have been a routine recession into the Great Depression by slashing the amount of money in circulation at exactly the wrong time. Their second mistake arguably turned what might have been a containable liquidity problem into a major banking crisis.

It may be worth journeying back in time to the days before the Fed was formed in 1913, a period incidentally during which there had been many bank crises, with the last major one occurring as recently as 1907. In those times, should any small bank get into difficulty the larger banks would rally round to bail it out, recognising that bank runs were hugely irrational things and could easily spread to larger banks, no matter how well capitalised they were, should depositors begin to panic generally.

It should be noted, by the way, that there was no government guarantee of bank deposits in the US until 1933, when it was established under the Glass–Steagall Act. Thus depositors could, and did, literally lose their money if a bank went bust while holding their savings. This is the Achilles heel of fractional reserve banking. It relies on something approaching a confidence trick, albeit one that is designed to serve a benign purpose. Everyone knows that the bank would be unable to repay all its deposits if everybody asked for them at once. Thus the system only works if the bank can persuade its customers to believe that it is never likely to need to. Yet as soon as a queue starts to form outside the door then a feeding frenzy will rapidly develop, as nobody wants to be last in the queue.

Note that in this situation a bank is rarely insolvent. It will be holding, as assets on its balance sheets, loans which it has extended to customers. In time these paper assets will turn into cash either as the loan is repaid or as it is sold on to another bank. Yet banks could not tell their depositors to go away and come back a few weeks later. As is graphically portrayed in *It's a Wonderful Life*, US banking law was very clear. As soon as you were unable to honour a demand from a customer to pay cash across the counter you had to close your doors.

So in practice the big banks helped out the small banks. They did this partly by extending them short-term credit, and partly by occasionally unilaterally imposing deposit lock-up periods under which depositors had to give a certain number of days' notice if they wished to be cashed out. One of the first executive acts of President Roosevelt, who actually took office during a bank crisis, was to impose a three-day bank holiday, with all banks remaining closed to their customers, allowing them all to put sufficient cash funding in place to meet depositor demand.

What happened if contagion started to spread even to the big banks? Well, big business factions like the Rockefellers and the Morgans would step in, providing both financial and moral support where necessary. After all, the last thing any big business combine wants is an unstable financial system.

The Federal Reserve system, with its twelve regional offices across the nation, was introduced in 1913, but was prompted by concerns within the business community (prominent among whom was the original John Pierpoint Morgan) raised by the 1907 crisis. The system was actually dreamed up by a group of commercial bankers, including Strong, in 1910 but it took three years before it could be enshrined as an Act of Congress. In a fascinating foreshadowing of later events, the bankers knew what had to be done but the politicians did not trust them to do it, while the politicians claimed to want to solve the problem, but restricted themselves to press conferences and campaign speeches.

While the Aldrich Plan, as the bankers' proposals were dubbed (named after Senator Aldrich, a member of the extended Rockefeller family), had to be kept largely secret for fear of instant rejection by the politicians, Strong, who seems to have been Morgan's de facto representative, would have been clear that the Fed was intended to play the sort of role that the larger banks had done in the past whenever bank failure threatened. After all, if that was not to be the case, then what real point would there have been to the Aldrich Plan? Its architects, chiefly Warburgs, Morgans and Rockefellers, were not known as men who enjoyed wasting their time.

In the event, perhaps another consequence of Strong's untimely death, it did nothing of the sort. On the contrary, it pursued what became known as a 'liquidationist' policy, allowing banks to go to the wall, unless of course they could produce 'real bills' against which additional funding might be advanced. For most this was simply not an option, particularly not when dealing with a tidal wave of desperate depositors and, as we have seen, several thousand went to the wall. While there are good arguments, which we have already explored, that allowing banks to fail can make good sense, there is little doubt, as is now acknowledged by Ben Bernanke, that in the early 1930s the Fed both made a bad situation far worse and failed in its avowed task of maintaining an orderly banking system.

We have made a somewhat lengthy excursion into these events because they illustrate an important and disturbing trend that has been identified by many academics who have researched financial crises across different countries and centuries. In most cases, certainly in modern times since the introduction of central banks such as the Fed, the prime cause of the crisis can be traced back to mistaken policy by the central bank. As we have seen, the Fed itself now admits that it played a major role in causing the Great Depression. It has been criticised more recently for its over-lax monetary policy, which is said to have been the prime cause of the present crisis. There are also various other examples. For example, the Bank of England's conduct since 2008 may already have sown the seeds of the next financial crisis.

There is a Latin phrase, *quis custodiet ipsos custodes*, which means 'who will guard the guardians themselves?' and it encapsulates a point which, in the context of financial crises is of crucial importance. Central banks are usually part of the problem, not part of the solution. The point that Friedman makes above in theoretical terms has been subsequently borne out by academic research. Bear this in mind as we continue our discussion of recession. Much of the time the situation could have been dramatically improved by doing *exactly the opposite* of what the central bank actually recommended and did. So, the next time you see someone from the Fed or the Bank of England on the television, try looking at them as one of the bad guys who gets us into messes, not one of the heroes who gets us out of them.

Recessions, then, seem to occur naturally as a result of inexorable, regular cycles of boom and bust. So regular, in fact, that in the nineteenth century they were seriously considered to be caused by similar cycles of sunspot activity. This will presumably continue to be the case (the recurrence, not the link with sunspots) way into the future, despite Gordon Brown's Canute-like claims to have successfully halted the economic tide.

There have been many attempts to explain why this might be so. The most likely answer is probably that the basic market principles of supply and demand do apply, though in a much more complex way than the likes of Adam Smith and David Ricardo might have imagined, and with a number of other factors operating upon them, not least fiscal and monetary policy, international factors, interference with the operation of free markets and inflation.

Clearly negative growth must involve a fall in aggregate demand, relative to output. We should also be ready to recognise changes in the nature of demand, with consumers and firms alike becoming more cost-conscious in difficult times and, in really difficult times, eschewing certain types of goods and services altogether.

The consideration of demand relative to output raises a further important point, which was made by John Kenneth Galbraith in his book *The Affluent Society*, which was published as long ago as 1958 but which remains as relevant today as it ever was.

By the time Galbraith was writing, Abraham Maslow had already published his famous hierarchy of needs,[4] which is still taught in business schools and psychology faculties today. This states that humans are concerned first to satisfy their most urgent needs, such as food, water and shelter. Having done so, they move onto the next category, which he categorises 'safety needs', at which stage they start being concerned with the security of their property and their employment. Then they move onto the next category, which deals with things such as love, friendship, family and relationships, and so on through five categories of needs in total. Though some may quibble with the precise definition and ordering, and question his methodology (he looked at only one type of society, and only a very narrow stratum within it), the basic theory appears impeccable; a man who is dying of thirst is likely to prefer a bottle of water to a new suit.

Galbraith points out that as a society we long ago stopped producing what we need: basic housing, food, clean water, and public transport, perhaps. We then move onto producing not what we need, but what we want: say, new homes, consumer brands, elegant clothes and motor cars. There comes a point even beyond that, he says, when we no longer produce what we want, but what we must be induced to want. Since there is no naturally occurring demand for such items, then demand or, rather, desire must be manufactured.

This is where the advertising industry comes in. They will promote a product as aspirational, or even competitive. We buy it not because we want it for itself, but for what it says about us. We buy this year's model of a car even though our old one is still serving us faithfully not because we need it, but because our neighbours have one and we do not want to be less discerning or, the ultimate horror, less rich. We buy a new mobile phone not because we need it, but because we want to be able to show our friends that we are up to the minute with new technology. We buy expensive branded clothes not because we

---

[4] Originally published as 'A Theory of Human Motivation', *Psychological Review*, Volume 50, Number 4, 1943.

want them, but because we seek to emulate a film or music star who wears them on screen.

We have created, says Galbraith, a society that is obsessed by production, a society in which increased production can only be possibly viewed as a good thing, even if it means more pollution, or faster consumption of the world's natural resources. Increased production can only be justified by increased demand, yet production levels long ago outstripped natural demand. So increased production can now only take place if those who have charge of production pay others to create artificial demand, which justifies some extra production, which raises the money to pay to create more demand, and so on.

If this extra, artificial demand were not created, he queries, would the world necessarily be a worse place – except perhaps for all of those in the advertising industry who would be thrown out of work? Production levels would be lower, which would inevitably lead to less employment, but might many people not be happy to adapt to a shorter working week, less income, but much more time of their own?

Whatever view one comes to on any of this, and to be fair Galbraith is clearly trying to provoke a debate, not propose the immediate adoption of a radical new socioeconomic approach, one thing must be beyond argument. As soon as we create the sort of affluent society that Galbraith describes, then we have created an economy that is highly likely to catch cold. We have no choice whether we buy bread or potatoes; if we do not buy them we will starve. We do have a choice whether we buy champagne or designer clothes or a new car. Thus we have created an economy that is likely to be much more volatile, to go up and down to a much greater extent, than would be the case with a basic subsistence model.

Thus, to pursue a whimsical approach, if Gordon Brown had been serious about wanting to eliminate boom and bust, it might have been interesting to know if he ever contemplated massive indirect taxes on luxury items and a total ban on advertising except of a basic informational nature ('Sainsbury's have baked beans at 50 pence this week').

The Austrian School of economists believe that cycles of boom and bust are created by central bank interest-rate policy. The government tries to stimulate the economy by fixing low interest rates. This encourages business to borrow and build production for new or extra goods. As economic activity grows, the government steadily raises the interest rate to try to halt inflation and now consumers start saving rather than spending, and firms stop borrowing. Producers find themselves with manufacturing capacity they no longer need and loans they cannot now afford, and what would otherwise be a modest fall becomes a serious recession.

So, whatever the reasons, and no matter the extent to which we may have made the severity of the condition worse by our own actions, there is general consensus that recessions occur naturally and regularly. The next question which arises, and a highly topical one given the current economic situation, is to what extent can we and should we (so perhaps two questions rather than one) seek to try to counteract them, to make their impact less severe or to shorten their duration?

There are two schools of thought on this. The interventionists take a robustly Keynesian approach, arguing that increasing government spending can boost economic activity and thus reduce unemployment, as can increasing the money supply. The problem with the former is that Keynes never envisaged this being done by a government that regularly ran a deficit as a normal state of affairs and would thus be already heavily indebted. Since the current Cameron-led coalition government is committed to reducing, rather than increasing, public spending then this option is no longer available, though, frighteningly, various politicians from the Labour Party are calling for it to be used notwithstanding Britain's existing debt mountain. However, as we will see below, this may in any case be a rather sterile debate.

Perhaps to compensate for their disappointment at not being able to use the traditional politicians' friend, borrowing and spending more money, the government and the Bank of England have instead massively boosted the money supply through successive rounds of quantitative easing. Technically the purchase of existing government bonds for cash, in practice this has the effect of printing more money and pumping it into the system.

The non-interventionists argue that because cycles of boom and bust occur naturally and regularly, then being in recession is rather like having a cold. It is very unpleasant at the time, but if you wait long enough then you will get better of your own accord. Neither increasing the money supply significantly nor boosting public spending is likely to have much more effect and in some cases may even make things worse.

Friedman, for example, feels that trying to control economic cycles either in a Keynesian (tax, borrowing and spending) or a monetarist (interest rates and money supply) way is counterproductive. By the time economic data is pointing in a particular direction, the economic cycle has moved on and will be ahead of whatever point is currently being indicated. The government then has to decide what to do based on this already out-of-date information. This takes more time. Whatever action the government decides upon then takes still more time actually to implement. Thus by the time the action actually bites, the cycle may be more or less at the opposite point to that indicated by the data relied upon. This often has the effect of making things worse, boosting activity during the up cycle and restricting it during the down cycle. For this reason some writers have called for any economic smoothing undertaken to be based upon different indicators, such as asset prices.

A good example of the sort of time lag Friedman has in mind was revealed by a report from the Institute of Fiscal Studies in early 2012, which pointed out that only 6% of the cuts to current services that the coalition government announced when it took office in May 2010 would actually have been implemented by April 2012, nearly two years later. This not only suggests that Friedman's views on the length of time between consideration, announcement and full implementation of government fiscal policy are broadly correct, but also throws into question the alleged correlation between public spending and economic growth. In early 2012 spending on public services was still the highest it had ever been in real terms, yet the economy was teetering on the brink of full-blown recession. This hardly argues for increasing such spending yet further as a sure recipe for boosting the economy.

Another example may help to illustrate this point still further. In the three years between 1929 and 1932 the Hoover administration increased US federal spending by about 50%, running deficits in order to do so. Precisely the action, in other words, that a Keynesian would recommend to avert a recession. During the same period, up until the very last three months, the Fed steadily slashed rates, which should have had the effect of increasing, not diminishing, the marginal propensity to consume, and thus increasing aggregate demand. Again, classic Keynesian stuff. Yet none of this seems to have made the slightest difference. America still headed into the longest and bleakest recession in history.

At the very least this is deeply inconsistent with the Keynesian belief that the government can seek to regulate economic activity through accelerating and braking with spending, borrowing and interest rates. At worst, it seems completely to disprove it. It may well be that all those times when success was claimed for such an approach, the economy was simply going its own sweet way all along. Further, if Keynesian policy measures *did* have any effect, then because of time lag issues, they may have made the peaks and troughs of the economic cycle more extreme, rather than less.

Of course, Keynesians would presumably argue that nobody has ever really tried to put pure Keynesianism into practice, with the government running a surplus during good years to fund deficits during bad years, and that the world that Keynes modelled is in any event one now long-vanished, with its fixed exchange rates, responsible fiscal policy and deliberate omission of foreign trade. Perhaps this is some answer to the obvious intellectual bankruptcy of Keynesian measures that was revealed during the 1970s, when it had to deal with such unforeseen elements as continuous budget deficits, inefficient industry, rampant inflation, militant trade unions and an increasingly expensive welfare state.

A team of academics from a number of different universities on both sides of the Atlantic[5] recently conducted detailed research into the effect of the fabled Keynesian multiplier in forty-four different

---

[5] Ethan Ilzetsky of the London School of Economics, and Enrique Mendoza and Carlos Vegh, both of the University of Maryland.

countries between 1960 and 2007, using a newly available dataset. They modelled the effect of an increase in government consumption on output and came up with some startling results. In any country with floating exchange rates, the effect of the multiplier was effectively zero. In any country that was open to international trade, the multiplier effect was actually negative, both immediately and in the longer term. In any country that was heavily indebted (over 60% of GDP), then the multiplier was broadly neutral in the short term, but negative in the medium and long term. Nor, at least for developed economies, did it seem to matter whether government investment or consumption was being measured.

The UK is a country that has floating exchange rates, is open to international trade and has public debt of more than 60% of GDP. According to this research, increasing public spending would actually have a *negative* effect on the economy, particularly in the longer term. Thus the debate as to whether the government is right to be cutting spending is a sterile one as far as the possibility of recession is concerned and can only possibly be right as far as the budget deficit and national debt are concerned.

The message that you simply cannot borrow and spend your way out of trouble is unlikely to be welcome in political quarters. Nor have the authors of the report seen it given any great prominence, but then those who debunk established dogma are rarely congratulated warmly; Galileo came very close to being burned at the stake.

Of course, government spending will rise during a recession anyway as increased unemployment brings increased welfare payments in its wake. At the same time, tax revenues will fall as there are fewer people still in work to pay income tax and corporate profits fall, thus hitting the public finances with a dreaded double whammy. It is for precisely this reason that it is imperative to run a budget surplus during good times, to build up a buffer with which to ride out these fiscal shocks, and Gordon Brown's failure to do so between 2003 and 2007 stands starkly exposed by subsequent events.

One suspects that had the public finances not been in their present appalling mess, then the current government may well have fallen victim to the siren call of the Keynesian stimulus with, as the above research suggests, unfortunate consequences. Deprived of their traditional crutch, they have resorted instead to a massive monetary stimulus.

The alternative, to allow the patient to wrap up warm and get over his cold in his own sweet time, does not seem even to have been considered. On the contrary, there is an implicit assumption in everything the government has done that they do indeed have the power, like Canute, to hold back the tide, to interfere in the inexorable workings of the economic cycle and bend it to their will. This despite the fact that there is no clear evidence that any such approach has ever worked, anywhere, anytime.

Yet there is general agreement by every economist, no matter how much or how little they may believe in either a Keynesian or a monetarist approach, that increasing the amount of money in circulation must inevitably increase inflation in the medium to long term. Indeed, this fact is so self-evident that it is even enshrined as one of Mankiw's famous Ten Principles: 'prices rise when the government prints too much money' (a surprisingly unequivocal stance for Mankiw).

Well, in the three years from the end of 2007 to the end of 2010, M4, the government's own measure of money, increased by over 40%,[6] partly driven by £200 billion of QE, which resulted in the government buying a staggering 30% of its bonds that were previously in private hands.

Remember, $MV = PQ$. If M has risen by over 40% yet GDP (which is assumed to be the same thing as PQ) is stagnant, then V has fallen significantly. It must follow that if V returns to anything like its former rate and if the capacity of output (Q) is fairly fixed, at least in the short term, then prices (P) must also increase significantly. Hence Mankiw's principle: 'prices rise when the government prints too much money'. Yet here the government has printed not just more money, but enormous amounts of new money. Surely this can only lead to very high inflation in the medium to long term?

---

[6] Author's calculations based on HM Treasury monthly data.

In other words, in throwing more money at the recession, the government has succeeded simply in buying future inflation for no discernible compensating benefit. Once again, the government and the central banks are part of the problem (or at least tomorrow's problem), not part of the solution. Once again, politicians have chosen the short-term cosmetic fix over the long-term national interest.

Nothing daunted, the Bank of England announced in early 2012, by which time the total spent on QE had already reached £275 billion, to inject (print) at least another £50 billion. Of course the Bank claimed that the QE already undertaken had 'a notable positive effect on Britain's economic output'[7] between 2009 and 2010, but then they would say that, wouldn't they? In fact, British industrial output at the end of 2010 was at an index level of 89.1 according to official Treasury figures, compared to 97.0 at the end of 2008. That's a *decrease* of over 9%. Some 'notable positive effect'.

The Bank does grudgingly admit elsewhere[8] that QE is likely to boost inflation, though it seems to be linking inflation changes largely to asset prices and interest rates rather than the boring old cost of living that people have to pay for their food, clothing and housing. What they do not mention is that the government, upon whom we rely to protect us from inflation, actually has a vested interest in creating and increasing it.

First, any heavily indebted government has an interest in inflation being as high as possible for as long as possible, since it means they will be able to pay their creditors back with devalued money; inflation is bad news for lenders but great news for borrowers. Second, the British government actually levies an overt tax on inflation. This point has been made before, but is such an important one that it bears repeating. Capital gains tax is a tax on inflation. Thus we have a situation where the government is able to influence inflation through public policy, ostensibly has a duty to society to keep inflation as low as possible and yet has a direct financial interest, as the recipient of CGT, in keeping it as high as possible. So, not just one but two blatant examples of why,

---

[7] Reuters, 1 February 2012.
[8] See for example its Q3 2011 quarterly report.

once again, the government is part of the problem, not part of the solution. Not that politicians are likely to concern themselves unduly about such a thing, but CGT must be the most deeply and offensively unethical tax ever levied.

Oscar Wilde once said that the truth is rarely pure and never simple, yet here it is both. The real enemy is not recession, but inflation. Recession has an unpleasant effect on the economy in the short term yet, as we saw in Britain during the 1970s, inflation has the potential totally to destroy it if allowed to rage unchecked, exactly as it did in Central Europe during the 1920s. The government is trying to cure someone of a cold which, if left well alone, will get better of its own accord, but in the process is administering a noxious poison that may well end up killing the patient.

Recessions come and go. So, though they do not like to be reminded of the fact, do governments. It is government policy to try to stop recessions from occurring. Yet much of the time it is government policy that many researchers have claimed to be the prime cause of recessions. We live in a Kafkaesque nightmare world where everything is topsy-turvy. The government claims to be trying to cure the current downturn, but not only are they likely to be unsuccessful in the attempt, they are almost certainly ensuring that the next cycle of boom and bust will be even more extreme.

Politicians would do well to read *Alice in Wonderland*, in which Alice says: 'If one drinks much from a bottle marked "Poison", it's almost certain to disagree with one sooner or later.'

# SIXTEEN

# Democracy and Totalitarianism

While hesitating to use what has become such a hackneyed buzz-phrase, it is the proper role of government that represents the elephant in the room whenever the present crisis falls to be discussed. A constant theme of this book, which hopefully by this point will require no further justification, is that it is impossible to understand any aspect of anything by looking at that subject alone. On the contrary, the required approach is almost always interdisciplinary. It has been possible to pursue our story this far only by looking at areas as apparently diverse as finance, economics, history, philosophy and, of course, politics.

Thus what may at first appear a fairly simple and narrow range of enquiry ('what can we do to solve our economic problems?') in fact prompts a whole range of deeper questions, some of which raise very fundamental issues as to what sort of society we wish to inhabit, and within what sort of system we want our politicians to operate. This chapter will attempt to address some of these concerns. What is the proper range within which government should operate? How might we deal with politicians who may be conflicted between their own short-term interests and the long-term national interest? What really is 'sovereignty', who should exercise it and can it be given away? How should we seek to define and protect the relationship between the state and its people? Above all, to what sort of society do we really aspire?

Some of these enquiries range far beyond the initial question as to the proper role of government, and will require an honest appraisal of how much responsibility we as individuals are willing to take for our own actions and the world they create by cause and effect. Most of them are also interrelated so that it is difficult to discuss them in strict isolation. However, the proper role of government may make a convenient starting point.

Ever since the early Greek philosophers, government has been a recurring subject of debate. There is general agreement that it exists to protect its subjects, but beyond that there is little unanimity. Adam Smith, for example, believed that it should simply protect the nation from military attack, provide the rule of law internally and supply essential infrastructure such as roads.

It is difficult to come to this subject without a great deal of intellectual baggage. Few people in the Western world would suggest that democracy is not the best form of government, nor that autocratic government is tyrannical and wrong. Yet the world's second-largest economy, which just happens to include more than 1.3 billion people, would not agree. If 1.3 billion people disagree with us, can we really be so sure of our convictions? There again, can we even be sure what we mean by 'democracy'?

Tony Blair won his landslide victory in 1997, gaining an overall majority of 179 seats, despite the fact that less than 31% of the electorate as a whole actually voted for him, and went on to take the country into an unpopular and, many believed, illegal war despite mass demonstrations against it. His successor, who was never elected prime minister at all, and inherited a government for which only 21.6% of the electorate voted, was able to give away British sovereignty to the European Union without calling a referendum.

A few other points are worthy of note. In that 2005 election, nearly as many people voted Conservative as voted Labour, and more than 54% of voters actually backed the other two main parties. As for the war and the transfer of sovereignty, the monarchy, the traditional ultimate check and balance of Britain's unwritten constitution, completely failed to function. Two conclusions might be ventured. First, this may be many things, but does not sound like democracy. Second, whatever sort of constitution Britain has, it does not seem to be working.

The result of these two things taken together is a form of government that has never formally been described, but may best be thought of as dictatorship by prime minister. Thus, any discussion on reforming our present political system is concerned with making it more democratic, not less, and is arguably both necessary and desirable.

Perhaps, as Aristotle suggested, we should concentrate not on classifying governments and putting labels on them such as 'democracy', 'oligarchy' and 'tyranny', but on whether a particular system of government is good or bad? Incidentally, many of Aristotle's views would not find favour today in what we might loosely classify as the Western liberal democracies. He believed, for example, that a true democracy would effectively turn into a tyranny of the disadvantaged, who would use their power simply to advance their own interest by soaking the rich. Equally, though, he recognised that an oligarchy might result in the moneyed classes using their power to advance their own commercial ventures.

Given this, he struggled to come up with an ideal form of government but eventually plumped for rule by those who were already wealthy enough not to fall prey to corruption and had a record of participating in judicial and administrative processes out of a sense of public duty. This may sound rather alien to a modern ear, but could be argued to be broadly how Britain was governed in the latter half of the nineteenth century, with lists of cabinet ministers reading like a roll call of aristocratic society.

If we were to follow Aristotle's approach, then how might we decide whether a particular system of government was 'good' or 'bad'? This task is itself fraught with intellectual peril, since any such assessment would first require us to agree on what the proper tasks of government might be, and here subjectivity must necessarily intrude. However, it may be possible to find areas of common ground on which an audience drawn from the Western liberal tradition might broadly agree.

At this point, however, a very important caveat must be entered, for it has a huge significance for what comes next. The word 'liberal' completely changed its meaning in just about forty years or so, the first forty years of the twentieth century, in fact. Changed so dramatically that it came to mean precisely the opposite of what it had originally meant. So few people understand this that it creates massive misunderstanding whenever such matters fall to be discussed.

In the nineteenth century and before, 'liberal' derived its meaning from 'liberty'. Thus a liberal was someone who believed in the absolute primacy of individual freedom. This meant that the government's role was to stay out of human affairs except to the extent necessary to protect people from physical attack, and their property from being damaged or destroyed. If we widen this definition to include the establishment of a system such as the courts to resolve disputes between its subjects, then this may loosely be called the rule of law. It was the government's duty to provide and maintain the rule of law, but to be very careful to go no further than this, since to do so would inevitably be infringing some individual freedom and this would already have been done to the extent necessary to provide the rule of law, for example taking away the right not to turn up to court when summoned to do so.

Of course, the nineteenth-century liberals were treading a dangerous line here. They all believed that the society of the day was unfair to the disadvantaged and should be changed. Yet their ultimate faith lay in the freedom of the individual and where any conflict between the two arose, then they chose libertarianism. There was a second, but related string to their bow, though. They believed in free trade, and the operation of free markets generally.

'Related' because they believed that political freedom could not exist without commercial freedom, indeed that each was a prerequisite of the other. Provided that markets, including for such things as labour and housing, were allowed to operate freely they would find their natural level, but this could not happen unless individuals were allowed to exercise their own self-interest, as advocated by the likes of Smith and Ricardo. Conversely, any interference in free markets would be a political act intended to deprive at least one individual of at least some of their freedom. The introduction of a minimum wage, for example, deprives employers of their freedom to employ people at less than the minimum wage. Thus political freedom and commercial freedom go hand in hand.

Of course this rather simplistic assumption was proved false, first in fascist Italy and Germany and latterly in China, where in each case a large degree of commercial freedom coexisted with a complete absence of political freedom. In fact, in just about every country today there will be neither political nor commercial freedom in the views of the purists. Any country that has either a minimum wage or rent control, for example, would not qualify on either ground.

Then the goalposts moved. Hayek argues that this was because social progress in nineteenth-century Britain and America (particularly Britain) was too slow. Germany, by contrast, had universal secondary education, a welfare system and pension funds in place well before the end of the nineteenth century. The result was that many people changed their views, believing that social change must be enforced, rather than encouraged, even if this meant restricting, through statute, the rights of individuals to act as they chose.

For the liberals, this was a disaster, and an unacceptable one. As Friedman is careful to put it: 'As liberals, we take the freedom of the individual, or perhaps the family, as our ultimate goal in judging social arrangements ... a major aim of the liberal is to leave the ethical problem for the individual to wrestle with. The "really" important ethical problems are those that face the individual in a free society – what he should do with his freedom.'[1]

Government moved in a different direction, however. A raft of legislation on both sides of the Atlantic profoundly affected all aspects of life, both social and commercial, all in the cause of creating a fairer society. A true liberal would, of course, argue that a society cannot be 'fair' unless it is free, and so there is an inherent contradiction in what a government has achieved. Is it 'fair', for example, as in the case of leasehold enfranchisement, to take away property rights that were freely agreed by consenting adults in full possession of the facts? Is it 'fair' to prevent people from using brighter light-bulbs in their home if they are happy to pay for the extra electricity that they consume?

It is not necessary to resolve these questions, only to note the fact that they exist. For they brought about a radical change in the meaning of the word 'liberal'. As we have seen, initially a liberal advocated laissez-faire government, in other words government that allowed individuals to get on with their own lives and did not seek to intervene

---

[1] Milton Friedman, *Capitalism and Freedom*, Chicago, University of Chicago Press, 2002, p. 12.

in their everyday affairs save to the extent necessary to guarantee the rule of law.

However, those who brought their reforming zeal to the service of the disadvantaged in the early twentieth century also called themselves liberals. In Britain, for example, much of the lobbying and campaigning for this was done by the Liberal Party. Thus, instead of believing in the rights of the individual taking priority over social advancement, which would occur naturally albeit gradually, people calling themselves liberals now believed that social advancement had to be pushed along at a faster pace, even though this could only be done by restricting individual liberty.

Whereas a liberal had previously believed in laissez-faire government, they now promoted paternalistic government, intervening decisively to regulate how people should behave in everyday situations. It is this about-face in the meaning of one simple word that has understandably caused much misunderstanding. When people hear the likes of Friedman, Hayek and Ayn Rand, whose novel *When Atlas Shrugged* explores this theme extensively, describe themselves as liberals, they are confused. What they fail to realise is that the word is still claimed by some in its original, nineteenth-century sense. In the interests of avoiding such misunderstandings in the pages of this book, let us agree to use the word 'liberal' in its modern, paternalistic, freedom-restricting sense and 'libertarian' in the traditional, laissez-faire, freedom-enhancing sense.

Why is it that the notion of individual liberty should have formed the starting point of the intellectual journey of so many of the great economists: Smith, Ricardo, Hayek and Friedman to name but a few? Partly, doubtless, because they saw individual freedom as the most fundamental aspiration of any civilised society and were puzzled that others apparently did not. Partly because they recognised that it is impossible to disentangle the question 'what sort of society do we want?' from 'how are we going to pay for it?'

Partly too because the question of individual liberty is the flip side of the nature of government. Under a libertarian system government is a supportive friend, ready to protect you when necessary; under a modern 'liberal' paternalistic system, government is more like Big Brother in Orwell's *1984*, with a view into everybody's life and a rule ready for every situation. This all seems a very far cry from Smith's vision of government, which was that it should protect its citizens and their property from foreign aggression, provide for the rule of law, and provide the essential infrastructure that life and commerce require in order to strive.

We encountered a number of separate but related questions at the beginning of the chapter. They all circle back to one: do we want big government or small government? Which would we prefer? Which can we afford? Whichever the case, are we happy that we are getting value for money? The great economists have recognised that sooner or later these questions must be answered and that therefore they are best addressed straight away. The lesser ones, and here we must sadly include Keynes, at least the Keynes of the *General Theory* (which contains not a single section on individual rights or the role of the state), start with numbers or mechanics.

Yet unless you know what sort of environment it is that you wish to create, protect or work within, how can you really understand what you are doing, and why? A socialist economist who believes in public ownership of enterprise, a centrally planned economy and full employment is likely to model the world very differently from a libertarian free-market monetarist. Surely, then, it is incumbent upon you to start by deciding whereabouts on these various continua your beliefs fall, and then test them rigorously?

The great economists do so, recognising that they must define and justify their worldview at the outset. They see their role as encompassing not just an explanation of what is happening but an analysis of what *might* happen, perhaps even what *should* happen, were things to be done differently. It is sad to relate that this view has been treated with grave suspicion by much of the economic community. In particular, it is almost as if there has been a determined effort to erase Hayek and the Austrian School from the pages of history.

Nor has this effort been honourable or worthy of any intellectual respect. Hayek's failure to distinguish between fascism and communism, pointing out, reasonably enough, that neither is a desirable outcome, has been held sufficient then and since to treat him as the equivalent of some sort of child sex offender, to be shunned by decent society and placed on a register of deeply deviant individuals. The fact that Friedman's monetarist theory did not appear to work when put into practice has been held sufficient to ignore his other work, for example on the nature of government. Yet Keynes, despite the fact that it has similarly proved difficult to validate his theories in practice, particularly his views on full employment and the economic multiplier, remains (rightly) a revered figure.

Hayek in a television interview would later ruefully reflect that once upon a time he and Keynes were the two best-known economists in the world, but then Keynes died and became a saint, while he (Hayek) published *The Road To Serfdom* and became a pariah.

It is right, then, that a modern audience, who may not even realise that these matters have ever been debated, should be given an opportunity to consider the rival arguments. Whether Hayek or Friedman got it right is not the point; it is unlikely that any two or three people would agree entirely on this in any event. What is important is that they have the right to be heard.

As we have seen, all libertarian economic thinkers have taken the freedom of the individual as their starting point. From this it follows that government should play as small a role as possible. Anytime that government intervenes in the working of what would otherwise be a free market, then individual liberties are infringed; Friedman gives the example of exchange controls in Great Britain after the Second World War infringing the freedom of its citizens to travel abroad. Thus government should only intervene in markets where it can demonstrate (1) that the market is not operating freely and (2) that it can solve this problem while limiting its involvement both in time and degree to the absolute minimum required. Anytime that government intervenes in everyday affairs it is similarly repressing individual freedom; regulations that limit the height from the ground at which works can be carried out on a ladder removes the freedom of a man who cannot afford scaffolding to make repairs to his home. Thus government should only intervene if it can show that the benefit of any such regulation outweighs its cost, taking both financial and social issues into account.

This is what we mean when we talk about small government and big government. Small government is permissive and laissez-faire. Big government is restrictive and paternalistic. Small government aims to protect its citizens from others. Big government aims to protects its citizens from themselves. Small government believes that a free market is the best mechanism for any socioeconomic interaction, since its result will always be a fair one. Big government is deeply suspicious of free markets and seeks to 'protect' its citizens from their outcomes, no matter how fair these may be.

Hayek's point was that once government started to infringe personal freedom, then it was impossible to stop, partly because of the constant need to sweep up around the edges to clarify and extend restrictions, and partly because government would simply grow ever more drunk on its own arrogant belief that it always knew best. Thus you either had a totally free society or you were on the road to serfdom, hence the title of his book. Being free is rather like being pregnant: you either are or you are not. You cannot be a little bit pregnant.

It is impossible to consider the question of small or big government without also asking some very fundamental questions about ourselves as individuals and what role the individual should play within the state. One question in particular runs through most of the issues raised by this book: to what extent do we expect individuals to take responsibility for themselves and (if appropriate) their families?

Readers will notice that this is arguably a rewording of the point from Friedman quoted above and begin to understand why such an apparently non-economic passage should have been extracted. What Friedman has the perception to realise is that it is with regard to this very important question of the role of the individual within society that we must base our economic thinking. If individuals are neither prepared nor expected to take responsibility for themselves, then big government becomes a necessary requirement, with obvious implications for the public finances.

Incidentally, those who have spent any time living in America before returning to Europe, or indeed vice versa, will be all too aware that very different attitudes exist on each side of the Atlantic. In America, it is taken as a given that the individual has primary responsibility for themself and that the rights of the individual, often enshrined in the constitution and clarified or delineated by rulings of the Supreme Court, are paramount. In Britain, cosseted for so many decades by the warm embrace of New Jerusalem, individuals seem much less willing to take responsibility for themselves, and the government much less willing to force them to do so.

Of course, there is a certain line beyond which government is obliged to act. For example, government will intervene to force criminals to accept responsibility for their acts. Yet this in turn raises the question of how 'criminal' should be defined. An individual stealing a newspaper is criminal, whereas the Bank of England failing to control inflation is not, no matter how serious the results. Unknowingly driving a car with a non-functioning brake-light is criminal, whereas a senior banker mismanaging their bank into insolvency is not. Clearly, therefore, however 'criminal' is defined, the question of potential damage to society is not a factor. Yet surely this would be a better yardstick for justifying government intervention than whether or not a particular act was classified many years ago by Act of Parliament as 'criminal'?

Hayek essentially raises the same issues as Aristotle, but framed in a slightly different way. For him, whether a government is good or bad is determined by the extent to which it is totalitarian. This in turn is determined by whether it infringes individual liberties; if it does, even to a certain extent, then it is totalitarian. Like Aristotle, he thought that the quality of government is far more important than its type. If you are being repressed, then do you really care whether the people doing the repressing are wearing communist or fascist uniforms?

Poor Hayek! He must have thought that with the world being consumed by a war against an evil totalitarian regime, then the postwar world would be fanatical about preserving and protecting personal freedom. Yet, in Britain at least, the socialist dream was at its height, with Attlee's government moving towards public ownership of all industry and a centrally planned economy. What Hayek, who described socialism as 'a new form of slavery', would have viewed as an Orwellian nightmare, Attlee and his chums saw as a collectivist nirvana. For them, anybody who failed to realise that a tyranny of the left was essentially different from a tyranny of the right must be a dangerous social deviant, and so Hayek's ideas were loaded into the cattle trucks and packed off to intellectual exile. Though he would belatedly win the Nobel Prize in 1974, he would be honoured by his own country (he became a British citizen in 1938) only ten years after that and his work remains largely unknown today, even to those within the financial community.

Of course there is one element of Hayek's thinking that he would probably change if he had the opportunity to come back from the great debating chamber in the hereafter and rewrite his book. He never quite grasped the fact that in practice government could be nominally democratic but still totalitarian. He does debate the point,[2] but seems to come down in favour of the idea that Parliament would only ever seek to restrict individual freedom 'where true agreement exists', and that everything else would 'be left to chance'. Later he makes it clear that he envisages this happening only where agreement 'was likely to exist in a society of free men'. Perhaps inevitably for an exile grateful to be welcomed by Britain from repression elsewhere, he took a somewhat rose-tinted view of the Westminster model, failing to realise that what it really represented was dictatorship by prime minister.

Like it or not, if we apply Hayek's test then every government in the world is totalitarian and we would only be discussing the degree to which, in each case, they restrict individual freedom. Such a sobering realisation is perhaps the best pointer of all to just how completely the insidious notion that government always knows best, and thus is always justified to intervene in everyday affairs, has invaded our thinking. The idea of a society based on individual freedom has become a dreamy utopia, and any aspiration to achieve it the mark of a dangerous idealist.

---

[2] Friedrich Hayek, *The Road to Serfdom*, London, Routledge, 2001 (see for example page 73).

Of course our subjection to the tyranny of big government has another reason too. Aristotle rightly conjectured that each form of government would be likely to promote the interests of the sector of society that it represented, hence his preference for some sort of meritocracy. What neither Hayek nor Popper, whose *Open Society* was published almost immediately afterwards, ever noticed from the viewpoint of their ivory towers, however, was that politicians once in government promote not necessarily the interests of their own socioeconomic tribe but *their own personal interests as career politicians.*

The price we pay for democratic representation is to force our politicians to think and act within the straightjacket of elections every four years or so. None of this might matter if government was carried on by self-sacrificing individuals who might not even want to be in government very much, but do so out of a sense of public duty. Sadly, however, such people do not enter politics or, at least, have not done so since the nineteenth century. Indeed, the most depressing common theme which runs through this book is that of politicians subordinating the long term to the short term, and the national interest to their own.

Thus this analysis of government, to which we have been led chiefly by Hayek, throws up two clear conclusions. First, whether it be a good thing or a bad thing, we currently have big government rather than small government. Second, our political system seems to make it inevitable that government will be motivated by the short term (ideally things that happen within the lifetime of a single Parliament), rather than the long term. Of course there are, and will continue to be, exceptions, of which Margaret Thatcher was probably a notable example, but these propositions seem to be generally true. The main objective of most government ministers, perhaps understandably, is to get re-elected.

So we seem to have two quite separate problems with government. The first is that we have big government without really understanding why, and certainly without ever having asked for it. The second is that we force our politicians to make decisions that have long-term implications within a system that rewards or blames their actions only in the short term. Let us look at each of these issues in a little more detail before considering what might be done about them.

Big government has been driven partly by the demands of New Jerusalem. The more units operated by the National Health Service and the more benefits offered by the welfare state, the greater the number of civil servants required to administer them. The same is true in general of the reach of the public sector as a whole. However, this is itself directly influenced by the amount of legislation and regulation in existence. Each new package of rules governing that civil servant's nightmare, an area of human activity currently devoid of supervision, requires additional civil servants to police it, sometimes even a whole new section or department.

This is a point that is so obvious that it should not require to be made and yet few seem to have noted it. Regulation comes at a significant direct cost, as well as the frequently incalculable indirect costs of businesses and investors being forced to operate less efficiently. The dreaded *OJEU*[3] tendering requirements, for example, make it impossible for public-sector investors such as pension plans freely to choose their investment managers. At the risk of repetition, it should be for those who advocate regulation of a particular area to convince the individual of its absolute necessity, as well as its continued desirability when subjected to rigorous cost/benefit analysis. It should not be for the individual to justify why regulation is not required.

Most worryingly of all, much regulation of recent years seems to have been driven directly by the diktat of the European Union, and while the direct costs of EU membership are recorded (Britain's annual contribution to EU funds), the indirect costs, including the expense of imposing and policing this blizzard of rules, are not. Some of these indirect costs, such as the potential economic effect of parts of the financial services industry possibly moving away to escape what they may regard as unnecessarily repressive EU regulation, could yet prove deeply damaging to the British economy. The chief executive of HSBC recently announced that the bank's value

---

[3] *Official Journal of the European Union.*

had been permanently reduced by no less than £18 billion as a result of regulations.[4]

Bigger government obviously means greater public spending. Civil servants do not give their services freely and nor do public-sector contractors. It also imposes other, indirect costs, though these are much more difficult to quantify. Since the public sector destroys wealth while the private sector creates it, then the larger government (the public sector) is relative to the private sector, the greater the strain it imposes on the national economy. Thus, quite apart from the ethical debate about individual freedom, it would seem clear that it is for those who advocate big government to justify its existence, rather than the other way around. Even those among us who may like big government are forced to ask the question 'yes, but can we afford it?'

Curiously, however, this debate seems never even to have occurred, much less to have been resoundingly won by the big government lobby. Has any politician ever gone out on the hustings on a platform of justifying the present number of civil servants? No, the point simply goes by default.

As for the direct conflict that often arises between long- and short-term considerations, a few examples drawn from current and recent events in the UK will suffice.

The coalition government decided effectively to use executive theft to take money away from the banks to invest in private companies. The word 'theft' is used advisedly. You cannot take money away from a business without decreasing the value of its shares and there was no legal precedent for penalising shareholders in this arbitrary way. On the contrary, it could be argued to be directly contrary to the rule of law, under which a government has an obligation to respect and protect property rights. However, let us leave such considerations to one side.

The government wishes to put money into private companies in order to boost the economy. So far, so good. Should that indeed be its objective, then there is very clear evidence of exactly where such

---

[4] *The Sunday Telegraph*, 4 March 2012.

money should go: early-stage venture capital, of which there is almost none in professional hands in the UK compared to, say, the US. This despite the fact that economic theory holds that the only two ways to generate significant growth in a developed economy, such as the UK, are through a more highly educated workforce, and innovation, the latter being the preserve of start-up companies funded by early-stage venture capital. Despite, too, ample evidence that this idea really works in practice. A recent study in America[5] showed that, while annual venture-capital investment represented only about 0.2% of US GDP, companies that either were or had been venture-backed now generated 21% of that same US GDP.

The facts, then, are incontrovertible. If you are really serious about generating significant long-term economic growth, then the only logical place to put that money would be in early-stage venture capital, administered by professional venture-capital firms. However, the government is clearly *not* serious about generating significant long-term economic growth because it has chosen instead to put the money into what the private-equity industry would call development capital, the taking of minority stakes in established businesses. Yet such capital is already professionally available. So, not only would any such companies that were deserving of funding be able to get it anyway, but there is also the very real risk that this large pool of money, investing for political rather than commercial reasons, may actually produce a false market, not that this is something that the government tends to worry about.

So why has the government acted in such an apparently illogical way? In order to answer this question you have to learn to think like a politician. Yes, venture capital provides the stimulus of a massive economic multiplier, as the American figures clearly show. Yet it takes a very long time to feed through: probably at least ten years. That is no good for politicians. They need something that can show results, or can at least be convincingly spun as having shown results, within the lifetime of a single Parliament. So, better to set up something that

---

[5] NVCA, *Venture Impact*, 5th edition.

merely supplements and might well end up 'crowding out' the private sector, and put a 'growth' badge on it to help spin the requisite message. For politicians, form is all-important, and substance irrelevant.

Similarly, the government knows that one of the yardsticks by which it is measured is GDP growth, though we have examined elsewhere how this is not any sort of valid measure of economic health, as opposed to activity. This is a convenient state of affairs that no government is about to disturb, since a government is able directly to influence GDP by simply increasing government spending. Usually, that is. Not if you have publicly undertaken to reduce the budget deficit. Now the throttle that you would normally pull wide open has been locked in the halfway position.

The government starts to panic. The media are starting to talk about recession and the opposition are saying this is all the government's fault (well, they would, wouldn't they?). Unless something positive starts to happen to GDP, then the government may be in danger of losing the next election. Well, if the Keynesian throttle is not available, then the monetarist one will have to do instead. Flood the system with new money through QE and, if that doesn't work, then do it again and again until it does work, or at least appears to.

We have examined elsewhere the wisdom of increasing the money supply to counteract the effects of recession. At best, it is unproven. It is quite possible that those instances where it appears to have worked were instances of coincidence rather than causation. Certainly if its intention was to boost lending, this has not occurred. The Treasury's own figures show that M4 lending has reduced dramatically over the entire period of QE.

Yet at what cost has the government been prepared to buy so little. At what risk have they gambled for such a small, perhaps even an illusory advantage. As we examine elsewhere in the book, every economist of any school of thought whatever would agree with the principle that the more money a government prints (which is effectively what QE does, though the new money is actually created digitally by being credited to banks' accounts), the higher inflation will be in the medium to long term. Remember the equation $MV = PQ$?

If M (money) increases dramatically, then sooner or later so must P (prices), unless there is a positive explosion in economic activity (Q). The only reason that inflation has not already started to soar is presumably that V (velocity) has dropped dramatically, as the banks lend less and consumers spend less and save more.

Another classic example, then, of the government being prepared to mortgage the future, in this case by pumping enormous long-term monetary inflationary pressure into the system, to pay for a short-term political advantage. An advantage that, tragically, may not even transpire.

Interestingly, QE, while being widely praised by central bankers on both sides of the Atlantic (in other words, those doing the QE), sits oddly with the advice and recovery measures imposed by the IMF during the Asian crisis that began in 1997. They advocated high interest rates thus *reducing* the money supply. There again, they also recommended allowing troubled banks to fail.

So the concerns we should have with the government are clear. The government presents itself as the bringer of solutions to our problem whereas in fact the government is itself part of the problem. First, we have big government, which every year is destroying large amounts of the wealth created by the private sector. Second, the government is composed of career politicians who are likely always to pursue their own short-term political interests in preference to the long-term national interest. What can we do about this?

Clearly these are difficult questions to be answered in isolation, and what follows should be read in the context of what appears elsewhere in the book as part of the discussion on reforming the national finances. However, certain principles may perhaps be extracted.

If we reduce the number of civil servants responsible for providing any particular service, then the most logical outcome is that the standard to which that service is provided will fall. Thus, it seems sensible to seek instead to reduce the number of services. Instead of feeding individual civil servants into private-sector employment, whole departments and offices could be closed at a time. This would be akin to what Thatcher described as 'rolling back the frontiers of the state', although, with the notable exception of the previously nationalised industries, she failed in this particular task. As Friedman ruefully observes, she and Reagan 'were able to curb Leviathan, but not to cut it down.'[6] We will explore later what specific areas might most usefully be targeted.

It is also Friedman who points out that, while the government ostensibly protects the individual, it is actually the government itself from whom the individual most needs protection. This points us towards a possible solution to our second problem. How might the individual be protected from the arbitrary self-interest and short-termism of politicians?

The answer is simple. We must take away from politicians the right to make such decisions, or at least force them to make them only within given, predefined parameters. We the people must reclaim the political process and make sure that it is operated for our collective long-term benefit, rather than to maximise the government's chances of re-election.

The citizen's right to a balanced budget is fundamental and should be enshrined as such within a proper written constitution. In this way, the government would be physically incapable of running a budget deficit and would be forced to live within its means. It could, however, be allowed to run a deficit as Keynesian 'abnormal spending', but only to the extent that it had built up a cumulative surplus in former years. Absolute restrictions could be placed upon an inflation-adjusted amount of public debt and strict definitions applied to bring all contingent liabilities onto the public balance sheet.

Politicians are, of course, slippery customers, so let us burden them with a constitutional court and make sure that it requires a heavy Parliamentary majority combined with a referendum to alter our constitution.

Once we accept the basic principle of simply removing certain possible causes of action from our politicians, then the possibilities in regard to other constitutional restrictions are almost infinite. Some

---

[6] *Capitalism and Freedom*, op. cit.

may, for example, have a strong desire to include provisions relating to military action or transfers of sovereignty.

Needless to say, such proposals will find little favour with politicians, who will gaze at us reproachfully and say 'but surely you trust us?'

To which we should, of course, reply 'no, and never will again'.

# SEVENTEEN

# The Great Pensions Disaster

It is almost time to begin pulling together individual components of the present financial crisis, which have so far been considered, so far as possible, independently. However, we must first deal with one that is, at least for the moment, largely confined to the UK, namely the collapse of the British occupational pension system. Before exploring what this is and how it came about, it may be useful to set out some of the background and terminology, since there are many different types of pension provision and those of us who are not pensions professionals tend, quite understandably, to find it all rather confusing. As we will see, however, even though this particular aspect of the problem is a peculiarly British one and even though we are treating it separately for the sake of convenience as a self-contained little problem of its own, it does actually relate and interact with the wider issue of national debt, which runs through this book like a leitmotif.

Broadly speaking, there are three different types of pension provision, one of which can be broken down into different categories depending both on the status of the institution responsible for the pension fund ('sponsor') and the way in which the amounts provided by the fund as pension benefits are calculated. Though different words are used by different people, for the sake of avoiding misunderstanding, let us refer to them as state, private and occupational.

A state pension is provided by the government and in the UK is what is generally referred to as the old age pension and is dependent on National Insurance contributions (income tax under a different name) having been paid for a minimum number of years. Incidentally, UK pensioners are particularly badly served in this regard. As a percentage of average earnings the UK's state pension is by far the lowest in Europe; the second-lowest being double the British level.

To make matters worse, the link between the pension and the real price of inflation (RPI) has been discontinued, which means that the value of the British pension will fall further and further in real terms with each passing year. Instead, indexation will be against civil service pretend inflation (CPI), which excludes the costs of housing, presumably on the basis that pensioners do not actually need to live in a house; they could instead choose to live in a cardboard box under a railway arch thus saving themselves rent, council tax, home insurance and utility bills.

Given that those over the age of sixty constitute such a large part of the electorate, it is interesting to wonder what might happen if they were to set up their own political party specifically to promote their interests. Unless and until this happens it seems unlikely that any significant improvement in their conditions will occur. In fairness, it should be recorded that various proposals have been put forward both to increase the level of pensions (slightly) and to de-link them from a contributory requirement, but it remains unclear exactly how or when these might be implemented, not least because various government departments do not even seem able to agree on any of this among themselves. Given the current state of the public finances, however, it can be stated with some confidence that it simply is not possible that there could be any significant increase to the sorts of levels seen in other European countries.

Incidentally, this is a good example of an obsession with equality of outcome. Does it really make sense that someone who relies solely on the state pension and perhaps lives in an elderly, energy-inefficient house, requires the same level of state provision as someone who also already enjoys an occupational pension or may have significant investment capital?

Of course there are a number of considerations to be taken into account when designing a state pension system. The government allegedly has a commitment to encouraging people to save for their retirement and would rightly wish to avoid a system that acted to discourage that. Yet some measure of coercion as regards contributions during working life (as already happens in many other countries, including Australia and America) could address this point very simply. There again, so could a system that actually encouraged saving in the first place.

Remember that under Keynes's model savings take away money that could be used for consumption. They are, in other words, the enemy of economic growth, or at least economic activity as measured by GDP. Since GDP is one of the dials on the electoral dashboard by which politicians are measured, largely because everyone seems too intellectually lazy to abandon it in favour of something more meaningful, it follows that politicians must discourage saving. However, they must at the same time espouse the cause of people saving for retirement in order to justify the paltry level of state pension provision.

In case you are wondering how and why the government should praise something in theory but discourage it in practice, then a career in politics is clearly not for you. By taxing savings income you can ensure that the post-tax income will always be significantly lower than inflation, and thus that any incentive to save is removed, since any saver is guaranteed to lose money in real terms for every year that the money sits in a savings account. Thus you can quite safely trumpet the need for people to save for their retirement, confident that even if they are stupid enough to take your advice then they can only possibly lose money. By that time, of course, you will be enjoying your gold-plated MP's pension.

So, conscious of the fact that state provision is woeful and likely to remain so, successive governments have adopted the line that of course the state pension was only ever intended as a final safety net and that it was always assumed that people would be making their own provision for their retirement, either by saving or by contributing to either a personal or an occupational scheme. It is worth pointing out for the record that none of this ever featured in Beveridge's recommendations and that many who did save diligently for their retirement were wiped out by the inflation of the 1970s. Worth pointing out too that politicians only ever began to show even the slightest interest in this area *after* it had become apparent that the occupational system they had encouraged and regulated had failed its potential beneficiaries dismally, with scheme after scheme closing its doors to new members, but then it is never wise to test political statements too deeply. Let us turn instead to these other possible sources of retirement income.

Personal pension provision has gone through nearly as many bewildering legal and regulatory iterations as personal savings schemes, with the government constantly changing the rules, presumably in an attempt to deter people from actually making use of them, since all involve, to at least some limited extent, deferred payment of tax. It is therefore preferable to talk not about the specifics, for these will surely quickly change yet again, but about the general principles of how these schemes work. Briefly, the individual pays a certain amount into a scheme every month and not only do these confer a certain amount of income tax relief on the payments themselves, but once within the scheme the money may accumulate free of tax both as regards income and capital gains. Note, however, that both the amount of tax relief and the amounts that may be paid in are limited, the latter both annually and in total. The government wants you to make provision for your retirement but only up to a certain level. The Treasury's constant demand for tax revenue in the short term, as always, overrides all other considerations. Note also that there are significant disadvantages when you reverse the process on retirement. Not only do most people have to buy an annuity (see below), but you will now be taxed on any income which it produces.

The vast majority of people will allow the scheme manager to make the investment decisions and indeed many such schemes are ranged alongside or as part of a mutual fund business, thus meaning that even if certain discretion is left to the individual it is normally a very limited choice and restricted to funds managed or offered by (and thus earning fees for) that particular manager. It is possible to have a self-invested scheme where all investment selection decisions are left to the individual, though even in this case there are certain types of investment that are forbidden.

Though there may be differences in the way in which the various schemes are run, they are identical in what happens when retirement occurs. The pension 'pot' is turned into cash by the sale of all the investments within the scheme and the individual is then required to use either all or most of it in the purchase of an annuity. Note the word 'required'. Government does not trust us to look after our own money. For most of us, we *have* to buy an annuity.

What is an annuity? An amount of money that is paid for a certain number of years or during someone's lifetime. Provided they have a partner still living, most people will opt for a 'joint life' annuity, which will pay an amount every month until the second of the two dies. So far, so good. What could possibly be wrong with that?

Well, annuities are provided by life insurance companies. This is not exactly a great hardship for them. Indeed, it is actually something that does them an enormous service. So far as their main business is concerned, the later someone dies the better, since it delays the moment the company has to pay out under a life insurance policy. So far as providing an annuity is concerned, however, the *sooner* someone dies the better, since it brings to an end the obligation to make annuity payments. In other words, this is a perfect natural hedge, the risk of one business perfectly offsetting the risk of the other. In fact it is probably about the only perfect natural hedge that exists anywhere. This dramatic reduction of risk is of great commercial value to the insurance company, yet none of this value is shared with someone who purchases an annuity. Perhaps because it is little understood outside financial circles, this point has never been pursued by any champion of consumer or pensioner rights.

It is only right that life insurance companies should be subject to rigorous requirements of capital adequacy. They currently carry so many liabilities, particularly pension-related ones, that any failure of a major player would be catastrophic, probably far more so than in the case of any bank, at least other than in the immediate short term. Unfortunately this means that they are more or less forced to hold their assets in government bonds (not least because there are EU regulations known as Solvency II that make it difficult for them to do anything else), and the rates for these are held artificially low by many types of institutional investors being forced by the government to hold them.

Just as in the case of annuities, the government has created a 'market' that is a market in name only, because it is populated by parties who have no choice but to buy, almost regardless of price. In recent years, bonds have frequently been offering a negative real return and

Adam Smith would say that this could only be a temporary market abnormality, which the invisible hand would swiftly correct, returning the market to equilibrium. Yet because there are forced buyers, this has not happened and institutions have continued to buy even though they are guaranteed to make a loss. Anyone who purchases a bond in such circumstances is effectively paying the government to hold their cash for them, which naturally suits the government just fine, and of course the higher the rate of inflation, the greater the benefit the government will reap, yet another example of the principle that the government has a vested interest in inflation being as high as possible.

All of which is very bad news for purchasers of annuities, because the annuity rate, the percentage of your capital sum that is paid out to you every year, is closely linked to the bond rate and when the latter is at historically low levels, as it currently is, then so must be the former. If, in addition, you want a joint life annuity, and to index-link it to protect yourself against inflation, then the annuity rate will shrink still further. As we will see in a moment, this should now also be of vital interest to many people who hold an occupational pension. Remember, too, that this is a contract. The annuity rate is fixed at the one prevailing at the time you buy the annuity and cannot later be changed, even if the annuity rate might double or triple in the meantime. You cannot, for example, phase your annuity in over several years to lock in different rates or ask for a weighted average over time.

This might all seem rather silly. After all, if the annuity rate is so low then why not allow people to invest their pension pot for themselves, perhaps across a range of assets or in an investment property and achieve a much higher rate? First, because the government assumes that you are an idiot who cannot possibly be trusted to look after your own money. Second, because the more money that is used by individuals to buy annuities, the more money life insurance companies have with which they will be forced to buy government bonds. Once again, the government is itself part of the problem. Indeed, the government is the cause of the problem. It is almost as if the government's only concern is to see that, sooner or later and directly or indirectly, all private wealth is consumed by the public sector.

So, let us turn finally to occupational pensions; it is predominantly these that you will have been hearing about on television and radio when people mention 'pensions' or 'the pensions crisis'.

Occupational pension schemes are those provided by an employer for the benefit of their employees and they are generally grouped into two different classifications, though both function in the same way. The distinction is based on the status of the employer (known in pension terms as the 'sponsor'): corporate (a business entity) or public (a government body or local authority). In other countries, such as the Netherlands, whole industries have sometimes grouped together to provide pension provision but the basic process and concept remain broadly the same.

Both employer and employee make contributions to the scheme, the money so contributed being invested by the trustees. The government allows this to happen largely free of tax and after retirement the employee receives a certain regular payment based on some percentage of their final salary, usually index-linked for inflation protection. Such schemes are known in some countries as final salary schemes and in others as DB (defined benefit) schemes. Incidentally, this is a highly complex area in reality, which is being deliberately greatly simplified for present purposes. What is important is that we should grasp the principles, not the details.

Readers will be all too aware that this basic model has completely disintegrated, at least in the UK. Pension funds have found that their assets are inadequate to provide final salary provision and so this has been withdrawn, at least in the case of corporate schemes, sometimes in respect of new members entering the scheme, and sometimes in respect also of existing members. There is, for example, not a single remaining FTSE 100 company with an open final salary scheme.

In the public sector, where the government will to tackle the problem has been unequal to the scale of likely resistance by trade unions, the funding deficit simply hangs over the public finances as an enormous off-balance-sheet liability. It is effectively a guarantee by the taxpayer to members of publicly sponsored pension schemes. It is difficult to get any agreement on the precise amount involved but one estimate puts this at about £1.3 *trillion*. Given the potential worthlessness of such a guarantee, the government is to be congratulated on having recently persuaded the Royal Mail pension scheme to accept just such a promise in return for £28 billion pounds of assets that can actually be sold for real money.

Final salary provision has been replaced by what is called either money purchase or DC (defined contribution) depending on whether you speak English or American. In this scenario, the basic contribution and investment mechanism stays the same but on retirement a very different form of pension provision ensues. Instead of being paid an amount by the scheme every year based on final salary, the pensioner is put in the same position as that of a personal pension holder, being required to go out into the market and buy an annuity, at which point they become subject to all the issues we have just explored.

The difference between the two different forms of provision is profound and not yet properly understood. The writer has calculated elsewhere[1] that in many cases pensioners might receive under a money purchase arrangement only about one-third of what they would have been entitled to expect under a final salary scheme. The consequences are clear and stark: the bulk of the British people must begin planning for an impoverished retirement.

The effect of this change is to transfer the burden of paying pension benefits from the trustees of the pension scheme to the annuity providers (the life insurance sector) and to transfer the investment risk, the chance that the size of an individual's pension pot may not be sufficient to provide an acceptable level of pension, from the trustees of the pension scheme to the individual. This latter development is, of course, hugely unfair since in many cases the individual is given little or no choice by the trustees as to how their money should be invested and so is forced to take the risk of something over which they have no control, but then when did the government ever care about fairness?

All of which prompts an obvious question: how did the funding shortfall come about in the first place?

---

[1] Guy Fraser-Sampson, *No Fear Finance: An Introduction to Finance and Investment for the Non-Finance Professional*, London, Kogan Page, 2011.

The answer you will receive to this question depends on who you ask. Pension trustees blame pension consultants for not being prepared to commit themselves to any definite advice and being generally negative on the idea of investing in anything other than blue-chip domestic equities and prime government bonds. Pension consultants blame pension trustees for lack of understanding and failure to take their advice. Both eagerly point the finger at anything and anyone who may deflect blame from themselves: government policy, increased life expectancy and volatility in financial markets all form part of the usual suspects. In much the same way, the weather is invariably offered as a reason for poor trading by retailers in their annual report to shareholders. They would always have performed so very much better, we are told, if it had not been quite so hot, cold, dry or wet (delete whichever does not apply this year).

In truth, all of these three factors have played a part, but the pensions industry can only have any legitimate complaint about the first, since the other two were entirely within the scope of their own analysis, planning and management. However, in order properly to understand what has gone wrong it is necessary first to take a brief excursion into the realms of pension plan theory. This is a highly complex area populated largely by actuaries, a profession generally noted neither for its imaginative thinking nor for its communication skills, but what follows is a simplified and hopefully readily comprehensible summary.

As the Thatcher era progressed, two practical problems began to become apparent. Both were caused at least in part by rising equity values, which sparked briefly as a result of the Barber boom and then picked up again with the growing prosperity and new equity culture of the Thatcher revolution. In a sense, one of them was a good problem to have while the other was a bad one.

Both the 'good' problem and the 'bad' problem sprang from the fact that many occupational schemes were suddenly fully funded. How, might you ask, could a scheme be 'fully funded' if its liabilities stretch out into the future so that nobody can really be sure what they are likely to be until they actually occur, in some cases in fifty or sixty years' time?

The answer to that lies in a compulsion to calculate things that runs through the history of modern thought. Funnily enough, some of the greatest thinkers of all time, not least Plato and Aristotle, were content to discuss the great issues of philosophy in purely conceptual terms, relying on logic and dialogue to reach conclusions that would then in turn form the basis for further discussion. Gradually, however, the mathematicians started to take over, until things reached a stage where some thinkers believed that mathematics was the only basis for truth. The logical positivists, for example, believed that unless something could be reduced to an algebraic logic proposition then it was not a valid subject of enquiry. Their wunderkind, Wittgenstein, is reputed to have said that there was no such thing as a game of football, only the rules by which it was played.

Sadly, rather than pointing at him in the streets of Cambridge and laughing as he passed, far too many people felt it expedient to pretend to think all this was terribly clever, and the cult of 'mathematics as truth' was born. Aldous Huxley, the author of *Brave New World*, whose father and brother were both famous scientists, was moved to remark sadly in a letter to a friend in the 1930s (to be strictly accurate, to his wife's female lover whom they were both trying to persuade to become his lover as well since it would make weekends away so very much more convenient) that science simply ignored anything that it could not calculate.

So, rather than simply accepting, as Aristotle undoubtedly would have done, that a string of liabilities existed that stretched into the future and that their actual occurrence was unpredictable (or, as Aristotle would have said, unknowable), it seemed sensible to accept that these future liabilities should be measured in some way. There is a way in which the world of finance can do this, by using what is called a discount rate to reduce a string of future cash flows to a single present value, and this is what was done. Incidentally, this method is perfectly valid, though it can involve some very subjective, and thus unscientific, methodology.

So now pension funds could place the present value of their liabilities against the market value of their assets in order to know how fully funded they were. The more attentive reader will at once spot several flaws in that last statement. First, you are not comparing apples with apples. You are placing a market-price valuation, which can go up and down daily, but is nonetheless a real value, against a totally artificial number that is the result of a mathematical calculation based on hypothetical future numbers. Furthermore, the liability value will go up and down according to a number of factors, including most importantly bond yields (on which the discount rate is based), inflation and life expectancy.

Clearly, therefore, this process cannot result in you knowing how fully funded you are. It can at best result in you having some idea of how fully funded you might be given certain assumptions remaining valid. To suggest otherwise would be absurd. This has, however, not prevented this view from being adopted as official government policy.

So, pension funds performed this neat little calculation and discovered that they were fully funded. Yet how was this a problem? Why, because the contributions that the employer, the corporate sponsor, paid into the scheme were fully tax deductible. There were concerns that an unscrupulous employer might use a pension scheme to park some profits one year and then take them out again when times were harder, or tax rates lower. Naturally, all this could have been dealt with quite simply by legislation making such actions illegal. Instead, Thatcher, who regularly trumpeted the virtues of using good times to put something aside for a rainy day, effectively prevented pension plan sponsors from doing this by the use of hugely adverse tax penalties to punish them if they continued to make payments into fully funded schemes.

Thus, 'contribution holidays' became the norm and when the rainy days came schemes had much less money available with which to meet them than would otherwise have been the case. The situation was made still worse by many schemes raising the scale of benefits payable in a desperate attempt to *increase* their liabilities and thus stay under the magic funding level. This combination of circumstances would fatefully go on to hit schemes with a double whammy just when they could least afford it. Incidentally, the same effect could have been achieved by a prudent revision upwards of life expectancy, but this does not seem to have occurred to anybody, which was to prove a further tragic error.

So, the government chose to deal with the first problem in a way that suited its own short-term interests (increased tax revenues today) but was hugely damaging to the long-term interests of pension fund members (less money in the scheme to pay out benefits tomorrow). What of the second?

The second problem might be said to be the same as the first, but viewed from a different angle. It is clearly desirable that all companies, particularly public companies whose shares are traded on a stock exchange, should use the same accounting procedures. If they do not, then valid comparison and analysis becomes impossible. The particular problem that arose here was that, largely because this situation had never been envisaged, nobody was clear exactly how pension fund surpluses should be represented for accounting purposes, and individual public companies were adopting a variety of different approaches in discussion with their auditors. Some showed the surplus as a company asset on their own balance sheet and the situation was complicated by the precise legal wording of individual scheme documentation being capable of different interpretations. Then again, how should a contribution holiday be handled? Should an adjusted figure be shown to take account of the fact that but for the holiday the profits would have been lower?

The solution adopted was exactly the one outlined above. It is difficult to criticise this as an accounting measure. Clearly there had to be consistency of treatment, and as a means of finding a number to plug into an audited balance sheet this approach is at least as sensible as any other. It was duly introduced as an international accounting standard and adopted as a British one.

So far, so good. It is impossible to blame the government for this. Where they went wrong was in allowing not only the pension industry but also various public bodies to adopt and use this accounting measure for purposes for which it had never been designed. Rather than at best a guideline, it was adopted as representing a scientific certainty of funding adequacy, when it was clearly no such thing. For one thing, it would change dramatically with rising longevity (life expectancy). For another, it insisted that the bond rate should be used as the discount rate, but why this rather than a target rate based on what the fund's portfolio actually contained? For yet another, it took no direct account of inflation, save how this might be reflected indirectly in changing bond rates. When this was made the basis of a whole new regulatory regime starting from about 2001, the last nail was driven into the coffin of occupational pensions.

All such discussion was swept aside and would now become a dead letter. Henceforth, a pension plan ceased to be a portfolio of assets that should be managed so as to be able to pay future benefits, and became something to be managed so as to minimise any fluctuation between the sponsor's accounting numbers for pension assets and liabilities. Even today, the pension industry and its inevitable body of regulators seem to remain largely ignorant of the fact that these arrangements were never intended to govern the investment policy of pension funds, but only the accounting treatment of their sponsor.

As a final act of lunacy, this desire to ensure no change in the balance-sheet figures was pursued even where schemes were in deficit, which many increasingly were as consultants reluctantly and belatedly began increasing longevity assumptions. Yet the only way in which this could be achieved, it was argued, was by holding the scheme's assets in bonds (things have recently become more sophisticated, but much too late to make any difference). Since the bond rate was used as the discount rate, by holding bonds then the two figures could be held always in balance (in fact, this is wrong since it ignores things such as changing life expectancy). Many gave fancy names to such an approach, such as liability-driven investment, which reminds one of a question in a history exam, 'the Glorious Revolution was neither glorious nor a revolution – discuss', since it was neither investment nor liability-driven. It was at this time that wags began suggesting that actually pension consultants were just bond salesmen in disguise.

Again, in retrospect it seems remarkable that such an obviously flawed system should have been so widely and readily accepted, not least because bonds, with their very low returns, could never possibly plug the funding gap. Investment managers attending pension conferences would often return bemused, convinced that they had just wandered into a parallel universe where pension consultants seemed completely uninterested in their clients' investment returns, but only in an artificially calculated accounting figure. Incidentally, the same firm of consultants tended to act both for the scheme and its sponsor, a potential conflict of interest that readers may think would be difficult to sustain under the scrutiny of financial regulation. The government therefore obligingly made sure that pension consultants were not subject to regulation or oversight by the FSA, for reasons which neither the government nor the FSA has ever made clear.

Two final pieces of government policy remain to be mentioned.

In the mid-1990s, a major overhaul of pension legislation was carried out in the UK. The main thrust of this was to implement the process referred to above as a legal requirement known as the minimum funding requirement (MFR) and provide for all schemes to ensure that they were at least 90% funded by April 2003. Interestingly, sponsors of funds that showed up as fully funded were now expressly prohibited by law from allowing further contributions, rather than simply deterred by excessive taxation.

By 2003, however, the world was a different place, the FTSE 100 index having fallen from a peak of nearly 7,000 to below 4,000. It was now that an aspect of the new legislation that had not been properly appreciated began to come into play. The sponsor now had a legal obligation to ensure that the scheme was fully funded. However, the sponsor was also free to close the final salary scheme down and replace it with a money purchase one, in which case, as we have already seen, the funding obligation of the sponsor falls away, save as to the making of pre-agreed contributions, and the risk of inadequate retirement benefit passes to the individual member.

This was what the Americans call a 'no-brainer'. If somebody is hitting you over the head with a hammer, but has also given you a gun with which to shoot them any time you like without penalty, then anyone in their right mind is going to shoot their assailant as quickly as possible. Corporate sponsors pulled the trigger, in all cases closing their final salary scheme to new members, and in some cases to existing members as well.

Then there was Gordon Brown's notorious tax raids on pension funds in 1997, which took away their tax-exempt status with regard to company dividends. There is general agreement that this has cost pension funds about £5 billion *every year* from that point onwards. This move has been almost universally condemned and it seems hard to believe that it did not contribute to the closure of some schemes that might otherwise have stayed open. Yet again, the long-term interests of pension plan members were sacrificed on the altar of short-term political expediency, the hunger for current tax revenues displacing any strategic consideration.

In fairness and by way of balance it is not suggested that trustee and consultant incompetence played no part in this. It did, and a major one, and it remains one of the scandals of the modern era that those responsible have been allowed to escape censure. To take but three obvious examples, why did it occur to nobody to question the fact that trustees were insisting on handling the investment of pension plans themselves, rather than appointing professionals to make these decisions, that trustees were not required to obtain even a basic financial qualification before investing money held on trust for third parties, or that actuaries were being allowed to give investment advice?

Finally, in a yet further example of both (1) British politicians being told what to do by foreigners and (2) ill-considered regulations that take little account of practical considerations, the European Union is currently proposing to impose its own solvency requirements on British pension funds, the same regulations it already applies to insurance companies. This despite representations from the National Association of Pension Funds that many corporate sponsors will not be able to meet its requirements, so that it may lead both to corporate bankruptcies and the closure of most or all remaining DB schemes, perhaps even to existing members.

Perhaps no step so clearly demonstrates the deeply illogical and inconsistent framing of public policy. Having prevented sponsors from making payments into schemes when they could, the government is now going to insist that they do make payments when many of them cannot. Small wonder that the pension industry long ago despaired of any intelligent response from the government on pension-related issues. Just to rub salt into the wound, the government did commission and receive (in 2001) the Myners Report: it made wide-ranging recommendations on how the investment of pension-scheme assets should be conducted, but sadly these proved far too sensible to be adopted.

So in the private sector, final salary pension schemes have gone the way of the great auk and the Caspian tiger, condemning many to a miserable retirement. Just to remind ourselves, it is possible that people may receive under a money purchase as little as one-third of what they would have been expecting under a final salary one. Those holding a personal pension scheme are likely to share a similar fate, at least unless annuity rates unexpectedly and dramatically improve.

In the public sector this has not yet happened, though the imperative to convert all publicly sponsored schemes into money purchase ones for both new and existing members is obvious from the point of view of the public finances. Though nobody can agree on an exact figure, the estimate given earlier in this chapter is roughly equivalent to a whole year's GDP and would by itself more than double the official figure for national debt, taking it to about the same level as that of Greece as a percentage of GDP.

The reason is simple. Any government seeking to implement such a measure would be hugely unpopular with public-sector workers, who are, after all, voters, and would risk almost certain failure to be re-elected. It would risk major public unrest and the need directly to confront mass industrial action. Worst of all, it would mean that politicians would have to give up their own pension scheme, which just happens to be by far the most generous in the country.

# EIGHTEEN

# 'New Ideas From Dead Economists'[1]

As we draw towards the end of our journey, it is time to take stock. We have seen that five quite separate, but related, problems have come together to create the current crisis and that three different schools of thought have governed the approaches that have been taken in trying to deal with them.

Let us remind ourselves of the five issues. There was the credit bubble that resulted in the banking crisis of 2007–08, and its after-effects as they affect the situation today. There has been the problem of permanent deficit funding adopted by the government and the consequent burgeoning national debt. There is the threat of recession, and possibly sustained low growth thereafter. There is a crisis in pension funding. There is the problem of our system of government.

These all operate upon each other to produce what is at first sight a bewilderingly complex picture, as even a few examples will demonstrate. Deficit funding, the cost of bank rescues and pension liabilities all have an adverse impact on the level of national debt. A government focus on short-term outcomes means that things like recession and national debt are seen, and dealt with, as political rather than economic issues. Measures taken to attack recession have important implications for the cost of government debt, as well as for the level of annuities received by pensioners. In fact, each one of these five issues operates to at least some extent upon each of the other four.

Before we draw together our thoughts on how to deal with these, it may be helpful to recapitulate the three belief systems that we have reviewed.

First, there has been the socialist model, pioneered by Marx, which believes in state ownership of the means of production, the elimination of private enterprise and a command economy. This model

---

[1] The title of a hugely enjoyable book by Todd G. Buchholz.

persists in isolated enclaves such as Cuba and North Korea, but was seen to fail spectacularly in the case of the Soviet Union.

Second, there was Keynesian thought, which believed that the government could and should intervene to smooth the peaks and troughs of economic cycles. Keynes believed in private enterprise and the profit motive, but he also believed in full employment and that the government could stimulate employment by being prepared to accept higher inflation, and correspondingly could reduce inflation only at the expense of accepting higher unemployment. He believed that the government was justified in running a budget deficit during the bad times to increase public spending but that this was an abnormal state of affairs and should be put right by running a corresponding surplus during the good times.

Third, there was the Austrian School, whose work appears to have been largely suppressed and ignored. They argue that the government should not intervene in the economy, partly because it is unclear that Keynesian spending really does create any lasting economic advantage and partly because any government intervention must inevitably infringe some personal liberties, and individual freedom is paramount, including the right to be able to participate in markets that are allowed to function freely.

Some intervention will always lead to more intervention and thus any paternalistic government must progress slowly but inexorably towards a full-blown totalitarian state, 'totalitarian' here being used to mean any government that restricts individual liberty. In the process, the government becomes large and expensive, operating as a drag on the national economy as well as crowding out the private sector in areas where they intervene.

A government's function, they believe, is to provide the mechanisms within which markets can operate freely, and to act as the custodian of money, which is not, as Keynesians believe, simply a medium of exchange, but is also an economic good in its own right and thus subject to the normal rules of supply and demand. If a government wishes to smooth out the economic peaks and troughs, it can do this by adjusting the amount of money in circulation against rising or falling prices, thus squeezing inflation out of the system. Inflation is not a normal symptom of a healthily functioning economy, but a sign that something is wrong.

Neither the Keynesian nor the Austrian approach has ever been tried in practice. The prevalent model since the Second World War has been what might be called a bastard Keynesian approach.

Even at its closest to Keynes's original ideas, for example in the United States, it has been undone by the government's inability to balance the books. Drunk with the power of spending progressively more and more public money, the government has made deficit funding a constant of economic life, not the 'abnormal' state of affairs that Keynes described.

At the other end of the scale, for example in Britain, it has for much of the time been mixed into a composite Keynes/socialist approach, which not only ran constant deficits but also took much of the national industrial base into public ownership and tried to run a centrally planned economy. This has at various times been called 'the 'third way' or 'the 'mixed economy', but 'bastard Keynesianism' is a much more accurate description. While much of state ownership was rolled back in Britain during the Thatcher era, the interventionist approach has survived unscathed, as the government has become progressively more totalitarian, with much of the new restriction of individual liberties now emanating from the European Union.

It is impossible to deny that it is this 'third way', practised in an unbroken line from 1945 onwards, which has created the current crisis. Though individual administrations have veered in one direction or another, they have all done so around the fixed and unchallenged core beliefs that government intervention is not only justified, but desirable, and that the government is immune from the normal rules that govern both living within one's means and sustainable levels of debt.

Though it may have pandered to the instincts of many post-war politicians, particularly those in the Labour Party who believed that socialism was basically a desirable system (Denis Healey's 'we'll give you *real* socialism next time' sticks in the mind) if only a few of its sharp edges could be rubbed off, the much-vaunted third way has collapsed under the weight of its own follies, inconsistencies and downright contradictions.

As the great Austrian economist Ludwig von Mises pointed out in 1958: 'The idea that there is a third system – between socialism and capitalism, as its supporters say – a system as far away from socialism as it is from capitalism but retains the advantages and avoids the disadvantages of each, is pure nonsense.'[2]

It seems clear, therefore, that in charting the way ahead we must discard this outdated method of political and economic government that has inflicted such terrible damage, not least upon the retirement prospects of many currently within the workforce. Tinkering around the edges will no longer suffice. The whole rotten edifice must be swept away and replaced with something that at least *may* work, as opposed to the present system, which we know from bitter experience cannot possibly be expected to do so, regardless of what politicians may tell us to the contrary. They have had nearly seven decades within which to convince us that their system works, and the facts speak for themselves. They will always prefer their own short-term interests over the long-term interests of the nation as a whole.

Socialism has already been tried, and has failed. That leaves two possible approaches: that of pure Keynesianism as originally envisaged by its founder and that of the Austrian School.

Keynes is one of the great figures not just of economics but also of modern history. He was right about the Versailles settlement and Weimar inflation. He came up with a model that seemed to explain the economic world in which he found himself. He was in addition a profoundly good human being, with whom even those who disagreed with him, such as Hayek, became close personal friends. Whether Keynes and Hayek did ever share fire-watching duties on the roof of a Cambridge college, as popular folklore now maintains, is immaterial. What is much more important is that it was Keynes who intervened personally to obtain lodgings for Hayek and his wife when

---

[2] Lectures given in 1958 but not published until 1979 as *Economic Policy: Thoughts for Today and Tomorrow*, Chicago, Regnery Gateway.

they were evacuated from London (where Hayek was teaching at the LSE) to escape the bombing.

So it would be fascinating to attempt to put his ideas into practice and see if they actually worked. However, we must beware of our hearts ruling our heads. Everyone knows that Keynes was a nice man who got a raw deal. First his ideas were ignored when they might quite possibly have alleviated a lot of suffering. Then they were appropriated after his death by unscrupulous politicians and used to justify things such as permanent deficit funding with which he would never have agreed, as would have been apparent to anyone who took the trouble actually to read his work. Because he was a nice man who got a raw deal, we may have a natural inclination to give him a break and set the record straight, but this should not blind us to economic realities.

His system may or may not have worked in the 1930s. We will never know, because nobody tried it. Yet even if it might have done then, there is significant reason to doubt that it would do so now. The world that he modelled was one of relatively closed, domestic economies and he expressly confessed that he was not sure how to treat international trade. Yet today's economies operate on a global scale and international trade is hugely important. He operated within a system of fixed exchange rates, whereas we have for many decades had floating exchange rates. He assumed that the amount of money in circulation would be limited at least to some extent by reference, ultimately, to gold. He never envisaged deficit funding as a permanent means of financing government expenditure. Perhaps if he were alive today he would come up with some new model to explain the new economic reality, but instead the world has moved on and left his model behind in the process.

So, while it would be tempting to roll back the clock and attempt to put Keynes's ideas into practice, it hardly seems feasible. Indeed, remember the research that strongly suggests that to attempt to do so in the UK's present economic circumstances would be positively harmful. However, let us take a leaf out of the book of all those politicians who have over the years picked the chocolate biscuits out of Keynes's box and left the boring old plain ones behind. There is at least one of his beliefs which remains as valid today as it was then, namely that government should, as a matter of course, balance the books.

This is richly ironic, of course, since politicians have been using Keynes for the last seven decades to justify running a budget deficit and getting away with it because nobody actually reads Keynes. In fact, as we know, Keynes suggested that this should only be done in abnormal situations and the difference promptly clawed back by running a surplus in the following years.

As we have already mentioned in an earlier chapter, this is such an excellent idea and politicians are so determined continually to ignore it, that surely this is a situation where we should force them to do the right thing whether they like it or not. Let us have a written constitution, hedged around with all sorts of protections to prevent politicians from changing it, which requires them to run a balanced budget. They could, as Keynes advises, run a deficit when abnormal times demand it, but only to the extent that they have built up a surplus in former years. Not the other way round, of course, or they will simply claim that this is an abnormal year and promise to run a surplus sometime in the future.

So, as we regretfully put Keynes's *General Theory* back on the shelf, we are left with the work of the Austrians, most notably Ludwig von Mises and Friedrich Hayek.

There is much more to the work of the Austrian School than it has been possible to convey in a book of this nature and length. For example, they advanced a whole new theory about pricing, value and the way in which markets work that has far-reaching implications not just for economics but for financial theory in general. For our present purposes, however, their relevance may be summed up in a well-worn phrase that can be criticised as both a generalisation and an over-simplistic summary, but which still serves neatly to encapsulate their beliefs: small government, sound money and individual liberty.

Individual liberty is really the starting point. From this springs both a commitment to markets being allowed to operate freely and small government. The fewer regulations the public sector has to police and the more areas of human conduct are left as matters of personal choice and ethical judgment, the smaller the public sector needs to be. The same holds true of markets. Where these are not allowed to operate freely, some form of government presence will be necessary to oversee the nature of the interference, whether this be price control, import tariff, restriction of market share, indirect taxation, regulatory supervision or any combination of these. All this requires more public servants, perhaps even whole additional departments.

The commitment to free markets goes way beyond a desire to limit the number of government employees, however. It is desirable both because free markets produce fair outcomes (though these may not always be to everybody's liking) and because economic freedom is seen as a prerequisite of political freedom. It is not sufficient guarantee by itself. The inhabitants of Nazi Germany had considerable economic freedom and the present day inhabitants of China enjoy at least some. Yet it is a necessary precondition.

This is a key element of the Austrian approach conveniently ignored by those who choose to brand its followers as monetarists and dismiss it out of hand on the grounds that monetarism was tried under Thatcher and failed. There is much more to the Austrians and, even so, some existing economists have a belief in money as more than just a medium of exchange.

No government since the war has taken as its basic tenet a belief in the freedom of the individual as an all-conquering quality that should sweep away all but the most vital regulation. Doubtless politicians and their advisers would mutter darkly of 'anarchy' at such a thought, but it seems hard to understand how being able to choose which herbal supplements to swallow, or which light bulbs to use in our homes, might sweep away civilised society as we know it. It would prove a fascinating exercise to be allowed to wander through the statute book and the wealth of regulation spawned even during the last decade and see how much might merrily be crossed out without causing any appreciable harm at all to the population.

For regulation comes at a double cost. Significant enough is the direct cost of the civil servants to consider, publish, monitor and police it. Perhaps more significant still in many cases is the unseen indirect costs to business of ensuring compliance, not least the myriad of consultants (often former civil servants) who spring up around each new outbreak.

In fact 'outbreak' is probably not the right word to use. Perhaps 'epidemic' might be more apt, and nor is this exclusively a European problem. According to CBN News, 50,000 pages of new regulations were issued in the USA during 2011 alone, apparently including a stipulation that every goatherd be provided with a mobile telephone. CBN estimated that even taking into account only the direct costs of regulation, these were equivalent to every member of the US work-force giving up 77 days' pay per year. CBN also estimated that if all US regulatory staff were combined into one body, it would be the third-biggest company in America and employ more people than McDonald's, Boeing, Ford and Disney combined.

In the UK, the coalition government has paid lip service to the idea of reining in regulation, obviously recognising that there are votes to be won from the business community, particularly from the owners and operators of small businesses. The Federation of Small Businesses (FSB) has, however, remained resolutely unimpressed, pointing out that the cost to European businesses of complying even with existing EU regulations (which the government has no plans to reduce) was estimated at €124 billion a year,[3] and noted that in the UK 'despite the rhetoric, the burden of regulation continues to get heavier'. A government report from April 2011[4] reveals that at that time no less than forty-six proposed new regulations were awaiting implementation, *not including* those arising as a result of EU and other international agreements, regulations, decisions and directives. The FSB paper pointed out that Britain ranked 89th out of 139 countries assessed by weight of regulatory burden. Finland, by contrast, managed to rank tenth, without having raised widespread concerns as to potentially high levels of herbal supplement overdose or light bulb dazzling, nor, presumably, of Finnish goatherds being unable to phone their mothers.

---

[3] FSB, *The Burden of Regulation*, Blackpool, May 2011.
[4] Statement of New Regulation, Department of Business, Innovation and Skills.

So, small government makes economic sense, greatly reducing the amount of wealth that the public sector destroys each year, both directly and indirectly. Yet to the Austrian School much more is at stake. Hayek pointed out that as soon as the state begins to infringe individual liberties then government has become totalitarian and the only difference between it and a socialist or fascist regime is not that it has been elected, but how far along the path towards total lack of freedom it has so far travelled. This was, and remains, an uncomfortable and unwelcome message. Certainly it is not one that any politician would acknowledge. Certainly it was responsible for Hayek being cast into the intellectual wilderness.

As for individuals, so with markets. Left to their own devices, markets will produce a fair result as long as they operate freely. What government seems to find difficult to accept is that while they are entitled, and indeed obliged, to intervene when a market is prevented for some reason from operating freely, for example where someone is abusing a dominant market position, this does not also apply when the market *is* working freely but they just happen not to like the result.

Where this latter, unjustified, type of intervention takes place, then the cost of it is frequently underestimated or even just not considered at all. For example, it seems logical to suggest that a minimum wage, which prevents the labour market from operating freely, is likely to tend to lower rather than higher employment, no matter how laudable the motive of trying to improve the circumstances of those on the lowest rungs of society. Similarly, rent control had to be abandoned in the UK when private-sector landlords refused to make any new housing stock available because they were unable to charge a proper commercial rent. We have already seen how something similar operated to help destroy Britain's once-extensive railway network.

Interestingly, Milton Friedman, writing back in 1962, more than four decades before this became apparent as a serious problem in the UK, picked out government compulsion forcing a citizen to buy an annuity on retirement as another example, alongside the more obvious ones of import tariffs and export restrictions. He also cannily singled out military conscription, which understandably proved extremely popular on American college campuses during the period of the Vietnam draft.

On one view, the examples given above may simply be instances of the law of unintended consequences, but they mask a much more fundamental difference between old-style liberals (libertarians) and new-style liberals. Libertarians believe in creating equality of opportunity. New-style liberals feel themselves compelled to create equality of outcome. Forcing schools and colleges to accept and treat equally applications from all students, such as occurred during the desegregation programme in the southern states of the US, creates equality and fairness where it did not previously exist. Forcing schools and colleges to award a certain number of places to students of par- ticular backgrounds, on the other hand, arguably does the opposite. Politicians should paddle in such waters with care, for they are murky and dangerous.

So much for the concepts of small government, individual liber- ties and free markets, all of which we have disposed of in far too little space properly to represent both their importance to the likes of Mises and Hayek, and to the world of economic thought generally, since they represent a strikingly different starting point from the mechanis- tic market models with which many economists begin their journey.

Since we have not had an opportunity to dig into the Austrians' view of market behaviour, this difference may not seem as profound as it in fact is. The Austrians believe that all economic behaviour is like the brief flashing of many different lights as lots of individuals buy and sell things, but with each individual being driven subjectively by their own emotional needs and perceived values. In fact, Mises refused to use the word 'economy', thinking that it smacked of a sort of machine driven by external levers, preferring 'catallaxy', meaning something that arises naturally as the sum total of many individual actions.

Under the Austrian view, markets do not automatically find their point of equilibrium at a price that all participants regard as fair and that clears all supply and demand at that price. Human beings, they argue, will only exchange something for something else if they value more highly that which they are obtaining than that which they are giving up. This decision will, in turn, be driven by the circumstances of the individual concerned.

To go back to our example of the man dying of thirst and a glass of water, he may well value that glass of water at more than a hundred dollars, whereas another individual in different circumstances would not. Then again, the 'utility' of the glass of water might decrease with each successive one. Would he value the fifth glass of water he was offered as highly as the first?

This approach throws off two important considerations, with both of which other economists have considerable difficulty.

The first is that since all market outcomes are the result of human behaviour prompted by perceived needs and values, it is pointless trying to measure and analyse them mathematically in order to predict the future because you would need to measure the human values and needs rather than market outcomes and these are not capable of mathematical calculation. Even if they were, then by the time you got around to measuring them, they would probably have changed; the man previously dying of thirst might by now have been offered many glasses of water. So deduction, based on conceptual analysis and discussion, is at least as valid as quantitative modelling. After all, the ancient Greeks deduced the existence of atomic particles without ever actually having observed one.

The second is that money is not simply a means by which the agreed price of a transaction is expressed, but is itself an economic good for which other goods are exchanged. Someone will only sell something if they value the amount of money being offered in exchange more highly than they do the utility of what they are giving up. Money is just like any other economic good in that there is a supply and a demand for it at any given time and these will decide its price, which in the case of money is represented by its purchasing power. The less money there is available the greater will be its purchasing power, and the more money there is available the less its purchasing power. Thinking back to the earlier chapter on 1920s inflation this may seem an obvious point, but there are still many, not least the Fed and the Bank of England, who need reminding of it.

There is a further point here, too, at least if we consider the work of Hayek's predecessor, Ludwig von Mises, and while it may be a point too far for some, it is worth stating. Mises believes that only 'commodity money' such as gold and silver is actually 'money' at all, since it is only these monetary metals that have any intrinsic value. Nonetheless, he says, there are various things we happily accept as money substitutes, with banknotes (which economists call 'fiat money') being the most obvious example.

While we should always have some reservation about accepting these in the place of real money, he says, their practical usefulness (being able to carry paper rather than gold) will in normal circumstances make up for their possible disadvantage (difference in value). Other money substitutes include things such as bank deposit accounts or loan facilities. We accept these too because of their convenience, in the first case because we can defer purchasing power to use in the future and in the latter case because we can use purchasing power today and return it (pay back the loan) in the future.

The problem with money substitutes is that their supply can be increased quickly and easily, unlike commodity money; the supply of gold and silver tends to be relatively stable, at least in the short term. Governments can print new banknotes or, as with quantitative easing, simply credit money balances to banks' accounts. Banks can themselves greatly increase the supply of money substitutes because, using fractional reserve banking, they can lend out much higher amounts than they hold as deposits. As the supply of money substitutes increases, then so its purchasing power must grow less. Put another way, it will buy less commodity money than its face value may suggest. Measured against gold, for example, the US dollar has lost about 97% of its purchasing power since 1971, when the Bretton Woods gold peg was abandoned.

So, whether you are what many would contemptuously label a 'gold bug' such as Mises, or a straightforward monetarist, such as Friedman, there is general agreement that the greater the money supply the greater the upward pressure on pricing, resulting in inflation. Whereas Mises would call the money supply the amount of substitute money in circulation and point to how much less gold each individual unit of substitute money would now buy, standard monetarists would fall back on the quantity theory of money, our old friend MV = PQ, and say that the same result would be caused by M,V, or both of them increasing. Really, both are expressing the same principle in different ways. Mises is measuring the purchasing power of (substitute) money against gold, whereas a monetarist would measure its purchasing power against total output (Q). In each case P (price) would rise, signalling a fall in purchasing power, in Mises's case against gold, and in the monetarist's case against the everyday cost of living. Either way, money today would buy less than it did last year, which means inflation. Either way, back we come to Mankiw's principle: prices rise when the government prints too much money.

Remember, too, that the Austrians have a rather different view of the boom and bust cycle, something we briefly touched upon earlier. Whenever either the government puts more money into the system or consumers save less and spend more or banks extend more loans, a surge in the money supply occurs. This leads to more money being spent and things being bought. This in turn leads firms to believe that they should increase production or perhaps change it to produce some new product for which there is suddenly new demand.

However, as the money supply rises, then so too do prices (as, usually, do interest rates). People are now no longer so rich relative to the cost of living. Consumption now returns to a more normal level and firms are left with this new production that they no longer need, and probably also with loans they can no longer afford. The investment they made was not really justified. It was what the Austrians call 'malinvestment'.

Thus cycles of boom and bust are caused by fluctuations in the money supply, which are in turn driven partly by interest-rate policy. The apparent 'boom' is fuelled by a phoney sense of being suddenly better off, while the apparent 'bust' is just things returning to normal but having to clear the effects of the malinvestment out of the system along the way.

The logical outcome of this view is that if the money supply could be precisely controlled, being increased when prices fell and reduced

when prices rose, as Benjamin Strong had advocated, then both inflation and these cycles of boom and bust might be squeezed out of the
system, or at least greatly reduced. This was the basic thinking behind
at least some of the policies of the Thatcher administration.

In fairness, it has to be said that the idea of using monetary policy
to control inflation is intellectually more attractive than the alternatives. Previous governments had either taken the view that inflation
was a necessary by-product of a growing economy and therefore not
something with which the government should be concerned, or had
played with price and wage controls, which as somebody once said, is
rather like trying to slow down a car by holding onto the needle of
the speedometer. Rising prices are a symptom, not a cause, of inflation.

Both in Britain and America it was found that reality was, alas,
much more complex than theory would have one believe. The original measures of 'money' did not take account of the new money
(money substitute, Mises would argue) banks could create by granting
loans. It also proved very difficult, if not impossible, to control this and
other types of credit. It had been believed that this could be achieved
by the use of interest-rate policy; witness the very high rates of interest
seen in Britain during the early part of the Thatcher era. However, in
the event, these proved something of a blunt instrument.

The best that could be said about this experiment is that it seems
that the operation of interest rates upon inflation is uncertain in its
degree and may also take a long time to have effect, particularly when
inflation has already been allowed to run out of control by previous
administrations. It is, of course, undeniable that in the end inflation *was*
squeezed down to manageable levels and it seems difficult to believe
that this could have been achieved without the high interest-rate policy, but debate continues to this day as to exactly how great a part this
played and the curse of economics is that it is impossible ever to come
up with definitive answers.

It is probably also true to say that pure monetarist theory probably
takes too simplistic a view. Two things in particular appear to need
revision. First, it seems hard to accept that velocity remains constant,
at least in the short term, as the quantity theory of money tends to

assume, so that more money must inevitably and immediately produce higher prices. In inflationary times, for example, surely people
will be tempted to spend their money as quickly as possible, knowing
that it will rapidly lose its purchasing power should they hang onto it.
Similarly, at other times both people and firms may be inclined to pay
off existing debts and even hold cash as savings. Second, whether as a
symptom of this variability of velocity or as a separate principle, prices
seem to be what economists call 'sticky'. They do not respond immediately to inflationary pressures, perhaps in part because firms may still
be using up existing stocks, and perhaps also in part due to a natural
disinclination of firms to raise prices until their competitors do too.

However, most economists, regardless of their basic belief
system, agree with the monetarist proposition in the long term
(apart, apparently, from those employed by either the Treasury or the
Bank of England). As Mankiw says, more money must sooner or
later lead to higher prices. The only dispute, then, is over what happens in the short term, and the last paragraph may help to explain
this. Whether that is the case or not, the present situation is clearly
highly disturbing.

As we have touched on already, nothing more clearly demonstrates
the intellectual bankruptcy of British government since the Second
World War than the dilemma by which the government is faced today.
For purely political reasons, they wish to stimulate GDP, artificial and
misleading a measure as it may be, in order to win the next election.
The traditional tool for doing this, borrowing money they don't have
and then spending it, has been used so often that it has broken. In fact,
not only has it broken, but it threatens the destruction of the whole
tool shed.

Mired in the accumulated mess of the irresponsible borrowing
of decades, additional spending, the traditional Keynesian remedy, is
out of the question (though nonetheless still advocated by a frightening number of British politicians). So they have turned instead to a
monetarist remedy, pumping more money into the system. Yet if they
believe in monetarist theory to the extent of trusting this to work,
they must also believe that in the longer term boosting the amount

of money in circulation will lead to inflation and that boosting the amount of money massively must inevitably lead to massive inflation.

Recent utterances by the Bank of England on inflation as they busily debauch the currency make interesting reading. There is much focus on price levels, the needle on the speedometer, but no mention at all of the large boot that is pressing the accelerator flat to the floor.

As economist and fund manager Liam Halligan pointed out in early 2012,[5] the UK's base money supply had already trebled during quantitative easing to date, even before the next round fell to be considered. A programme, let us remind ourselves, that has completely failed in its stated objective of boosting bank lending. The fact that, as many supporters of QE claim, the actual value of banknotes in existence has not changed, is disingenuous. The Bank of England has swapped paper instruments for account money that can (and is intended to be) 'spent' (lent out).

The reality is simple and brutal. Somewhere out at sea is building a massive tsunami of monetary inflation. A tsunami which sooner or later must crash ashore with terrifying consequences. Once again, the long-term national interest has been sacrificed on the altar of short-term political expediency.

The Bank of England would argue that what has been done can easily be undone, essentially by putting the asset purchase process (by which QE purchases government bonds for debt) into reverse, thus pulling money out of the system again. However this presupposes that they could spot *in advance* the precise moment at which to do so and this seems most unlikely, especially given that they would probably seek first to resort to the usual blunt instrument of interest-rate increases. Experience from the 1970s shows that once RPI inflation hits 6%, things can run very rapidly out of control and that once the inflationary toothpaste is out of the tube it is very difficult to put it back.

It may be worth injecting a healthy dose of reality at this point. The Bank of England's assigned task is to keep CPI below 2%. Given

---

[5] *Daily Telegraph*, 11 February 2012.

that this measure uses civil servant pretend inflation rather than the real thing, this should not prove an unduly taxing task. Despite this, the last time the Bank actually achieved its target was in November 2009. This hardly inspires confidence in their ability to play with matches and not get burned.

By the way, a clue to the apparent indifference of the Bank of England's staff towards inflation may be found in the fact that they, unlike the bulk of the population, enjoy index-linked final salary pension arrangements; 'index-linked' to RPI, by the way. This despite the fact that the Bank itself clearly believes that the pensions of all lesser mortals should have to make do with CPI, thus losing value in real terms with every year that passes. The trustees of the Bank's own pension scheme naturally rejected such a ludicrous idea out of hand.

# NINETEEN

Only a crisis – actual or perceived – produces real change.
When that crisis occurs, the actions that are taken depend
on the ideas that are lying around. That, I believe, is our
basic function: to develop alternatives to existing policies,
to keep them alive and available until the politically
impossible becomes the politically inevitable.

MILTON FRIEDMAN, 1982

# Getting Ourselves Out of the Mess

It is time to turn our attention to what measures might be taken to resolve the present crisis. Some we have touched upon already. Others are prompted by the analysis that has been performed in earlier chapters, some of which you may have found somewhat depressing.

Before proceeding further, it may also be useful to remind you of what I said at the outset. Much of what I have to say in this closing chapter may be considered radical, impractical or just plain ridiculous, depending on your point of view. I make no apologies for this. My conclusions are the result of logical analysis of the facts. My logic may be faulty, but it is sincere and honest. I have not drawn back from any of the unpleasant places to which it has led me. I have followed my thoughts to their logical conclusions, no matter how disturbing they might be.

Whether or not you will agree with any of my recommendations, you will at least hopefully agree that the preceding chapters demonstrate beyond dispute that the politicians of the last seven decades have led us to the very brink of disaster.

To proceed in the same way for any longer seems to me not only ludicrous but also deeply frightening. To suggest that change is required seems to me so obvious as to need no further justification. That the required change should be radical seems to me a simple restatement of the depth of our problems. A potentially fatal gunshot wound cannot be treated by the application of a sticking plaster.

If you wish to label my views impractical, I might to some extent agree with you, at least in the sense that I do not expect any of them to be implemented, or even seriously considered, by any existing politician. For they all have a vested interest in the system remaining exactly as it is – and it is that system which lies at the root of our problems. It encourages politicians to make decisions based only on their likely short-term outcomes and it gives them far too much scope within which to make such decisions, with far too little democratic mandate.

As I suggest towards the end, I believe that if any effective change is to come, then it will come from outside the existing system. It will come, or at least be driven by, what the Americans call 'we, the people'. As a society, we claim to believe that it should be the will of the people that prevails, democratically expressed. Yet we allow politicians to govern us on their terms, rather than ours. If this is to change, it can only be because we the people decide to change it and this in turn cannot happen without an informed debate.

This book is my contribution to such a debate, albeit necessarily a personal and introspective one. The real one, when it happens, will involve many people, hopefully enough people to make a real difference. It will almost certainly come to different conclusions, though I am vain enough to hope that at least some of my thoughts may be deemed sensible to at least some degree. I sincerely hope that those conclusions *will* be different. That will show that we are indeed living in a democracy, rather than treading the path to serfdom.

★ ★ ★

Let me recapitulate briefly the five issues I have been addressing; the after-effects of the banking crisis, budget deficits and sovereign debt, the threat of recession, the UK pension funding crisis and our system of government. To these I now probably have to add a sixth, namely the threat of future inflation, particularly as created by quantitative easing.

As for the economic schools of thought upon which we might draw for inspiration, I will rely heavily on the beliefs of the so-called Austrian School. This may seem unfair on Keynes, since his theories were never given a chance to be tried in their entirety, but it is true that the interventionist, paternalistic model of government that they imply *has* been tried, and has clearly failed; indeed, it is precisely this model that has landed us in our present mess. I shall, however, be drawing upon at least one Keynesian principle that seems eminently sensible, namely the restriction of budget deficits to what may be made good in other years by corresponding surpluses.

At the centre of this rather tangled web sits an arm of government, the Bank of England. Over this august institution the government has, with typical contempt for the intelligence of the electorate, cast a cloak of independence, a myth that should be punctured straightaway. The 'independent' Monetary Policy Committee (MPC) makes its decisions on the principle of one man one vote (there are currently no female members), and comprises nine members. Five are Bank of England officials and the minority four external members are appointed by the government. Thus the Bank's representatives can always force through any decision they desire. It is curious that the government did not make the external 'independent' members the majority, rather than the minority, and allow them to be directly elected by the public rather than appointed by the Treasury, but then perhaps that might have been carrying the principles of democracy a little too far.

The Bank sees its role as 'promoting and maintaining financial and monetary stability and its contribution to a healthy economy'.[1] If so, then the astute observer may spot that it must surely rank as one of the most unsuccessful organisations in human history, since we currently have neither financial nor monetary stability, nor a healthy economy. Perhaps wisely, the Bank's website does not elaborate on how these things might be defined, nor does it mention its failure to keep inflation under control.

The proper role of the Bank is, therefore, a vital question.

It would doubtless, were it forced to articulate its approach, argue that some entity needs to be in existence to try to smooth away cycles of boom and bust. It would certainly take for granted the old Keynesian idea that it is both right and necessary for the government to intervene in the economy by tweaking tax, spending and interest rates. Yet this assumption is highly questionable.

We know that cycles of boom and bust already existed by the nineteenth century at the latest, and this was long before any attempts were being made to manage the economy in any way, so it seems reasonable to assume that such cycles do, and will, occur naturally. We also know that many writers claim government (central bank)

---

[1] Bank of England website, accessed 23 March 2012.

policy can actually make these cycles more, rather than less, severe. In America, the Federal Reserve itself admits that its own policies made the Great Depression far worse than it need have been. If there is no evidence, despite the confident words of Gordon Brown that appear at the beginning of this book, that a government can eliminate cycles of boom and bust, and clear evidence that at least in some cases they can make things worse, then is this not a strong argument against any government intervention at all?

At best, the case for government intervention is 'not proven'. The 'bust' part of the cycle can occasionally turn into recession. Where this occurs, it occurs naturally and is rather like the economy catching cold. It is very unpleasant while it lasts but, left to their own devices and allowed to operate freely, markets will clear and growth will reappear. The government should intervene only if for some reason markets are not operating freely, in order to remove the obstruction.

It seems preferable for the Bank of England to be tasked with two objectives. First, the supervision of the banking sector and the operation of its payment systems so that banks can be allowed to operate freely and fail safely. We have already discussed how this may be accomplished. The second would be the control of inflation, but much would need to change here too.

First, the Bank needs to rid itself of the idea that inflation and growth are somehow linked, that one is a necessary by-product of the other. Given that much economic growth will in the future be driven by technology and innovation, which should make production more efficient and thus cheaper, there seems no logical reason for such a proposition. Rather than attempting (supposedly) to keep CPI at 2%, why should the Bank not be tasked with keeping real inflation (RPI) at zero? After all, we know that economic growth is possible without a direct link to inflation, since the effect of inflation is already stripped out of the GDP figures by means of something called the deflator.

Second, the Bank needs to accept the view that inflation is a monetary phenomenon and should therefore be manipulated by controlling the money supply, for which interest rates have proved a very imprecise and unreliable tool. A more efficient way must therefore be found of doing this. The basic principle, though, seems sound. Inflation is not caused by rising prices. Rising prices are caused by inflation, which is a drop in the purchasing power of money. Money is not just a medium of exchange but an economic good in its own right, subject to the usual laws of supply and demand. Too much money leads to a drop in its 'price' (purchasing power). Thus inflation can and should be controlled by controlling the money supply.

This might best be done by way of an overall system, making use of various levers, rather than the comparatively crude attempts made during the Thatcher era; one can nonetheless learn from that experience. One such possible system would consist of two linked processes.

The first might include the use of gold. This is an emotive subject, so let me clearly state what is, and is not, being suggested. This book specifically does *not* propose a return to the Gold Standard. For all sorts of reasons, this would be quite unfeasible. However, it might be possible to return to a system where all money in circulation has to be covered up to a certain proportion, say 30%, by physical gold reserves. This system would be comparatively simple to establish and operate. The United States' existing gold depositaries could act as global gold custodians and could make publicly available the amount of gold held to the account of any country at any time. At the same time, countries already publish their M4 (should this be the measure agreed upon) money supply figures and it would be a simple matter to calculate, perhaps on a quarterly basis, whether the 30% level had been breached and, if so, how much additional gold a government would be forced to buy. In this way, currency could once again be linked, at least partially, to a physical store of real value.

The other side of the system might be rather more difficult to achieve, but is nonetheless worthy of consideration. Each month the government could announce how much sterling bank lending it was going to allow and invite the various banks to bid for all or part of that capacity, stating at what interest rate they were proposing to lend it out, and allocating it in descending order. Needless to say, there would have to be a legal prohibition on banks lending it out at a lesser rate than the one upon which they had bid.

It is submitted that this is the missing link in the monetarist logic. There seems little point in attempting to control money supply through QE or its opposite, and still less through interest-rate policy, if the banks are free effectively to create new money any time they like by creating credit balances in customers' loan accounts. Instead, create a market for credit each month and allow it to operate freely by way of an open auction. A monetarist approach to controlling inflation surely deserves at least a fair trial, and this might be it.

The most obvious stumbling block to the successful operation of such a scheme is the question of foreign banks lending in sterling. This could perhaps be dealt with by way of international agreement, opening up the auction process to all comers, and withdrawing UK regulatory approval from any banks that try to stand outside the system. Another problem might be fluctuations in the exchange rate driven by interest-rate changes, but this could be dealt with by setting a standard savings rate, as to which see below.

At the same time, changes might be made to the way in which the government raises debt by issuing bonds, bringing this more into line with commercial lending by banks. To take but two obvious examples, government bonds could contain financial covenants, for example about balancing the budget and not breaching certain pre-agreed debt levels, and provisions for what lawyers call cross-default so that should the government break these arrangements then every single government bond in issue would simultaneously go into default. They might also contain specific arrangements as to what would happen in the event of default, perhaps giving the bond-holders the right to take possession of and sell certain state assets, or the right to have tax proceeds paid directly to themselves until the arrears are cleared. As a further thought, they could contain a provision giving the bond-holders the right to elect for repayment in gold rather than currency. Such provisions would force the government to behave with financial responsibility and would also protect the nation from the possibility of some future government being elected that would otherwise like to head back down the path of credit-fuelled spending sprees. So too would a requirement that, rather than issuing bonds with a fixed rate of interest, the government should only be permitted to issue index-linked bonds based on RPI. Now the government would have a direct interest in eliminating, rather than maximising, inflation. By making the coupons on such bonds tax-free without limit to UK citizens, the government could at the same time provide an irreproachably fair means for people to save for their retirement. Naturally, by the same token, capital gains tax would be either abolished or reintroduced in index-linked format.

The final piece of the jigsaw has already been suggested earlier. The introduction of a written constitution could create the right (as far as the people are concerned) or the obligation (as far as politicians are concerned) for the government to produce a balanced budget. Following Keynes, the government would be allowed to run a deficit but only to the extent that they had stored up a similar amount by way of a surplus in previous years. The government could allow costs to continue to spiral out of control only if they were prepared to introduce very high levels of taxation, and it is doubtful whether this would prove effective in our modern society in which people can, and do, move to live and work overseas. There would thus also need to be a constitutional provision preventing the government from taxing British citizens who live abroad.

All very well, politicians will say, but balancing the budget straightaway would involve massive spending cuts that would cause huge damage to the British economy and probably prompt social unrest. Rather than coming up with airy-fairy ivory tower solutions, how about descending to the level of reality and confronting the world as it is, rather than as you would like it to be? Fair enough. This is a perfectly valid challenge and I must rise to it.

It is difficult to be certain of the numbers, not least because we know that the vast majority of the cuts outlined by the government have not in fact been implemented, at least not yet (two years later!), but let us assume that the deficit (the amount that must be borrowed) for the year ahead as at the first quarter of 2012 is about £120 billion. By the way, to demonstrate further the scale of New Labour's mismanagement of the economy, Gordon Brown inherited a public sector borrowing requirement of about £5 billion, which was subsequently reduced to zero, not least by the sale of 3G mobile telephone licences for a windfall of more than £20 billion. In 2000, he began spending. By the end of 2002, he was announcing the borrowing of £20 billion, but predicting that this would once again return to zero over the next five years or so. Needless to say, it didn't.

Well, let's start with overseas aid. It may come as a surprise to many readers to learn that at a time when Britain is experiencing the worst financial crisis in history, it is giving away 0.7% of GDP to other countries to help them become more competitive with us, one of which (Brazil) has actually just overtaken us in the global economic stakes and another of which (India) is coming up fast on the rails. Nor, on this occasion, can the government claim simply to be toeing the European line. Britain gives several times more in aid per capita than any of our EU partners.

The Department for International Development (DFID), the department responsible for this folly, has a budget of £8.8 billion for the year to 2013, rising to £11.3 billion the following year.[2] Let me make this the first of our savings by eliminating Britain's foreign aid programme altogether, at least until we can afford it and, if and when it is reintroduced, make sure that countries that are our clear economic rivals, such as Brazil and India, are firmly excluded. By definition, axing the overseas aid budget can have no adverse impact on the British economy at all and is unlikely to cause riots in the streets.

As set out earlier, it seems sensible when looking to make cuts to the public sector, to cut whole areas rather than the degree to which something is provided, not least because the former approach could make possible the closing down of whole government departments. This can be accomplished, at least in part, by embarking upon a programme of repealing, as rapidly as possible, most of the regulation that has been introduced in recent years, all of which infringes individual freedom and little of which can be justified by cost–benefit analysis. Since much of this has been imposed upon us by the EU and could

---

[2] DFID official figures.

only be swept away with their consent, which will not be forthcoming, then let me grasp the nettle and propose withdrawing from the EU forthwith. Again, this is most unlikely to cause civil unrest. On the contrary, it is likely to prove wildly popular.

It is impossible to estimate the total cost savings that would be enjoyed, since so much of our cost of EU membership is indirect and hidden, but we can quantify the direct savings. Britain's contributions to the EU recently hit £9 billion, which one national newspaper[3] pointed out would have been enough to avoid either the recent increases in National Insurance contributions (taxes, despite their name) or the 50% rate of income tax.

I am still a long way short of £120 billion, however, and I hope that realisation will persuade people to be open-minded about what I propose next, rather than responding with exactly the sort of knee-jerk emotive response that we are bound to hear from politicians themselves.

Defence spending seems still to be running at well over £40 billion, despite the announced cuts. I suggest that it is no part of the role of a small, bankrupt island in the Atlantic Ocean to project its military power around the world and that it should therefore be possible to eliminate most of this, though it will naturally come as a shock to our politicians to learn that they will no longer be able to play with big boys' toys by letting off whizz-bangs over Libya (nor able to contemplate doing so over Tehran). Perhaps to soften the blow, the military could set up a shooting gallery in the back garden of 10 Downing Street and let the Cabinet have a few of their latest automatic weapons to play with.

What does Britain actually *need*? What is left of the Brigade of Guards for ceremonial purposes; their existence is surely justified by tourism income. Air-sea rescue operations, and some maritime patrol aircraft. Some fishery protection vessels. A few squadrons of fighters to protect our airspace. What else? Nothing, apart from perhaps some special forces for hostage-type situations. No blue-water navy. No submarines. No aircraft carriers. No infantry, armour or artillery

---

[3] *Independent.*

units. No strike aircraft. How much this would save is unclear but it could presumably be as much as £35 billion, perhaps even £40 billion a year on an ongoing basis. On a one-off basis, it should be possible almost entirely to close down the Ministry of Defence and sell off all its buildings and facilities.

Our politicians would cry that this would leave us defenceless, but most of our European partners are in exactly this position. Belgium could be successfully invaded any weekend by a mixed force of traffic wardens and lollipop ladies, but this does not seem to worry the Belgians unduly. More to the point, it would deprive our politicians of the opportunity to drag us into wars of dubious legitimacy at the behest of the United States. If all we could contribute to joint military operations was a mobile bath unit, how much less pressing might be the siren call of the Pentagon?

So far I have identified an amount probably in excess of £50 billion in savings, even on a conservative assessment, although of course there may be significant one-off costs associated with bringing them about. Nor can it be pretended that slashing the defence budget would not have an adverse effect on the national economy. Defence contractors would suffer. Some might even be driven out of business. At the same time many men and women, some of whom have risked their lives for their country, would be thrown out of work. None of this would be easy, economically, socially or politically, but then neither was allowing moribund industries to go to the wall during the Thatcher era. Nor, incidentally, is living through national bankruptcy.

Assuming that one did not wish to make inroads into the health or education budgets, the only remaining obvious place to make cuts would be the welfare budget and this is currently a point of great political sensitivity. It lies beyond the scope of this book to propose specific changes, not least because the writer lacks the knowledge or credibility to do so, but surely there has never been a greater imperative to attempt some sort of radical reform of the system, rather than the tinkering around the edges which the present government is proposing. The judgment of history will not be kind should they shirk that responsibility.

The critics of the present system allege that it has created a culture of scrounging on the taxpayer. That is perhaps unkind to the many genuinely disadvantaged people who would not be able to survive without welfare support, though it is undoubtedly true in part. Perhaps it would be more accurate to say that it has created a culture of entitlement. To see in March 2012 a single mother interviewed on television who expects her fellow citizens to pay her more than £40,000 a year to bring up her baby at their expense, and be comfortably housed in a desirable part of London while she does so, inevitably raises profound ethical questions. Similarly, the announcement during the chancellor's Budget statement in March 2012 that, even after some proposed reforms, 750,000 families would still be in receipt of child benefit suggests strongly that the welfare state is no longer about helping those who cannot work, but has become a means by which some of those in work can help themselves to a better lifestyle at their fellow taxpayers' expense.

It brings us back to the issue of whether individuals should take responsibility for their actions, and for the welfare of themselves and their families, and it is surely the responsibility of the government to bring such issues out into the open and make sure that they are fully debated. An effective welfare state will channel scarce resources to those who are genuinely unable to work, rather than providing a better standard of living for those who could or even do work and there seems general public acceptance that the present system does not achieve this.

I have dealt with the banks, the budget deficit and the threat of recession. I have also examined an alternative way of controlling inflation. There remains the question of the government's huge 'off-balance-sheet' liabilities in respect of public-sector pension schemes.

For once, the truth really is both pure and simple. On even the most ridiculously optimistic forecasts, this is not an obligation that the government will ever be able to fulfil. Yet this is a truth that the government is not courageous enough to tell, being guilty here too of tinkering around the edges rather than taking the radical action the situation demands.

I believe there really is no room for debate or disagreement here. The government must flick the switch that changes all public-sector plans from final salary to money purchase overnight. This must be done by Act of Parliament or statutory instrument so that it takes precedence over the terms of any pension trust agreement, and it should preferably take effect retrospectively so as to prevent an unseemly scramble for retirement before the specified date. The only decision that needs to be taken is whether to do this in respect of all members (including current pensioners) or only for those who are yet to retire. Naturally, this is likely to lead to severe industrial action, but sooner or later this will subside, just as the miners' strike did, and at least here politicians will be able to show that they have acted honourably for once by including their own pension scheme, and that of the Bank of England, in the new arrangements.

That brings me to the last of our five issues, namely the fact that we expect decisions with huge long-term economic implications to be taken within a system that will punish or reward such decisions entirely on the basis of their short-term political consequences. I have already dealt with the most pressing need in this regard, which is for a written constitution that would severely restrict politicians' freedom of action in these areas, in particular forcing them to run a balanced budget.

This would have the advantage that other matters, such as military action or surrender of sovereignty, could also be given clear constitutional treatment, perhaps being made subject to a referendum, and giving the Sovereign power to call a referendum on any such matter should the government fail to do so.

There are other clear improvements that could be made to the political system. For example, all voting in Parliament could be made electronic, confidential and anonymous, thus ending forever the power of the party whips and allowing MPs to vote according to their true beliefs on every issue. This would end the present system of tyranny by prime minister. Consideration might also be given to banning political lobbying, though this would be both contentious and difficult to enforce, as well as financial donations to political parties above a certain nominal amount. These could even be banned altogether and each party given a state grant pro rata to total votes cast at the last election.

As was stated at the outset of this chapter, I am not so naive as to expect that any of these suggested measures will be adopted by any of the existing political parties. They all involve the surrender of some aspect of power, whether it be the power to damage the economy or the power to interfere in every aspect of people's everyday lives. Asking a politician to surrender some of their power is akin to asking a turkey to vote for an early Christmas.

For something has gone profoundly wrong with our society. Instead of a political system which is operated by politicians for the benefit of the people, we have a system that is operated by politicians for the benefit of politicians. None of this is going to change unless and until we, the people, reclaim the process and repair it, before handing it back to the politicians in a form that it is safe for them to operate. It is time for the people to intervene.

This could perhaps be done by forming a People's Party that would contest the first available general election on a platform simply of taking power, making these changes within a single parliamentary term and then disbanding itself.

There seems no good reason why this should not happen. Clearly, the British people are deeply disillusioned with the political process; witness how many of them cannot even be bothered to turn up and vote at election time. Sadly, the traditional British reaction to such disillusionment has been apathy. Unless this can change, and quickly, the future seems bleak.

For as the ship heads steadily towards the rocks, the politicians on the bridge are giving press interviews while they ready their own personal lifeboat in the form of their generous index-linked pension funds, their seat in the House of Lords, their company chairmanships, their speaking engagements and their lucrative book deals. They realise, even if we don't, that the system is run for their benefit, not ours.

So do not look to politicians to get us out of the mess we're in. They are not the solution, but the problem. They always have been and, unless we do something to stop them, they always will be.

# INDEX